George Packer's

The Village of Waiting

"In *Out of Africa* Isak Dinesen writes of Kenya: 'Up in this high air you breathed easily, drawing in a vital assurance and lightness of the heart. In the highlands you woke up in the morning and thought: *Here I am, where I ought to be.*' Of my five-hundred-odd mornings in the Togolese highlands I woke up hung over, bathed in sweat, hungry, blowing on an extinguished lamp instead of turning off my alarm, mildly at ease, or mildly anxious. But never where I ought to be."

VINTAGE DEPARTURES

George Packer

The Village of Waiting

VINTAGE BOOKS

A Division of Random House New York

A portion of this text originally appeared, in slightly different form, in *Sequoia*.

Grateful acknowledgment is made to the following for permission to reprint previously published material:

Dissent: article entitled "Togo: The Dictator's New Clothes" by George Packer, which appeared in the Fall 1985 issue of *Dissent*, Vol. 32, No. 4.

Harcourt Brace Jovanovich, Inc.: excerpt from "Gerontion" from COLLECTED POEMS 1909–1962 by T.S. Eliot. Copyright 1936 by Harcourt Brace Jovanovich, Inc. Copyright (c) 1963, 1964 by T.S. Eliot. Rights outside the U.S. administered by Faber & Faber Ltd. Reprinted by permission of the publishers.

Library of Congress Cataloging-in-Publication Data
Packer, George.
The village of waiting.
(Vintage departures)
1. Togo—Description and travel.
2. Packer, George.
3. Peace Corps (U.S.)—Togo—Biography.
I. Title.
DT582.27.P33   1988   966'.81   87-45912
ISBN 0-394-75754-8 (pbk.)

Author photo copyright © Scheri Fultineer

Book design by Tasha Hall

Manufactured in the United States of America
10 9 8 7 6 5 4 3 2 1

Was even he perhaps another person, an unknown and still unmade young man whom chance and time had thrust down there under those yellow animal eyes, those black eyes of women and men and children . . . so that he might find himself in otherness, in the other-than-self, so that he might discover history outside of history, and time outside of time, and the original pain of things, and himself, outside of the mirror of Narcissus' pool, in men, on the arid earth?

—Carlo Levi,
Christ Stopped at Eboli

To be African is to be a bastard. The heart of Africa is metamorphosis.

—Breyten Breytenbach,
The True Confessions of an Albino Terrorist

For my mother

ACKNOWLEDGMENTS

There are several debts which I can't pay back but want to mention anyway. Kate Hovde was a part of this story in ways only she and I know. Michelle Burch and Tim DiLaura provided friendship throughout my time in Togo, and in Boston, David Miller shared an obsession with Africa and literature during difficult months of the writing. Nancy Packer and Gail Perez read the entire manuscript; they were as acute and supportive as any critics I could ask for. Becky Saletan of Vintage Books and Bob Lescher, my agent, took a chance on a book by a fledgling writer about an obscure place.

CONTENTS

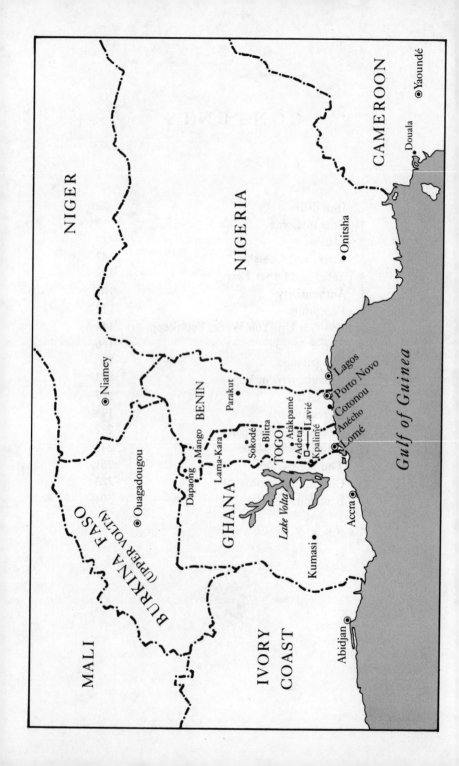

INTRODUCTION

Before clearing out of Africa, the European colonizers spawned a string of unlivable capitals in the swamps along the West African coast at the edge of the Gulf of Guinea. Like the others, Lomé, Togo, is oppressively humid and rotten with malaria, typhoid, and fifty other tropical diseases. But when I was in Peace Corps in 1982 and 1983, volunteers, tired of weeks in the interior without movies or chocolate or even electricity, flocked to Lomé and met at a restaurant called L'Amitié, on a busy dirt road near the Grand Marché. L'Amitié was shabby-modern: the menu had roast chicken, but if you ordered it you would probably hear the squawks of the bird being slaughtered in a back room.

One afternoon a Togolese boy limped in. His left leg was withered, shorter than the other. He dragged it along like a sack of cornmeal, one hand placed flat against his bum thigh and the other hand gripping the wrist to keep it firm. The deformity had twisted his upper body, but his broad shoulders were powerfully muscled. He was a familiar African type, barely distinguishable from the other cripples I saw in Lomé and throughout Togo, victims of polio or a nurse's wayward needle in the sciatic nerve.

He hobbled over to the table where a group of us Americans were complaining about the mosquito problem at the city's cheaper hotels. He might have been fifteen, or twenty-five. He wasn't handsome; there was something dull about his face, but also an openness, a frankness. He waited until our voices dissipated and he had our attention.

"Excuse me," he said in French. "I want to do you a favor."

He put his hands on his nose and began making noises through it. Pushing his fingers against the bridge and nostrils, and snorting out, he managed to close the air passages in just the right way to approximate a kazoo. He had perfected a full octave, and the tune couldn't be mistaken: he was playing "La Marseillaise." Some of us went red, others laughed helplessly, but he went on deadpan through several choruses. Then he played "When the Saints Go Marching In." By the end we'd stopped laughing and were listening, dumbfounded by his skill and by the way he stood before us, unflappable, performing on his nose. When he was done he gave a little bow, collected a handful of coins, and limped out. He hadn't smiled once.

Remembering the cripple at L'Amitié brings back the feeling I associate with much of the eighteen months I spent in Africa. The diseased body, the unnervingly dignified manner, and the thing he'd taught himself for a meager living—a street musician with only his nose to play—left me at a loss whether to answer with laughter, horror, money, or awe. The struggle to stay afloat took on endless variations in Togo. And the white foreigner who'd come on an enlightened mission, and once there managed to keep his eyes open, quickly lost his bearings in the face of it.

An English teacher, I was stationed in Lavié, a village of about two thousand people, almost all peasants—a dense maze of mud huts, some roofed with sheets of corrugated iron, some with grass, clustered at the foot of the low green mountains in southwestern Togo. *Lavié*, from a bit of local history at least a century old, means "Wait a Little More." A paved road bisected the village, and once in a while, from the coffee and cacao town a dozen miles down the road, a bush taxi—a Toyota pickup or Mitsubishi van—tore out of the hot silence, engine roaring and horn blaring, flashed through the village in ten seconds, and disappeared over the hill at the far end. These taxis came through as messengers from the modern world of money, bistro music, and functionary suits, a world in whose margins the villagers of Lavié, like the cripple at L'Amitié, survived. There they lived out a drama, always tragicomic, that is one version of the drama of Africa and the postcolonial world, and that Westerners know next to nothing about. Not the newspaper Africa of lunatic presidents and gimcrack armies and relief camps peopled by ghosts, nor the picture-book Africa of voodoo and looped earlobes and lion hunts. Between the closed borders of these two ideas there's a no-man's-land of which we have no picture, where the people of Lavié wait, with their cutlasses and their radios.

I spent a good deal of my time with them sweating, lonely, angry, diarrhetic, bored—though they would be surprised to hear it, since I didn't let them know. It was impossible ever really to know each other. Under one pair of Western eyes Lavié started as a mystery that became a threat and eventually an attraction, while never ceasing to be any of these. Some Africans whose stories are told here took me into their confidence at considerable risk to themselves. Accordingly, I have changed certain names and details of description. Others made the less dramatic sacrifice of kindness. This book is written in appreciation of both.

The Village of Waiting

CHAPTER 1

Lost in Lomé

I ARRIVED IN LAVIÉ ALREADY SICK OF TOGO, SICK OF Africa, wanting out.

When Peace Corps notified me at Yale in the spring of 1982 that I would be leaving for Togo in three months, I had to go to the library to consult an atlas. The country was still labeled with its colonial name, Togoland—a sliver squeezed into the West African coast among a crazy patchwork of borders. Over the following months, amid the distractions of getting my degree and saying good-byes, a sense of the place formed in my mind—startlingly clear, hopelessly abstract. The dozen species of venomous snakes Togo was famous for; the bit of wire I would hook to my shortwave antenna for better reception; the Camusian ex-colonials I'd find hanging around waterfront bars, muttering into their whiskeys about freedom and death. And farther out still, I imagined a young country that would be more vital than the money- and success-worshiping one I'd grown up in, struggling with life-and-death issues, forging a new literature that might put to shame our breakfast-table realism.

And then I pictured the tropical cliché. Endless miles of low green bush, with me somewhere in the middle of it, on a cot in a room where light and heat poured in, swatting at mosquitoes and drinking from a canteen. I had grown up in one university, then spent four years in another. I had done well; the future seemed secure enough. But I wanted to leave the path for a while. My reasons for going were not more idealistic or more defined than these. In fact, a few days before leaving I discovered I had no real reasons at all, and, briefly, I panicked.

It turned out there were no French existentialists hanging on in Lomé, just officials of the cotton company and their tight-lipped wives and stylish children who attended the Ecole Française up the street from the Peace Corps office. A few lime-green vipers flashed across my path. I saw no evidence of political or literary ferment at all. Politics, in the first weeks, seemed to consist of the banners stretched across Lomé's intersections, in Togolese red, yellow, and green, saluting the peace and unity of the rule of His Excellency President Gnassingbé Eyadema. Literature was the twelve-page government daily tabloid, saluting the same thing.

I spent my first three months in training at the junction town of Atakpamé, 120 kilometers north of the capital and 80 kilometers up the road from Lavié. It was a hilly, overcrowded place teeming with battered Renault taxis and women elbowing through the market—boisterous lighter-skinned southern women, remote Moslems from the north in makeup and scarves. We spent most of our time hidden away, first in a mud-hut suburb called Hiheatro down the road, at a cheap two-story hotel with bats in the ceilings, and then in a Catholic girls' school on a hill overlooking Atakpamé. There were about thirty of us: eleven new arrivals, five veteran volunteers to train us, a half dozen Togolese French teachers, and an assortment of young and old men who did our wash, cooked, and cleaned. The school-age workers latched on to volunteers in hopes of being given a permanent job and a place to live once we were dispersed to start teaching.

The idea of training was essentially futile. College graduates without a word of French or a day's teaching experience had ten weeks to learn French, something of Ewé or another local language, and English instruction within the French West African educational system before being packed off alone to teach in a village school. This while suffering from heat and dysentery, pining for letters from home, and wondering if we hadn't been flown to the wrong planet.

Throughout these early months Togo existed only for "cross-cultural" purposes. We learned to eat with the right hand (the left was set aside for the other end of digestion), and to give the proper greetings. On Saturdays we made group forays to the Atakpamé market. These were occasions of terror—the women pushing their way between stalls of tomatoes and imported soaps, with loads on their heads piled three feet high; the babble of Ewé, which sounded angry and directed at us; the heat of the indoor market, its stench of meat going bad and human sweat and its clouds of flies; my pathetic attempts, with my training-manual Ewé, to buy handfuls of peanuts or tins of Chinese mosquito balm from a girl who, along with her friends, burst into giggles. We were like a herd of prisoners being brought out in a cage for public inspection, looking through bars at the world around us and unable to make any sense of it, or to get away from its sounds and smells. A hundred black eyes stared back in.

One evening, when we were still in the village down the road from Atakpamé, our trainers arranged a meeting with the local village elders as a cross-cultural lesson. They arrived an hour ahead of schedule (our first lesson), a dozen aging men parading into the courtyard of the hotel. Hurriedly we arranged chairs in two rows, Africans facing Americans. Most of them had put on their ceremonial robes for the occasion. One ancient man wore a crown that might have been stolen from the props room of a high school theater, cardboard lined with green velvet and pasted with plastic gems; pinned to his robe was a small gold badge with a picture of President Eyadema. He was asleep before we could say *"Woezo"* ("Welcome") for the third time. The chief-regent had come, and the chief's secretary, the chief of the sister village, a couple of farmers in ragged trousers and shirts, a carpenter, and a stooped, lame old man with a cane, crooked teeth, and alert smiling eyes: the *gong-gongeur*, who beat the official cowbell that called village meetings.

The village chief himself had recently died. Our Togolese teachers had instructed us not to ask about him. It was customary to keep a chief's death secret for at least a year, and though all the villagers knew the truth, they went on pretending he was still alive.

We asked questions for an hour. The elder who spoke for the group was a muscular man of about fifty, in a black-and-white-checkered robe that left one shoulder bare, no shirt, sunglasses—Ray Charles as a Roman senator. Our questions had to be translated into Ewé by one of our Togolese English teachers, and from Ewé into the local language, Akposso, by one of our French teachers who came from this region. The elder's replies made the trip in reverse. He explained how a chief was enthroned and, if he was a bad one, destooled—which he would be if, for example, he took advantage of a woman with a marital problem who came to him and had to stay the night because the problem was too difficult to resolve in a day. He ticked off the central taboos of their society, each having to do with attracting evil spirits after dark: don't whistle between 6:00 P.M. and 6:00 A.M., don't pound manioc or yams after dark, don't drag a rope through the dirt at night.

Our questions inevitably came around to polygamy. "Of course the chief must have more than one wife," he said. "Powerful men are bound to have many wives, since women are like chickens."

Before our murmurs of protest could resolve themselves into a response, he was shooting questions back. Why weren't we polygamous? Why did the daughter's family pay the dowry? Why did some couples have no children at all?

It wasn't clear who our spokesman would be; we lacked the Africans' unanimity. Finally a woman spoke up. "We have only one wife because we think love is something that can't be divided up among other people," she said. "Love is a precious thing between two people. Sometimes those people don't want children because their love for each other is enough."

We all waited while this answer made its way from English into Ewé and then into Akposso. The old men sat forward and listened intently. When the translation was finished, they roared with laughter.

.   .   .

Training went by in a blur of sudden afternoon rainstorms, practice classes, pygmy goats and potbellied babies in the dirt roads, the *thwap-thwap* of women with baseball-bat pestles pounding yams in their great wooden mortars, endless games of Scrabble, a plague of winged termites, rushes to the toilet, humid nights under mosquito netting, bats squealing and rustling in the ceilings. In the first days here, with the heat, the food, intestinal troubles, and the sense of having been pulled up by the roots, I seemed to lose about 20 percent of my energy and never quite recovered it again. Some of the men shed twenty pounds in training. And toward the end, the rigid schedule and the long confinement with others rattled our nerves. The Togolese teachers, forced to spend every waking hour with Americans, grew irritated at our casual attitude toward work. One night after dinner a female teacher announced that we were going to sing a round of French songs we'd been learning in our classes. I must have curled my lip at the thought. Later a volunteer told me that this gesture said to an African what an American understood by a raised middle finger. There was an uproar among the Togolese, cool complaints to our director, explanations, apologies, mutual vows of goodwill, a week of tension. I imagined that preparation for war was a little like this: make soldiers wait long enough in conditions bad enough, and eventually they will crave combat. I craved a village of my own.

In Togo and throughout West Africa aphorisms were written on just about any surface available—the backs of buses, walls, school-books. Most of them were religious and slightly fatalistic: "God's Writing Has No Eraser," "God Alone Is Enough," "Who Knows the Future?" Others were more enigmatic: "He Who Betrays Me Wastes His Time," "Sea Never Dry." Some were simply nick-names, like "Lagos Boy." Over the rough-framed doorway of a building in Hiheatro, where a seamstress sewed clothes at a foot-pedal machine, someone had painted two English words that I had to pass by every day and that summed up the frustration of our summer-long limbo: "Do Something."

The chance came abruptly at the end of August. Training ended, we were shuffled down to Lomé for a swearing-in ceremony at the ambassador's residence and told to get ready for the trip to the villages that the Togolese government had selected as our teaching posts.

Lomé was a shantytown of a quarter-million inhabitants, sprawling neighborhoods of concrete-and-corrugated-iron shacks with a patch of paved roads and ministries and shops downtown, near the beach. Even in the commercial center, among the African airline offices, Lebanese houseware shops, and French business offices, you couldn't escape the smell of Lomé, my first and most enduring impression of the city: the burnt, heavy, acrid odor mixed with sea brine, of the cooking oil in which thousands of women on streets all over town were frying food to sell. The smell disappeared in only one place, on a stretch of beach between the four-star Hôtel de la Paix and Hollando's department store. Here the sand was used as an unofficial public toilet. Men came to face the sea and open their flies, women hoisted up their skirts and squatted, a pipe emptied the green slime of city sewage into the ocean.

I ended up waiting in Lomé for six weeks.

An obscure cabinet member who was an in-law of the president refused to sign the leases that allowed new volunteers to take up lodging. Togo had always paid for Peace Corps housing, but the economy was in a shambles, the word *crise* on everyone's lips. Now the *directeur du service de matériel* claimed that Peace Corps houses were too opulent (which was generally true) and dredged up instances of abuse by volunteers. From now on, he insisted, the U.S. would pay the rent. The nuisance dragged out into a stalemate. Peace Corps administrators talked of ending what was touted as a model program; the *directeur* wouldn't budge. If he had been anything other than a relation of the president, a bit of subtle blackmail would have won him over soon enough. Instead, aware of his power, he eventually stopped receiving the Togolese and American Peace Corps officials who made humble daily trips to his office.

We couldn't leave the city, since the bureaucrat might give in at any moment. I waited from day to day. Peace Corps had been good enough to lodge me with a few others at the house of our director. It wasn't far from the office, and a hundred feet from the Gulf of Guinea, in a wealthy diplomatic neighborhood full of Mediterranean-style villas with metal gates and generous palm trees. The household itself was an unreal and slightly disturbing memory of the old life: quilted bedspreads and frozen slabs of ground beef, air conditioning, cupboards full of cupcake wrappers and Oreos that came in by diplomatic pouch. The director's young daughters lay around watching the VCR, and whining; his wife mourned for the better days when they were in the Ivory Coast, fussed at Yao the housekeeper, and whined. As far as she was concerned, they had been in Africa at least one year too long: the broken freezer was leaking, the meat was going bad, the maid was unreliable, the humidity was unbearable. Like other wives in the foreign community she had no role here, and at times her complaints at the breakfast table seemed about to rise to a pitch of frantic despair.

The director—a short, fat academic whose hair ends were always damp with sweat—spoke perfect French and Swahili, wore the local functionary leisure suit in robin's-egg blue, and never whined. Every morning he was chauffeured the quarter mile through cratered sandy roads to the office, where he worked like a demon all day. He kept a controlling hand on every aspect of Peace Corps/Togo, coddling some volunteers, blackballing others, and was determined that the program maintain its model reputation back in Washington. At breakfast he smiled and chewed and explained how he was going to bring the *directeur du service de matériel* around. His wife demanded to know how he could be in such a good mood.

I learned to stay out of the house when the family was home. Unfortunately this was between twelve and three, when nothing was open and the heat was at its worst. As soon as I stepped out the door into the scratchy wet air—the road puddled with recent rain, the half-naked children staring and calling names—Africa replaced the unreality of the director's house with its own. I drifted between the two, waiting for some word, less and less sure of what I was doing here. The American Cultural Center, located past the Grand Marché in the city center, opposite the U.S. embassy, was a refuge of air conditioning and the latest American magazines, but it, too, closed at twelve; and anyway, it seemed the easy way out.

So I wandered around Lomé in the sun and noticed that my tongue was turning hot and prickly. My feet, in leather sandals, were filthy from the streets.

Sometimes I sat with a Coke or beer under an umbrella at the Benin Beach Club. Where the beach hadn't become a toilet, a few Europeans lay burning in the sun—women mostly, pink topless wives of businessmen or diplomats—but they didn't swim because of the surf's dangerous undertow. Nearby gangs of fishermen hauled in their nets in a tug-of-war with the gulf, and market women foraged with sacks for pebbles to sell to the concrete mixers in town. On these stretches of sand the sunbathers looked misplaced and slightly comical, like sunbathers on a rooftop in a slum. Lomé was too small and obscure to have developed a resort culture. Africans came to the beach to scratch up a living.

Downtown Lomé in these hours was deserted, except for the black-market money changers from Nigeria who played cards on the road by the Grand Marché, the cripples who opened office doors for a few francs or dragged themselves through the streets with rubber pads under their hands, and the small-time vendors. These last flocked to any white they saw, brandishing fistfuls of bracelets and garish imitation masks. When they hissed to get my attention, I hissed back. Taxi drivers tried to run pedestrians off the road, and I took to yelling obscenities in English, knowing they couldn't understand—until a Ghanaian driver heard me and returned the greeting.

Nothing was more unnerving than the children. About the first thing you noticed in Togo, after the cooking oil, was that everyone seemed to be under the age of ten; and immediately after, if you were white, that they were all yelling *"Yovo!"* at you. Sometimes it came in a kind of child's verse, chanted the way American kids chant "nanny nanny nanny goat": *"Yovo, yovo, bonsoir! Ça va bien? Merci!"*—five, ten, twenty times, until you were out of their sight. Other times it was a half-joking request for money: *"Yovo? Donne-moi dix francs!"* Or else posed as a question that could sound almost ontological: *"Yovo?"* Or simply repeated at will: *"Yovo yovo yovo yovo!"* *Yovo*, of course, meant "white." It was a child's version of *yevu*, of which I had various translations: "white," "stranger," even "peeled orange." Togolese friends insisted that the word—used all over Togo and by all ages—had no malicious overtones. It meant something good. An enormous papaya was a *yovo* papaya, the paved road was the *yovomo*, the *yovo* road. I would nod, unconvinced. Long after I'd left Togo, as I was browsing in the drafty, sober stacks of a library at Harvard, I found an article in an obscure African language journal about the various West African names for whites. There was the old word, *yovo*, from *yevu*; and *yevu*, it went on, came from *aye avu*, which meant "cunning dog."

The children were just curious, I learned, dazzled by *yovos* and eager to make friends. No doubt they were; I gave out my address the way basketball players give out autographs. The vendors near the Grand Marché were probably not malicious either, nor the taxi drivers, nor even the money changers who offered whites low rates and then shortchanged them by a third. At most they were pulling my leg, making a little fun, redistributing the wealth in the right direction. But *yovo* got into my brain and became an evil word, the single most evil word I heard in Africa, with a dozen nuances: derision, hostility, inanity, a mocking reminder of wealth, an unwillingness to learn my name, to see past my skin color. It was an introduction to being a privileged minority.

Yovos typically like to get things done and to master their situation. They don't always respond well to an environment of too much freedom and not enough to do. And the idle days in Lomé seemed to be dementing me slightly. I came to associate the city, and especially the hot midday hours—functionaries going home on mopeds, and the empty streets when downtown closed; soldiers eating bananas in their sentry boxes outside the deserted presidential palace on the beachfront, African pop blasting from bars, the heaps of fish drying on sidewalks, the scant shade, the briny smell, the deep sand—with an African void. This sense lay quiet for months at a time after I left Lomé, but I was never completely rid of it again. Spawned in idleness, it stayed with me even after I'd begun working, as if in the weeks of dangling I'd encountered something real and permanent about Africa, or me, or the combination of the two. It lingered, a memory and a possibility, like malaria in the blood: the feeling of being trapped, vulnerable, in a place where nothing had any meaning and I had none to provide. Toward the end of the wait, as my nerves wore thin, it became intense.

On the western side of the city there was a neighborhood called Kodjoviakopé—the swanky villas of diplomats, the German embassy, the Peace Corps office, and then, farther west, a collection of cheap bars and eateries with names like Don't Mind Your Wife Chop Bar, where more English was spoken than French. The border with Ghana was a hundred yards away. I took to wandering through Kodjoviakopé and drinking in the border bàrs filled with Ghanaians and a few Togolese and Nigerians. I liked to hear African English, I liked the international air; but something else appealed to me too. The Ghanaian men and women in these places worked in Lomé, but they spent the night across the border. Every evening at a quarter to six the bars, swollen at the end of the workday, were suddenly evacuated in the rush to make customs before the border closed at six. There were migrant workers, bargirls, houseboys, and a half-criminal element of smugglers and prostitutes. None of them had any legal right to work in Togo and they could be expelled at any time. Like me—though far less privileged and more at ease—they were marginal here, they didn't belong.

One afternoon a rainstorm caught me in a bar within sight of the border, with its chain link fence and the Black Star over the sign Welcome to Ghana. Two men at my table, print shirts unbuttoned to the navel, were speaking in an angry Ewé spliced with English phrases. "Bad job" and "quenched" kept surfacing. I caught enough to know they were talking about money somebody owed one of them. For a few minutes I was intrigued and tried to follow their conversation. The bar began to fill with people coming in out of the wet, soaked newspapers on their heads. The rain didn't let up. The conversation began to elude me and meander. The two men seemed listless now, and suddenly I no longer had the slightest interest in what they were saying. The chatter in the bar became loud, and indistinct and foolish as foreign languages always sound. What I really wanted was to be out of there, but that was impossible because of the rain. So I waited; and as the rain kept up I had an urge to run along the shelves behind the bar and smash every bottle in the place.

The Africans around me were talking and cracking jokes, in their vast patience. What thoughts, what emotions distracted and gripped them were opaque to me. Of course, my private sense of purposelessness was their daily routine; still, their equanimity in the face of it awed me.

One of the two men turned and caught my eye. He gave a friendly smile.

"*Yovo.*"

"*Ameyibo,*" I said. "*Nkonye menye yovo o.*" I'd learned the word for "black man," as well as a way to say I had a name and it wasn't *yovo.*

"Eh!" He turned to his friend, and both of them laughed and repeated what I'd said. I could see they were surprised and impressed. Perhaps if he'd then asked me what my name was it could have been an entry to a conversation, even an acquaintanceship. But he didn't; and now it seemed we were not much more than curiosities to each other.

There was a great commotion. As if on cue everyone was getting up and hurrying toward the bead-string door, including the two men. Damp newspapers were lifted over heads, people disappeared into the rain. My watch said quarter to six: the border was about to close on them.

In mid-October the *directeur du service de matériel* changed his mind, signed the papers, and released me. It was done hurriedly, without explanation, the way a taxi waited hours in the station without moving and then for no apparent reason started up and roared off. I had two days to buy a gas stove, frying pans, and a bottle of Jim Beam, enjoy a last *yovo* meal at the Italian restaurant, and pack my bags for the trip to the interior.

It was finally going to begin.

A woman was hacking at a branch with her cutlass, under a red-blossomed bougainvillea vine in the yard. She wore a sleeveless light blue frock with shoulder straps, and a piece of market cloth tied round her chest held a baby asleep on her back. She looked young, pretty, and very thin for an African woman—so thin, in fact, that I thought she must have had some sort of wasting illness. Above high cheekbones her eyes were darkened with pencil lines of black makeup; and this, too, was unusual in a village. Perhaps it was the makeup that fixed my first and lasting sense of Christine's eyes as wells of sadness. Though she—together with her husband and children—was to be my neighbor and to share the house in Lavié with me for fourteen months, I have barely half a dozen memories of her anywhere outside the yard. Everything that took place between me and the Agbeli family happened within that twenty-by-twenty-foot patch of dirt, as if everything were already contained in the moment I entered the yard.

My arrival didn't make a big impression. Christine looked up at my *"Bonsoir,"* smiled modestly, and went back to her chopping. I wasn't particularly interested in her at the moment either. I had my belongings to worry about. The Peace Corps truck had just left them and me at the side of the paved road. I'd been the last volunteer drop-off at the end of a long day's drive from the capital. The house was at the edge of the village, facing away from the road—a faded concrete building painted yellow, with a pitched roof of corrugated iron, bars on the windows, doors and shutters painted blue. Between the drab house and the grass-and-bamboo hut on the other side of the dirt, the bougainvillea with its bright red flowers, creeping up a crude trellis in the middle of the yard, looked luxurious, foreign, and fragile.

At our house the dwellings of Lavié stopped and the bush began again—now, after the rains, an impenetrable green jungle of trees, vines, and grass. The light was failing, and clouds had moved in over the low mountains behind the village.

I had a little kerosene-powered refrigerator (stored upside down to get the Freon moving), a mobylette missing its chain, wicker baskets full of clothes, textbooks, and mosquito netting, the dozen garishly colored cushions I'd bought from an old seamstress in Lomé, and the *yovo* gadgets—manual typewriter, camera, Sony Walkman, and shortwave radio—I'd bought on a last spree in the States, all stranded at the roadside. And no key. I went back up to the road.

A couple of teen-aged boys had appeared and were staring in something like amazement at my goods. As I approached, one of them said, "It's going to rain, *monsieur*." I was at a loss, unsure of the next move; for the first time in four months in Africa the next move was up to me. In my confusion I thought for a moment that the thing I had to do was keep it from raining.

There was a sound of distant voices, singing—faint, from the top of a hill in the village center, then louder as the singers descended into view. At least a hundred people were walking my way. They were mostly women in bright patterned *pagnes*—bolts of imported cloth—and scarves, swaying a little with their song; a few men were in back, bedraggled in shorts and torn shirts, and a number of boys and girls. The voices of the women carried loudest. It was something like a chant, church music—the African gospel in Ewé that the radio played evenings, slow and high and strangely cheerful.

Then I noticed the coffin men were carrying near the back. It was carved out of mahogany, painted red and blue and embossed with brass—probably the equivalent of two months' income to the family of the deceased. As they drew even with me, a few of the older women in front were sobbing. Others sang, or walked along expressionlessly, or smiled and chatted. Some took notice of me and my boxes.

A man emerged from the procession and hurried toward me, hand out. Middle-aged, with the top of his head bald and his shiny forehead high and dignified, his nostrils flaring, he—unlike the other men—was dressed in *kente*, a traditional robe sewn from strips of brilliant orange, red, and blue squares. The *kente* was draped around his body and tossed over one shoulder like a toga. Quickly I decided he must be the village chief. He was beaming.

"Mon-sieur Georges! En-fin! Bonne ar-ri-vée! Woe-zo!" He pumped my hand, almost inarticulate with delight.

"Yo!" I answered with a little bow.

"Oh, *très bien*, you have already learned Ewé. You will do well." He spoke good French. "You haven't been waiting long?"

"Only a few minutes."

"And no one here to greet you!" He shook his head and smacked his lips in displeasure. "No, that's not good."

And immediately he was ordering the boys to move my things to the house, and another boy to fetch the keys. We were drawing a number of curious stares from the mourners.

"You have arrived on a sad occasion," the chief said. "The village has lost one of its daughters, a student at your school. She was in her last year. A great pity."

"I'm very sorry. How did she die?"

He shrugged helplessly. "Ah—who knows? She got sick and then her stomach blew up and she died. Oh, Monsieur Georges, but you are here! We've waited so long! Your arrival will be auspicious in Lavié. The village is going to see changes—some real changes! Welcome! *Woezo, woezo!*"

It did not strike me as auspicious. I imagined one of the older women near the front of the procession coming back to shake her fist at me: Is nothing sacred to you *yovos* with your *yovo* things in full view while we bury one of our daughters? A wind kicked up. The sky was nothing but gray clouds. The funeral hurried by, the chief shouted more orders at the boys. The keys arrived, and we ducked into the house with my boxes as the first drops plunked like stones on the metal roof.

The chief dismissed the boys, who were standing in the living room, still admiring my mobylette. I reached in my pocket for change. "I want to thank them for their help." The boys started to bow and take my tip.

"No, no," the chief said, "you mustn't give them anything. It's their duty. Money will only make them *voyous*." The word, used commonly, meant "hoodlums." The boys went out unhappy into the rain.

A little light was left outside, but in the living room I couldn't make out a thing beyond the bulky forms of my belongings and a couple of low armchairs. The floor seemed to be bare unswept concrete, and the room had a dank smell about it, as if a bucket of water were standing in a corner. I couldn't see the chief's face either, but I had the sense that he was waiting for me to say something. The moment seemed to call for some sort of speech. I had none. And so for half a minute there was one of those awkward silences, filled with goodwill and incomprehension, that kept intruding on my first weeks in Lavié.

"The frigo is inverted, I believe—" he began, but then there were two quick claps outside the door through the noise of the rain. Clapping took the place of knocking in the villages, where mud and thatch huts used to have no doors and some still didn't.

"*Excusez?*" Two damp men stepped inside. The older of them, a big man with a jovial moon face, raised a hand and stuttered in English, "W-Welcome to our Am-m-merican teacher!"

"Thank you."

The chief said, "Monsieur Georges already speaks Ewé. You don't need to use his language, he has mastered ours."

The man congratulated me, switched from English to Ewé, and delivered a short speech that was wholly lost on me.

I could see he was a teacher. His corduroys looked new, the sport shirt fit his large belly, and when he finally used the one language we had in common, his wasn't the chopped, spat French of villagers. It came out in a rapid, dense stutter. The other man looked barely older than I. His eyes, low on his face, stared dully out of deep black skin, his front teeth stuck out crookedly, and his shoulders and arms were powerfully muscled. He gave the impression of youthful menace. In his shorts and flip-flops, a cutlass in one hand, he looked to me like an illiterate peasant.

The chief introduced us all. Our handshakes ended, African-style, with finger snapping. The older man was Agbefianou, a history-geography teacher. The man in shorts, Aboï, was the school principal. He seemed to note my surprise, without smiling.

"*Soyez le bienvenu,*" he said solemnly. "Monsieur Packer, you will excuse my appearance. I've just come from the fields. I cannot tell you how happy we are to have you among us at last. Truly, the school and the professorial corps have suffered without one of our English teachers. The children have been inquiring after you. Ah, they've been so anxious! Every day, 'Has the American arrived yet?'

Therefore, when I heard I came directly from the field with no time to dress appropriately. You will forgive my attire." He handed me a half-dozen letters that had been waiting for me and glanced around the dark room. "You have some interesting possessions."

Aboï's French was a complete surprise. He spoke it slowly and with elaborate care. It was the stiff, official French you heard in African airports and government offices, left over from the colonial administration. I'd never heard anyone speak bureaucratic French in private before. I associated it with paperwork and a fondness for rubber stamps; sometimes it seemed the thing the Togolese had retained best from colonialism. I could hear the thud of the rubber stamp in Aboï's voice, but when he was silent he still looked like an illiterate peasant youth.

We chatted for a few minutes, about school, about the reason for my long delay, about the rain, which was letting up. The chief and Agbefianou occasionally turned to each other in midsentence and switched from French to Ewé, then back to French. But with Aboï, whom they called *"Monsieur le Directeur,"* they only spoke French. I wondered if he was not from the region, not an Ewé. Perhaps a Kabyé, from the northern savanna. The Kabyé were blacker, and I thought I saw an uncanny resemblance to the face of President Eyadema, who was Kabyé. Aboï stood stiffly, a little ill at ease, hands clasped behind his back, clutching the cutlass.

The rain had stopped. Outside it was completely dark. In the tropics the sun goes down in fifteen minutes. Aboï asked me to start teaching within three days, said good-night, and went out. The chief, after more handshakes and *woezos*, followed him, assuring me he would have a lamp sent over so I could see. Agbefianou lingered a moment. He was pointing at something in the dark.

"It's a M-M-Motobecane?"

He meant the mobylette. I said it was.

"At the end of your service here, could you sell it to me?"

"I'm sorry, it belongs to Peace Corps." He made a small noise of disappointment. I said, "Aboï is so young. How did he become principal?"

"Ha ha!" he laughed. "That is a story. The last principal ripped off the school treasury and ran to Ghana. He never came back or else he'd go to prison. That was two years ago. And Aboï had the highest qualifications on the staff—he had his *probatoire* and had gone to the Ecole Normale Supérieure. So he was chosen by the authorities."

Because he'd finished the second-to-last year of high school, had gone to the new teacher-training college in Atakpamé, and had a smattering of education theory, Aboï—brand-new, and probably not from the region—had stepped in ahead of the entire staff. Agbefianou seemed to be grinning. When I asked how things had gone under Aboï, he laughed again and the smile stretched across his round face.

"W-W-We are trying."

Before Agbefianou left I learned something else. The girl who was buried today, a star student in the *3ème* class—the last of four years in the CEG, the Collège d'Enseignement Général, roughly equivalent to junior high school—had gotten pregnant. He didn't know by whom. Some people said one of the *voyou* students, others were whispering about a member of the teaching staff. A pregnancy and childbirth would have meant the end of her education, in the year of her chance to pass the *brevet* exam, the BEPC, and enter high school. She'd gone to a village herbalist—whose identity was also unknown, though plenty of rumors were circulating about him as well—and taken medicine to induce an abortion. That was what had killed her.

Agbefianou left, swallowed in pitch blackness. I was learning fast about nighttime without electricity. I stood helpless in the middle of the room, hardly able to see the hand I held out to feel around before taking a step. Through the barred window that looked out on a grove of bushes and the paved road, I saw a couple of dull orange flames, kerosene lamps, swaying up the hill toward the village. Beyond them, the low uneven outline of the mountains was just visible in the moonlight. An hour before they were lush, green, inviting; now they loomed rather ominously. Over the far side of them the world had disappeared.

Shouting rang out in our yard—Christine snapping at one of her children, who answered in a small defensive whine. In a minute a light appeared at my door. Christine stood in the doorway holding the handle of a lamp, a covered enamel bowl in her other hand.

"*Ago.*"

"*Oui, entrez.*"

She stepped in. "*Pardon, monsieur,* I told the child but he forgets. *Vous allez manger le fufu. Voilà la lampe.*"

Another surprise: Christine spoke French. The lamp was throwing great shadows across the walls—flashes of blue, of little clots of mud in the corners of the ceiling. She set it down on the floor with the bowl, smiled, and went out without another word.

It was *fufu*—pounded manioc—a steaming, shiny white blob like bread dough floating in a greasy pool of reddish pepper sauce. I only managed to get down a few fingerfuls before I felt nauseated and had to throw the rest out between the bars of the back window into a banana tree. It wasn't the *fufu*. By now I was used to local food, even getting to like the taste. It was exhaustion, rawness, the incoherent stream of images running through my head—the woman chopping wood, rain, a girl swallowing herbs and her stomach blowing up like a balloon, the coffin, Aboï's dull eyes, Agbefianou's stutter, the chief pumping my hand, the dark mountains, the dank smell. The pressure of letters in my back pocket. Letters from home. Normally I tore them open as soon as I had my hands on them. But home was farther away than ever tonight. I decided not to read them yet. I could taste how lonely they'd make me; I wanted to give myself a fighting chance to get used to this isolation. It was a new feeling tonight—not entirely a bad one. Lomé was behind me. I was on my own, in the village—where I had thought I wanted to be.

Outside, in a body of water that seemed to surround the house, frogs were raising a tremendous racket. Then I heard singing from the village. The voices came loud in the dark, and when they stopped there was the rapid tapping of drums. The same words seemed to be sung over and over: first the single voice of a woman, then the echo of a group. This was not the high-pitched church music of the burial. Driven by the drums, these voices were vibrant; they exulted. I imagined a crowd of dancers.

I hadn't seen the rest of the house. Where was the bedroom? I held up the lamp and went through an open door into a smaller room. A bed frame took up most of the floor space; a window gave out on the yard, half blocked by a bush.

"Monsieur!"

The woman's voice again, from the yard.

"Faut fermer. La porte—faut fermer. You must shut the door. There are thieves and snakes at night."

I went into the living room, shut the door and bolted it. Back in the bedroom I undressed and sat on the bed. Sharp bits of straw poked through the mattress. I raised the glass ball of the lamp, smudged with ash, and blew out the flame. In the sudden darkness a thought came to me and I leapt out of bed. The lamp was out, no matches. I hesitated, then ran my hands over the rough mattress to make sure none of the twelve species of venomous snake was in bed with me before I lay down to spend my first night in the village.

CHAPTER 2

Manioc

IT HAPPENED TWICE A DAY DURING MY FIRST WEEK in the house: the *clap-clap* outside the front door, the sudden appearance in my bedroom of one of the Agbeli children, *"Mama dit . . . ,"* the steaming bowl of *fufu* placed on my writing table, the little bow, the stolen glance around my room, the wordless backstep out. Once, I'd gone out to talk with Aboï and found the bowl waiting for me when I got back.

Manioc, a hairy tuber, grew in clumps around the fringes of the village, long shoots capped by a large leaf like an open hand. Peeled, sliced, boiled, and pounded, it achieved the consistency of bread dough and probably had less nutritional value. I always knew when the bowl was about to come over. Preparing lessons in my bedroom, I would hear Christine's cutlass whacking a branch, then smell the woodsmoke of her fire. After a half hour came the sharp, high-pitched orders to her kids, and then the sound of their pestles pounding away—the squishy sound of wood driving into boiled chunks of manioc, and as it softened up, the hollow suck of *fufu* absorbing the blows. The sound came in a three-beat rhythm: *Thwap! thwap! thwap! . . . Thwap! thwap! thwap!* At my desk I pictured three children, hardly taller than their pestles, standing around the mortar, pounding in sequence, pausing to throw water on the *fufu* when it began to stick, and murmuring as they debated whether it was finished.

In these first days I saw the Agbeli family less than I heard and imagined them. As I set up house, cleaned the floors, knocked out the nests of mud wasps from the walls, made a water filter from plastic buckets and chalk sticks, hooked up the butane stove, and wrote my first lesson plans, they were the African family out in the yard or on the other side of my kitchen wall: Christine and her countless children.

She had eight. I learned this from her husband, who stopped by on my third night to give a formal welcome and introduce himself as the man of the house. His wife hadn't bothered to introduce herself, and no one did it for her; she'd simply sent over the *fufu* and reminded me to shut my door. Shining a lamp, the man of the house came into the living room, where I was reading: belly-first, fleshy-cheeked, balding, with eyes set wide apart under a high forehead. His eyes were red and his smile loose, as if he'd been drinking. I knew immediately that this was Benjamin, Christine's husband, the younger brother of the chief—my *patron*, as others called him, since he and the chief were landlords of the house. He looked like a smudged copy of the chief: the same large brow, but bulbous instead of noble; the same sad, underslung eyes, but where the chief's were hard and clear, these were heavy-lidded and bloodshot. Benjamin slurred when he greeted me.

"*Bonne arrivée, Monsieur Georges!* I would have come by to see you last night but my taxi is *en panne* and I was in Kpalimé getting it fixed. Always, it's work, work! Never any rest. I leave at five in the morning—I take my bath first—and I come home sometimes ten, eleven, even midnight. Work never ends. God made us to work."

I invited him to sit and offered him a cup of Jim Beam. He'd never tasted bourbon and was interested.

"It's good, the whiskey of the *yovo*."

Benjamin, a taximan, made the route from Lavié up to the top of plateau and back when the vehicle was operating. He rambled on about the lack of passengers and freight now that the rainy season was coming to an end, and then about his children. "I have too many. In the old days I could have afforded it, but now, with the *crise économique*, life costs too much. I won't have another. If I had more money I would have married a second wife, like my brother. But what can one do, as a taximan? Now even the wife I've got is too much. For the African, *monsieur*, there must be wives and children. If a man has just two children, or three, he can be rich and powerful, but he is nothing. He is not considered. Me personally, I have eight. When I lived in Abidjan I saw the French there with no wives and no children. For the African, this cannot be understood. You, *monsieur*, you yourself have how many?"

I acknowledged my state of disgrace. He reassured me that I was still young and had plenty of time to produce. As a matter of fact, there were village girls here who would be delighted to mother my children. I changed the subject back to his.

"I think I've seen all of your children except the oldest."

He fairly spat. "Lucien. Because he's never home. He's a *bandit*, a *voyou*. He is good-for-nothing. He goes off at night who knows where without a word. Sixteen years old! Still in *sixième*!" Benjamin drained his cup of bourbon.

"I was going to ask if he wanted to be paid to do my laundry."

"He ought to be beaten instead. *Bandit, voyou.*"

Shortly afterward Benjamin left, promising to fix the pump of my cistern so I could have water in the shower; it took three months.

The next night the glob of *fufu* sent over was the size of a monkey's skull. I'd just polished off a plate of eggs and potatoes I'd fried up on my gas stove; but "cross-culture" had taught us that sending back a meal without making a good dent in it was an insult. I forced down half a dozen fingerfuls. The red palm-oil sauce was so peppery that it had my scalp itching, my nose running, and my shirt damp with sweat. I went to the back window and chucked the *fufu* out for the Agbelis' stray chickens and goats. Part of it ended up on the window bars and back in the living room. It didn't occur to me until the next morning, when I heard the younger children rummaging through the thickets behind my living room, exclaiming and laughing, that the family might have put it to better use.

I decided that I would thank Christine and tell her that I would be able to cook for myself from now on. It was time to meet these neighbors. On the fifth night I crossed the yard—we had a generous date palm by the bougainvillea, a grapefruit tree, a banana tree, and several papaya—and clapped outside her kitchen. The sun was diving down over the plateau and the frogs in the swamp were warming up.

Christine was sitting on a tiny stool amid billows of smoke from a wood fire, slicing manioc into a black pot balanced on a horseshoe-shaped clay stove. Her children were sitting around the dirt floor. The kitchen was thatched; bundles of sticks were tied together for walls, and the rising smoke filled a bamboo platform under the ceiling to dry out stacks of corn ears and manioc roots. I had to crouch to get in. Aside from the family, there was nothing inside but a few dirty bowls, blackened rags, *fufu* pestles, an earthen jug of water, and a couple of stools. Christine told one of the boys to bring me one, then greeted me.

"Fié nawo." ("Evening to you.")

"Fié," I answered, and went on with the Ewé greetings I'd picked up in training. "How is the household?"

"They are there."

"And the children?"

"They are there too."

"Your husband?"

"He too."

"Today's work?"—meaning that the last time we saw each other was today.

"The work of today."

The children raised shouts of delight. A few words were enough to convince them I had achieved fluency. I looked around the hut. By fading sunlight and firelight six small faces were staring at me—curious, thrilled, terrified. Aku, the perpetually dozing baby, was asleep on Christine's back. Thrill belonged to the four middle children: Claudie, ten; the eight-year-old twins, Emma and Markie; and Dové, five. Atsu, at fourteen the oldest after the absent Lucien, was too polite to show anything but curiosity. He had a high-pitched

voice and a face splotched yellow with a fungus that peeled away
the skin as though he'd been in the sun too long. But for Mawuli,
a two-year-old boy, the new *yovo* brought pure terror. Whenever he
saw me staring at him, he turned his face in the other direction or
simply burst into tears. On my first morning, as I sat on my stoop
boiling water over a charcoal grill for safe drinking, he had come
ambling across the yard toward the kitchen with nothing on but a
shrunken T-shirt, the little penis sticking out under his swollen
belly. When he became aware that I was looking at him, he pulled
the shirt up over his head and continued walking.

Mawuli had an Agbeli face, the face of the chief: the large forehead
and receding hair, the low eyes that seemed pulled down by his
cheeks. The others all had Christine's high cheekbones and dark
features. By the light of the fire the family looked astonishingly
beautiful.

We went through the names until I could recite them on my own,
to their cheers: Atsu, Claudie, Markie, Emma, Dové, Mawuli, Aku.
Christine. Then, one by one they repeated mine, and somehow
along the way it turned into "Georgie," pronounced "Judgie"; and
then a *Fo* was put in front of it, and I became, with overtones of
respect, Brother Georgie. The loathed nickname of my elementary
school days caught on here, and I liked it. After Lomé and *yovo* it
was like music. Eventually I acquired a number of names in the
village. The Agbeli children, and most other villagers, called me
"Fo Georgie," though older people and market women dropped the
respectful *Fo*. Christine called me *"monsieur"* for almost a year, until
I prevailed on her to use what her children used. To the chief and
Benjamin I was always "Monsieur Georges"; the teachers called me
"Packer," or more nearly "Packah" or "Puckuh," though Aboï took
the liberty of calling me by the Frenchified version of my first name.
My own students used "Mistah Puckuh"; other schoolkids and unmarried girls called me *"monsieur"* unless they were teasing or flirting, in which case they lowered it to "Fo Georgie." And with a few
villagers, especially small children in the far corners of Lavié who
rarely saw me, I never got past *"yovo."* I accepted all the various
names. Their proliferation seemed appropriate. My identity frag-

mented along the lines by which the village itself was fragmented, and for different villagers I seemed to be different people.

Tonight in Christine's hut we spoke a broken mixture of French and Ewé. The older children, especially Atsu, had learned some French at school—the stiff singsong that came out of children's mouths after a few years of education.

"I wanted to thank you for the meals, Christine."

She laughed a little and nodded.

"It is very kind of you to keep thinking of me. But I can cook my own food."

"You?" She looked incredulous. The children giggled. "A man?"

"Well, you see, *chez nous* . . ."

Whenever I heard myself saying *chez nous*, I realized the ground for communication was slipping out from under me. She interrupted.

"The *fufu* isn't good?"

"No, it's delicious."

"The sauce is too hot?"

"Not at all! Only I don't want to . . ." I didn't want to take their money: that was it. And now that I knew, I didn't know how to go on. I looked at the expectant faces in the dim light.

"Only I can't eat *ameyibo* every night—some nights I have to eat *yovo*."

"Woo-eee!" Christine laughed, and the children joined her, and in a second we were all laughing. Eventually little Mawuli was laughing harder than anyone, even though he hadn't understood.

Christine's French was simple, restricted to the present tense and full of direct translations from her own language that didn't quite make sense at first. But among married village women, most of whom were without any education, she was one of the few who could communicate with me in French. Our conversations had drastic limitations and always seemed to arrive at a crucial moment, on the verge of some revelation, when language collapsed and left me hungry to know more. Not just language but also Christine's deep reserve and perhaps even my own impatient need to know erected walls daily. But we could speak a kind of French together, and that fact decided a great deal. She might have been simply my African landlady, instead of the person I came to know better than anyone else in Lavié.

Christine's French came from the market women of Abidjan, Ivory Coast, where the family had spent some years. She was a woman of real beauty: the high, shiny cheekbones that give some Africans an Oriental look; dark, underslept, abstracted eyes; a full and expressive mouth; skin the color of rosewood. At thirty-five, after nine children in fifteen years (a twin of Atsu had died), her body was thin and strong and exhausted. Sometimes when she wasn't wearing a scarf, and her long hair was unbraided and uncombed, she had a wild gypsy look. And something about that look, and her shouts during the day at the children, and the nighttime quarrels with Benjamin that I began to overhear, usually about money, and then the tired smile she put on for me the next morning, said that she wasn't happy here.

She was born in the mountain village of Agou, thirty kilometers by road on the other side of Kpalimé (Mount Agou, the highest point in Togo, was just visible from Lavié on clear days). Her parents died when she was small, and a dentist named Tutuaku and his wife, from Agou but living in Lomé, adopted her. So even though she grew up in the capital, with its automobiles and crowded markets, she was among her own. By puberty she was selling green oranges on the street, then took up sewing. If she had gone to school at all it was only for a year or two, and this was a source of bitterness. "Me, a teacher!" she once exclaimed. "If I went to school, today I can be a teacher. But."

But when she was still in her teens—a ripe age here—she met and married a taxi driver, followed him to his home village, and began producing children. She had an aunt in Lavié, but Christine was an outsider, and it seemed fitting that she lived in the house at the edge of the village. A few women always came by during the daytime to gossip for a while, but there wasn't the constant socializing in our yard that went on in other compounds. She was even scarce at Sunday church services and the all-night funeral dances that drew hundreds of villagers. Other village women, who wore simple *pagnes* tied round their waists and often left their breasts bare, were fleshy, hoarse from breathing smoke, and strong enough to throw me to the ground. Christine looked delicate, almost elegant, in her Goodwill lace camisole; and with me, at least, she had a soft, withdrawn air. Her neighbors called her by her African name, Abra, or else *"Lucien no"* ("mother of Lucien"), but she insisted I use the French name. She wasn't neurotically restless here, no Hedda Gabler among the mud huts; she wasn't, after all, a foreigner. Ewé was her language, and life hadn't shown her much besides children and hard work. But she seemed to hold back, as if this village weren't enough, weren't where she belonged. And almost from the beginning there was that bond between us.

The branch in the stove had died to a glowing coal. Mawuli was asleep with his head against Dové's back. Christine said, *"Ezado"*— "Night has arrived." She said it solemnly, like a formal end to the day. Lulled by the warm fire at my back and the sleepy faces around me, I'd been slipping into a trance.

Claudie, the ten-year-old, was nibbling at a piece of boiled manioc. That day I'd learned that the word for "manioc" was the same as their name, *agbeli*. Grasping my first chance to make a joke in Ewé, I said, *"Agbeli le agbeli dum"*—"Agbeli is eating *agbeli*."

Their faces were blank.

I pointed at the manioc in Claudie's hand. "Isn't this *agbeli*?"

"Ah!" Claudie exclaimed. *"Agbeli le agbeli dum!"* Now they had my joke and were laughing. Ewé, like Chinese, is a tonal language— to me it always sounded like a workingman's opera, music from the gullet—and one syllable, given ten inflections, can have ten different meanings. I'd mispronounced the word and changed its sense. Atsu set me straight.

"Our name isn't from manioc," he said. *"Agbeli* also means 'there is life.' "

Life happened mostly outside, in the dirt yard between the house and Christine's kitchen hut. Mother, children, and animals milled around in it all day and often slept in it at night. I once made an inventory of things scattered around the yard at the end of the day: a flowered enamel cooking pot with two peeled oranges in it, a peeled orange that had been sucked dry and thrown in the dust, a few pairs of shorts and dish towels hanging from the wire laundry line that stretched from the house to a thick branch planted in the dirt, a stool, two galvanized metal buckets and an enamel basin for fetching water and washing clothes, a knee-high mortar and two pestles leaning against the twisted sefofo tree by the house, a litter of blossoms fallen under the bougainvillea vine (they fell with any hard rain or wind, and the bougainvillea itself always looked as if it were on the verge of blowing off its crude trellis, and once did), an oil drum for catching rainwater off the corrugated roof, a piece of cloth lying in the dirt, scraps of notebook paper, one child's flip-flop. In the morning the yard was always clear again. The first sound outside my window at dawn, after the echo of roosters across the village, was Emma or Claudie or Atsu sweeping the yard, quick scrapes across the dirt with a bundle of straw.

If I had to make a list of all the family's possessions, it wouldn't be much longer than this yard inventory. I had been given two-thirds of the block house; the ten of them occupied one-third. No one in the family, no one in the village, ever suggested that this arrangement might be unfair. I had my living room, bedroom, kitchen, and a dank little spare room I found no use for, as well as a toilet stall and tiled shower. They had an oblong front room and two small bedrooms behind it; their latrine was at the side of the house, by the cistern—a seat of mud over a hole surrounded by a stick fence; their shower, for which they used buckets of water, was a slab of concrete, hidden by a screen of sticks, under the sefofo tree near the door. The smaller children washed themselves in the yard. Inside their three cramped rooms were two or three chairs, Benjamin's bed and mattress, the straw mats Christine and the children slept on, a couple of wicker baskets full of clean and dirty clothes, school notebooks lying in a heap. The prize possession, aside from his lame taxi, was Benjamin's shortwave radio. By village standards they were fortunate that the main house had a concrete floor, plaster walls, and wood doors. By every other standard available to me, they lived in squalor. Excluding the pieces of furniture, their belongings could fit in the trunk of a compact car.

When an exhibition of African masks and artifacts was mounted at Harvard University's Peabody Museum in 1986, I had the chance to make a rough comparison between Liberian village housewares from 1928 and a Togolese family's a little over half a century later. The comparison is worthless from almost any point of view, since it involves two different tribes and countries and considers nothing of trends or causes. So my interest was only personal when I noted how similar Christine's possessions would have looked alongside the artifacts in glass display cases. The difference between "Liberian 1928" and "Togolese 1982" would not have been in the quantity of items, or even in their quality and convenience, but in type. Next to Christine's enamel basin for carrying firewood (imported from Europe), her Dan or Mano counterpart's wood-and-straw apparatus; next to Christine's print *pagne* for carrying Aku on her back (imported from the Ivory Coast), a Liberian mother's backpack made of sticks and animal skin; next to Christine's kerosene lantern (imported from China, with kerosene from the West via Ghana), the Liberian's palm-oil lamp. Fifty-four years of development had replaced a set of locally made items with their imported counterparts.

But in the chores that filled every hour, day after day—collecting wood from the forest, chopping it, pounding *fufu*, cooking in dense smoke, washing clothes at the stream, carrying water from the stream—it was hard to imagine that anything had changed.

Nothing was ever wasted. Each child had two or three sets of stretched or ragged clothes, to which nothing new was added for a year. From scraps of worn-out cloth Christine sewed book bags for Atsu, Claudie, Markie, and Emma to take to school. My garbage never failed to turn up useful items. Before dumping it in the rubbish heap behind their kitchen, where it was pecked or nibbled by chickens and goats for weeks and then burned, one of the kids rescued an empty Quaker Oats can for storing corn flour, a nearly clean sheet of paper for homework, a moribund White Elephant battery for God knows what. A tin that had contained chocolate pudding from Cameroon metamorphosed into a tiny sailboat. Plastic bags bought at the market for seven cents carried things to next week's market.

At every market in Togo an area was set aside for the Goodwill

clothing brought in on ships from the West: faded jeans and corduroys with the ridges worn off, heaps of T-shirts announcing "Harvard Law" or "The Incredible Hulk," summer dresses, laceless
shoes without mates. The clothes fetched good prices for the men
who had paid bribes to oversee their unloading at the Lomé docks,
then for a succession of middlemen, and finally for the traders—
usually Moslems from the north or Niger—who sold them in the
villages. Charitable donations became the hottest fashion here.
Items as ridiculous as fur-lined winter hats with earflaps were
snatched up. Coming from overseas, they carried the prestige of the
yovo. In fact this minimarket had the name "dead *yovo* market"—
since no one still alive and in his right mind would actually give
away perfectly good clothes to people he didn't know and would
never get money or thanks from.

My garbage, and eventually my clothes, kitchenware, and a small
portion of my monthly allowance from Peace Corps, turned me into
the living "dead *yovo*" next door.

Next to the Agbelis I was fantastically rich—richer than I will
ever feel again. The extent of my wealth was probably inconceivable
to them, since even my two hundred dollars a month from Peace
Corps amounted to a peasant family's annual income. When Benjamin began to neglect his conjugal and fatherly responsibilities, my
eight dollars biweekly in exchange for laundry, sweeping, and two
meals a week filled the breach for food money. It was always received
with dignified gratitude. To me it seemed miserly. "Cross-culture"
had warned us about the perils of giving away money and having
poor Africans dependent on us. Eight dollars for a few tasks was
some sort of compromise between pay for service and patronization.
I knew it was either too little or too much. I'd never had this power
and responsibility; it awed and depressed me, and I didn't always
handle it well. Other villagers, and especially functionaries, with
whom there was less intimacy and less at stake, "borrowed" money
from me; when I left the country I had credits amounting to several
hundred dollars. Of course, we all knew it would never be paid
back, but we tacitly understood that the loan was a sham to keep
them from looking like beggars and me from looking like a sucker.

It dawned on me that few Togolese held any perceptible rancor against the whites who came into their country with government-issue Yamahas to lift Africans out of poverty. Traces of a self-mocking envy, perhaps, but no sense that it wasn't fair, let alone that our huge wealth had anything to do with their poverty. Even functionaries who had studied Marx at the Université du Benin and called themselves socialists didn't have the bitterness or insight or experience to translate theory into what they saw of white lives. It may be that they were too polite to show their feelings. But to the Togolese I knew—especially the villagers—wealth seemed natural to *yovos*, a part of our constitution, like stomach disorders and nasal voices.

And it was easy to forget how poor the people of Lavié were. A village—especially a village where you live for months on end—doesn't show its poverty like a city. Lomé, with its crowded shacks and canals full of gray bilge, always reminded me of African misery, mainly because there were steel-and-glass government ministries and whitewashed diplomatic residences within sight. Rural Alabama, the poorest region of the U.S., hadn't depressed me as the slums of New Haven had. The villagers of Lavié were poorer than shanty dwellers in Lomé, but after a while I didn't think of them as poor. Even the swarms of potbellied children stopped looking malnourished. Partly it was habituation, but it was also the physical appearance of rural life. Garbage was easy to hide and burn. The omnivorous bush provided most villagers with a latrine. And the village was a great leveler. I knew, intellectually, that a field laborer or a mason who made a little over a dollar for a day's backbreaking work suffered from extreme poverty. But when I saw him walking up the hill past my house at the end of the day, exchanged the evening greetings, and accepted a sip from his jug of palm wine, he wasn't one of the wretched of the earth but a village yeoman missing two teeth. Aside from my own strange presence, there was nothing to compare. Everyone lived in a small house, mud wasn't worse than concrete, thatch was actually cooler than iron. Anyone could clear a plot out in the bush. No one looked poor. And the villagers seemed happy.

. . .

There was life. That—at any rate, to an American raised on the LA Lakers, Shakespeare, and ice cream—was the incredible thing. Among the fallow wastes of the bush, the look-alike rectangular huts around look-alike dirt yards, the heat that began to burn at nine in the morning and only let up after you were asleep, the nutritionless blobs of manioc, the yellow-eyed scavengers, life was going on.

The village was laid out like this: A maze of houses, roofed with grass or corrugated iron but nearly all walled with mud, ran roughly west to east along either side of the Kpalimé-Atakpamé road for about a quarter of a mile, with no house farther back from the road than a hundred yards. A few families, most of them recent transplants from the north, lived in isolated clusters a mile or so down dirt tracks that meandered south through the flat grassy bush away from the road. On the northern side of the road, where the dirt was an orange clay, the plateau started almost where the village ended. There the last compounds began to rise and the paths between houses turned into trails that led up to fields on the mountainside, some an hour's walk away. The plateau—cool wet jungle rather than the grassland to the south—ran the length of the village, a shrug of earth coursing across lower Togo from Kpalimé to Atakpamé, southwest to northeast, and as far back as the great waterfalls around Badou and the Ghana border.

Electrical wires, draped with creepers, went through the village and powered the main towns along the road from Kpalimé to Atakpamé. Outside Lavié there was a hydroelectric plant where a corps of Yugoslavian engineers had dammed up the Kpimé waterfall in the fifties; the plant electrified much of southern Togo. But Lavié, only two miles away, was passed over by the wires and had no electricity—no running water, either. The U.S. Agency for International Development, with an engineer from Lavié named Ahonsu and a Peace Corps Volunteer, was planning a system of clean-water taps around the village, bringing down water by gravity in PVC pipes from two rivers on the plateau into two chlorinating cisterns, and from there through a network of metal pipes to twenty faucets. When I arrived, village men had just finished chain sawing trees and clearing brush above the village for the cisterns, and were hauling up planks to make forms for the concrete pour. But the work went sporadically, materials from Lomé were in short supply, and the taps didn't flow for another year. In the meantime, women and children lined up, mornings and evenings, with their buckets and basins at the slow streams that edged the village. The Agbelis were lucky to live next to the bush: they only had a fifty-yard walk for water.

It seemed to me when I arrived that, in this density of dwellings, with the tropical bush all around and always trying to encroach, two thousand villagers lived as they must have for decades or longer. The rhythm was simple. Sun gave way to dark, work to sleep; larger cycles—the yearly one between rain and dryness and then the cycle of a single lifetime—were made up of hundreds or thousands of repetitions of these daily ones, which never varied. The same smells of woodsmoke, wet mud, human sweat, and excrement; the same noises of roosters, squalling babies, *fufu* pounding, insects, the rare taxi speeding out of nowhere. The village hardly seemed touched by linear time, by history—or, more precisely, had bumped up against it once around the beginning of the century in the form of German and French colonizers, received the bruises of church, school, and dispensary, and gone unscathed ever since. In this stasis there was life, and life seemed to boil down to two things, almost indistinguishable from each other: commerce and chat.

At the crest of the hill up from our house, where the road curved toward the center of the village, people came to drink in the bistro, the only store in Lavié. There were two dark rooms and a counter where Bière du Benin, Coke, and Fanta were sold—cool if the refrigerator was working, warm if not—as well as batteries, soap, pens, eggs, and aspirin. Most of the patrons—men whiling away the hot mornings, or drinking off fatigue at the end of a day in the field—couldn't afford the bottled drinks and took shots of distilled palm wine from a green glass jug. The walls were decorated with the usual "Guinness Is Good for You" soccer posters. Two brothers owned the place—one a primary school teacher, the other a man named Kodjo. Kodjo was not only uneducated but also one of the few truly stupid people I knew in Lavié. It took ten minutes to buy a drink from this man. After punching a few buttons on his calculator, he would mumble that the thing didn't work, add up my two bottles of beer on a scrap of paper, take my money, and then come knocking at my door fifteen minutes later to tell me he'd counted the change wrong, and listen dully as I showed him that he'd been correct in the first place. His wife Yawa really ran the store. Kodjo had two wives, but Yawa, a brittle woman, spoke French and could add on the calculator, so naturally she became the storekeeper. Whenever I came in and asked after her health, she smacked her lips and shook her head that she wasn't well. Kodjo and Yawa reminded me of the couple in the film noir *The Postman Always Rings Twice*—the amiable, dim shopkeeper and his clever, trapped wife stewing behind the desk.

The bistro was an outpost of progress; the village market antedated everything. This cluster of shaggy grass shelters stood empty all week, looking like a browsing herd of small woolly mammoths. But every Friday it came alive and swarmed with villagers, women from other towns who arrived by taxi and unloaded sacks crammed with yams, fruit, and basins full of cornmeal, women from the remote plateau villages who jogged down the hill trails before the sun came up, babies on backs and goods in baskets on heads, traded all day, and jogged back up at dusk, three or four dollars' worth of change jangling in their knotted *pagnes*, empty baskets on their heads, babies still asleep on their backs. At the peak of the market, around noon, when it filled with schoolchildren, you could hardly walk the paths between the stalls. Little girls circled with plastic buckets on their heads shrieking, *"Etsi glacé!"* ("Ice water!") Big smiling women, heads tied in scarves and breasts stretched halfway around back by the mouth of a baby, dangled the crusty carcasses of dried fish from Lomé—*"Akpe, akpe, akpe!"* Palm oil, thick and blood red, was ladled from vats into old rum bottles. One corner of the market was for manioc and yams, another for sacks of charcoal. Next to the dead *yovo* clothes a fetish priest spread out his *grigri* on the ground, jackal pelts and bird skulls and snakeskins, which gave off the sharp stench of dead animal. Everywhere the cries of women hawking goods and arguing prices, the heavy smell of cooking oil, the chatter of men who spent the day at a woman's drink stall swallowing calabashes of sweet, frothy palm wine and fermented millet beer amid a swarm of flies and laying bets on a game of lots.

Western politicians and economists have recently been saying that the salvation of African economies lies in the free-market ideology to which they are traditionally so suited. Before they incorporate all of their ideas into loan guidelines, these policy makers might visit the market in Lavié on a Friday. They would see five women sitting side by side, all selling bowls of the same cornmeal, at the same price, chatting, laughing, nursing, and making change for each other all day, never undercutting prices or otherwise trying to make their own cornmeal more desirable. Curiously, bread women were the only ones who competed, but even this marketing never went beyond shouts of *"Monsieur, monsieur*, buy my bread, what's wrong with my bread?"* Aside from the bread women, the only recognizable bit of free enterprise was the astronomical price quoted by every seller to whites, often four times the standard price. I got wise to this practice fairly quickly, and eventually it stopped. A lot of money changed hands on Fridays, but more than anything else the market was Lavié's weekly social occasion: a sort of shopping center, bar, restaurant, pool hall, and ladies' club packed under one cluster of grass roofs.

At least once a week I had a ritual conversation in Ewé with one of the unmarried market girls, a flirtation whose rules and script we both knew:

"Monsieur, what do you want?"

"Give me fifty francs of onions."

"Here, take these."

"These, for fifty francs? Do you think I don't know the prices?"

"It's the correct price!"

"No, it's too expensive. You ask this price because I'm a *yovo*."

"Never! It's the same price, *yovo, ameyibo. Monsieur*, you understand Ewé like this?"

"I try."

"It's good, it's good. Where is your wife?"

"No wife."

"No wife? Then let's get married."

"Us?"

"You and me. You don't like me?"

"I do, I do. When?"

"Tomorrow, Saturday."

"I'll see you in the church at eight o'clock."

"Here's one more onion for free—because you try."

Selling and socializing didn't stop when the market emptied on Friday at dusk. They continued all week, day and night. At midday, during the dead hours when shutters were closed and courtyards empty except for goats licking the pots left out from the noon meal, old men dozed in the shade on a rock outside the bistro. Facing them across the road, women sat under palm fronds and peeled green oranges while their babies slept at their feet. In the late afternoon, when the men woke up, the two knots of villagers—one male, the other female—drank and chatted on opposite sides of the road, indifferent to each other. Even after most people were asleep, a few women sat up in the public place—a dirt shoulder off the paved road across from the bistro—and huddled together around little tables by the light of paraffin flames, selling matches, pills, or cigarettes to people up late.

It didn't take long to see that women were the lifeblood of the village, not just in the chores they labored at but in their devotion to the ceaseless ritual of commerce and chat.

One evening not long after my arrival, I was walking down the hill toward my house when I heard a voice call out of the darkness of one of the yards: *"Fo Georgie! Va!"* A husky, smoke-scarred woman's voice. Complying, I stepped off the road.

At the back of the yard, separated from mine by bushes and bamboo shoots and a half-built cinder-block house, Ama was stirring a great black pot like a witch's caldron over burning wood. In it was cornmeal boiled into thick, stiff mush—after *fufu*, the village staple. Nearby she'd arranged her wares in a flowered enamel tray on a flimsy table: Gauloise and Marlboro cigarettes, in boxes and singly, bottles of aspirin, sugar cubes, canned pilchards, decongestants, a rum bottle filled with kerosene, another with distilled palm wine.

"*Fo Georgie,*" she repeated without looking up from the fire, "*nu-kata me va gbonye o?*"

I shook my head. In French I said I didn't understand. With mild disgust she pointed to her ear and flicked her finger in the air, as if to say, "How the hell am I supposed to understand your words?" She called out, "Etienne!" and a round-faced boy with startled eyes ran over to interpret.

"She says why haven't you come to greet her, *monsieur.*"

Ama said something else at length, indicating me with the wooden spoon, to which corn mush stuck.

"She says you are her neighbor and you must come introduce yourself. Have you heard something about her in the village, that she is not a good woman?"

I assured her I hadn't heard a thing. I'd been busy—just arrived—getting ready for school—no time yet. I was sorry.

Her son translated; she listened. "Hmm." Then, smiling for the first time, she told me I would have to do better in the future. I promised I would. She invited me to stay for corn mush.

Ama was Christine's sister-in-law. Her husband, the oldest of the Agbeli brothers, was a gaunt drunk who had a beat-up Toyota wagon into which he crammed illegal numbers of passengers and bounced them between Lavié and Kpalimé. Ama, at half his age, was about as old as Christine. From the neck up, Ama looked younger—she had a teen-ager's shiny round face and open expression—but her body had gone ahead fifteen or twenty years: short, heavy, and powerful, with the shoulders and biceps of a halfback, thick girth, vast bottom, and a walk that was somewhere between a waddle and a swagger. Unlike Christine she never bothered to cover her breasts, which were large and sagged halfway down her belly; but, in keeping with tradition, she almost always kept her head covered by a scarf. The most striking thing about her was her voice—deep, hoarse, throaty. When she spoke I could smell woodsmoke.

She cultivated me as friend and pupil. The first evening wasn't the last time I gave Ama offense. Periodically, if I missed a day or two, she would reproach me and demand to know if some gossip was filling my ear with poison about her. These lapses had to be atoned for with a loaf of bread from Kpalimé, or better yet, a bottle of Bière du Benin at the bistro: two missed days, two loaves, two bottles. Her interest in me had the smothering, chiding quality of a mother. She pressed me with invitations to supper and then nagged me to eat more, corrected my Ewé grammar and insisted I give the greetings in the proper order. My ignorance and lack of village tact led her to pin a name on me that stuck: I was *akla*—"bold," according to a teacher I asked, with suggestions of irreverence and even uncouthness. "If a head of state appears in public in his tennis shorts and knee socks," the teacher analogized, "they will call him *akla*." But since I was a *yovo* and didn't know any better, Ama took me in hand to instruct me in village ways.

She spent every waking minute selling or preparing things to sell— a tireless and remarkably successful *commerçante*. She rose at four every morning to boil rice and sold it between five and seven in the public place to students going to school and farmers setting out for their fields. During the hot hours she wove mats under a tree. In the evening, while she prepared dinner, a constant stream of passersby stopped to exchange the endless greetings and buy a cigarette, aspirins, or a shot of local gin from her enamel tray. On Saturdays she walked fifteen kilometers into Kpalimé for the immense outdoor market with a basinful of bananas on her head. She always had kerosene on hand in vats and rum bottles, in case the Ghana border closed and the Texaco station in Kpalimé ran out; she resold it at 50 percent profit. Once a month a local driver who made the daily trip to Lomé and back dropped off sacks of frozen South American steaks, which Ama cut up and grilled to sell on wood skewers. And somehow, when Christine had to buy food at the market and feed her children corn mush three times a day, Ama had enough manioc and yams from her own field throughout the dry season to make *fufu* and invite me over.

I once asked her about this. She reminded me that she had only four children to Christine's eight, and then explained that she planted her crops up on the plateau, a four- or five-kilometer hike along steep paths, where it rained better.

My explanation was more theoretical. Ama belonged to the village. She was born here, had family here. Lavié, with its unchanging patterns of cooking and talking and selling and sleeping, was enough for her. She wasted no energy chafing against the village because she was incapable of imagining any other life. She had never been the hundred kilometers to Lomé, much less Abidjan. She had the one word of mangled French even the octogenarian women knew—*Bonzoo!*—and one other, *Frigidaire*. It seemed to me that, in a sort of mystical way, her crops succeeded because Ama was profoundly attuned to the rhythm of life here. It was out of the confidence of this grounding, this centeredness, that she took me in hand and tried to make a villager of me. With Ama I was "Fo Georgie" from the start. Though her existence was constant drudgery she seemed content, laughed easily, was never alone.

The contrast with her sister-in-law, Christine, wasn't lost on me. Ama was like manioc, coarse and rooted in the village clay; Christine was like our bougainvillea, a transplanted flower, buffeted here. Over time a jealousy arose between them. When I came home from one of my first suppers at Ama's house, Christine was waiting for me in the yard.

"*Monsieur*, it's late, the night has come. Where were you?"

"Da Ama invited me to eat her food."

"You ate her food?" She smiled. "You won't eat mine anymore?"

"No, of course I will. But she invited me. Could I refuse?"

For an answer she gave a sarcastic snort. After that I was more careful. I made sure to bring back two loaves of bread from Kpalimé; and while Ama seemed to accept that Christine was closer to me, Christine could hardly tolerate the competition. We defused the tension by making light of it.

"If you eat Ama's food again," she would laugh, shaking her fist and rolling her eyes like Medea, "I will tear her hair out!"

I taunted her: "*Jalouse! Jalouse!*"

Ama's brother, Kumavi, was as typical of village men as Ama was of women, and at the heart of his typicality lay alcohol.

It was difficult to know how much booze the average village male consumed. Between calabashes of palm wine, shots of the gin distilled from it, and—on special occasions—bottles of beer at the bistro, it must have been something close to a half gallon a day. Some of the farmers and the older men—even if they spent the day working the fields—began drinking before the sun was hot, reached a peak of consumption when they stopped working during the dead hours, hit another peak when they returned home in early evening, and only stopped when they went to bed. For some the drinking, like their wives' selling, served as the rhythmic drumbeat to their lives. Yet I hardly ever saw anyone plastered. Alcohol saturated them until they sweated it, breathed it, and stank it, but their tolerance was tremendous, and getting smashed didn't seem to be the goal. They were after a kind of constant buzz, a mild stupor, perhaps like the Colombian farmers who chew coca leaves.

Other men concealed their boozing well, but with Kumavi it was apparent the moment I laid eyes on him. He looked a little like a *fou*, a village idiot: his shirt and trousers were always filthy and in tatters, his jaw was unshaven, and most strikingly, his eyes were a mass of broken blood vessels. Yet he spoke French and never slurred or stumbled. Whenever he looked at me I had the uncomfortable feeling that he was implicating me in some secret I didn't care to know about. His look and smile—unlike those of *fous*, who usually seemed benign—were faintly sinister. They seemed to say, "There's no use denying it, you know as well as I do what's going on." I never learned exactly what was going on, but I didn't stop believing he had a secret; and in the humid heat my imagination conjured up a scenario of Kumavi selling his soul to one of the forest gods in exchange for a lifetime's flow of palm wine and gin. Privately I dubbed him "Faustus."

The first time I met him was at Ama's. He was handling a boa he'd killed in the bush. A fire was going in Ama's clay stove, a spit set up over it, and Faustus was about to open the snake's belly with his cutlass. The thing was five feet long and at least a foot in circumference. He caressed the limp body the way you handle a prized rifle.

Without a greeting he said to me, *"On va la couper."*

He cut. It sounded like a steak knife ripping gristle. Blood welled up in the gash, and out of the swollen white belly a mass of eggs emptied onto the dirt, thirty or forty of them, the size of golf balls, floating in a yellow ooze. He placed the tip of the cutlass against an egg and punctured it. A sliver of a snake, no bigger than a worm, slipped out and began wriggling in panic at this rude birth; the cutlass descended and sliced it in two. I wondered if he would open all the eggs and then fry up the little black strings together as an hors d'oeuvre. But apparently his interest was only biological; he scraped the mass aside, and the eggs rolled away and collected a coat of dirt. Then Faustus cut off the mother's head.

"On va la manger."

While the gutted carcass was roasting on the spit, he explained that the head would be used in a ceremony. When I asked to attend, he laughed. This was not for *yovos*, or for women. And in fact Ama, turning the snake on the spit, was clucking and repeating, "Bad. Men are bad because they eat snake meat." Perhaps she found the whole thing as repulsive as I did, or perhaps she believed in the snake cult that still flourished around Lomé and the coastal region: the snake god's priests were women. I declined Faustus's offer of a morsel. In Togo I ate bat, bush rat lungs, bush rodent, even anteater, but I never overcame, as I'd hoped I would, my fear of snakes; it only intensified. Faustus ate with relish, tearing chunks of flesh from the skin, which he held with both hands like corn on the cob.

At the end of his meal Faustus said to me, "Tomorrow you will come see where I make s.d.b." The conspirator's grin. I accepted; I didn't ask what s.d.b. was.

We set out late the next afternoon—Faustus, Ama, Etienne, a few other children, and me. The forest began at the village's edge; off the road, any sign of human presence disappeared almost at once. Going out of Lavié east toward Atakpamé we had the plateau on the left; to the right, an expanse of grassy bush, an occasional baobab or palm, and the fantastic peaks of clay termite hills, like Gaudí's church spires, twenty feet high. It had rained, one of the last storms of the year, and the light, coming in low under the late-day clouds, washed the hillside in a pearly clarity and cast long shadows across the road, where branches and vines hung.

In the other direction, toward Kpalimé, monkeys inhabited the cliff above the hydroelectric plant, but here we only had snakes, birds, and bugs. The air was dense like gas and buzzed with insects. Men returning from the fields passed us and raised their cutlasses, their one and only tool, in greeting. At the crest of a hill a few men were lounging under a spreading tree next to a display of souvenirs— wooden statuettes, woven grass bags, miniature *fufu* mortars—intended for tourists who might happen by, though in all my months in Lavié I didn't witness a single sale. After a half mile we left the road and climbed a path up the plateau. Faustus thrashed with his cutlass at twigs and grass; the trail, overgrown, was treacherous with rocks and tree roots. Though the sun had already started to set, my shirt clung with sweat to my back. After a few hundred yards the ground leveled off. We came out into a clearing, a grove of cacao trees with unripe purple pods and banana trees with leaves hanging out of the middle like enormous tongues.

We were standing in front of a distillery.

Under a makeshift thatch roof a fifty-five-gallon drum was being fired with wood from below. A rubber hose ran out the top into another drum and continued on to a third; a small hose hung out of the last into the neck of a green glass jug, the kind men carried back on their heads at night to sell to Kodjo and Yawa at the bistro. Plugged with a cotton filter, the jug was collecting a trickle of distillate. The whole grove had the medicinal smell of raw liquor.

Beyond the still a pair of toothless, bleary-eyed old men lay among fallen palm trees, a gourd of wine between them. The palm trunks were bristling with reeds like the backs of bulls about to be slaughtered; the reeds had been inserted into holes to extract the wine. The old men lifted their calabashes and greeted us: *"Woezo!"* Amused by my presence, they insisted I sit between them and have a drink.

Palm wine flowed, the color of soapy dishwater. We all drank. It was a sweet, heavy batch. Flies buzzed around the lip of the gourd and floated in the surface foam. A flick of the full calabash got rid of the fly bodies and gave the ancestors their portion of wine in the same motion. I'd heard that the puddle's configuration in the dirt could be read like tea leaves to divine the future. When I asked him to read mine, Faustus stared at me and didn't answer.

We drank another calabash, and another. A glass jug was produced. Distilled palm wine is as close to grain alcohol as anything you can legally buy in the West—sickly sweet on the tongue, fire going down. With each swallow my throat rose. I chased gin with palm wine to clear the taste, and sat back against the palm trunk, looking up in the gathering dusk at the cacao trees, which slowly revolved against the sky.

Faustus was explaining how the gin got its name.

"The first white man from Ghana came here. He was English and when the Ewé gave him some s.d.b. to drink he made a face and said in his own English, 'So dat be. So dat be.' These Ewé were ignorant. They never heard any English before. And afterward, they always called it '*sodabi.*' In Ewé it is the same: *kpetessi.* But we don't use the Ewé. We say *sodabi*, s.d.b."

Except for the children, we were all drunk. I'd gone beyond the mild stupor permissible in the village, but out here it didn't seem to matter. We were in the bush; the rules didn't apply. And night was coming fast anyway. The sun was going down over Ghana, a perfect orange sphere in the heat mist. It would touch the horizon, and five minutes later everything would be dark. I lay in a daze, listening to Faustus and to the sounds of the woods. The branches were moving with creatures, hundreds of Faustus's snakes.

At night the forest filled with spirits. Every tree housed one; they lurked in the elephant grass and the hollow of dead palm trunks. Christine once told me of the god who wandered the woods outside our yard. She wouldn't pronounce his name after dark, but she told me that he could change shape from dwarf to giant, that his face was hideously scarred, that he gave you the pox, that you heard the *clop-clop* of his feet whenever he crossed the paved road, and that if you went into the woods at night and met him, he would stare you down until you were sick with confusion, lost your memory, could never find your way back home. As she spoke the children

listened in terrified silence. Whistling, or dragging a rope, or anything that might attract him at night, was forbidden. In daylight
Christine was willing to tell me this god's name: Sakpaté.

I was now about ready to believe. It didn't take a child or a neurotic
or an urge to go native to think the trees might be inhabited. An-
imism is the triumph of night over the mind. When the darkness
was total the woods closed around us. Even here, in the bush, there
was life, but at night it was inhuman, wild, threatening. It couldn't
be ignored, but as long as you stayed among people, in the village,
and respected the dead, they watched over you. The night traveler,
the man who abandoned his village for Lomé, or Abidjan, or the
yovo's country, was a lost soul.

Faustus made his liquor with palm wine, fire, and the forest spirits.
His alchemy worked because he believed. Bush, snakes, ancestors,
sodabi, spirits were all in collusion with him, bound up in a single
world alive with potential for good or evil, healing or sorcery. This
was his conspiracy: just this village I had come to. He and Ama
lived in its rhythm. Drunk, I lay there with them and waited for it
to overcome me.

I stood up. It was pitch-dark, and the *sodabi* was wearing off. What
was happening? I might have slept. Or Sakpaté might have found
me and led me astray. But hadn't he found me once already—led
me here, to Africa? How did the night traveler get back home?

Somehow we found our way to the village. Christine scolded me.
The woods were not fit for men at night. Didn't I see now that Ama
was not a good woman? She would tear her hair out! I collapsed on
the straw mattress as my lamp threw spidery shadows against the
walls.

In *Out of Africa* Isak Dinesen writes of Kenya: "Up in this high
air you breathed easily, drawing in a vital assurance and lightness
of the heart. In the highlands you woke up in the morning and
thought: 'Here I am, where I ought to be.' " Of my five-hundred-
odd mornings in the Togolese highlands I woke up hung over,
bathed in sweat, hungry, blowing on an extinguished lamp instead
of turning off my alarm, mildly at ease, or mildly anxious. But never
where I ought to be.

CHAPTER 3

Khaki and Goatskin

 HAD COME TO TEACH. FIVE DAYS AFTER ARRIVING IN Lavié, armed with a few rough lesson plans sketched in a thin copybook and a map of the U.S. from the American Cultural Center in Lomé, I drove my Peace Corps–issue moped off the *yovomo* onto a rutted trail, past the chants of the primary school, and into the grounds of the Collège d'Enseignement Général.

It was 6:45 A.M. The entire school was assembled on the field, the students in rows facing a flagpole, the dozen teachers in a knot to one side, under the mango tree outside the principal's office. Seeing me, a few teachers waved.

It was not yet hot but clear it was going to be. The grounds of the school were a rough terrain of dirt, cut grass, and fringes of shoulder-high grass that had grown up over the summer and not been cut back. The woods encroached on the far end of the grounds and seemed about to catch three adjacent classrooms of one building in its tangled branches and creepers. The buildings were ranged haphazardly over the terrain: three long cinder-block structures with window and door openings but no windows or doors, and corrugated iron roofs breaking out with rust. A pair of open-air thatch shelters stood alone in a field. The entrance to the principal's office next to one of the cinder-block buildings was paved with concrete and lined with flowers; behind the office stood a rutted dirt basketball court with a pair of netless hoops tilting precariously.

"Attention for the mounting of the colors!" a boy yelled as the sound of my moped died. Another boy began yanking a rope to raise the green, red, and yellow Togolese flag. I got off to lock my bike next to a Suzuki and a Kawasaki with a sticker on its gas tank: "Fifteen Years of Peace," it read, the words forming a halo over the image of President Eyadema in military dress.

Three hundred and fifty voices, so quiet I didn't hear them begin, were singing the national anthem. "La Togolaise" has a sweet melody, a little like the French children's song "Alouette," oddly free of the bombast of most anthems. The voices rose and fell:

> *Si nous sommes divisés,*
> *Nos ennemis nous vaincront . . .*

They stood, splashed by the pink light of early morning, in a dozen neat rows of twenty or thirty, a sea of khaki. Every boy wore khaki trousers and a long- or short-sleeved khaki shirt; with their flared collars and epaulettes, they looked like a troop of underage black recruits for some European desert battalion. Every girl wore a khaki skirt—which fell below the knees, sometimes to the ankles—and a white blouse. The girls' uniforms gave an inch of room for variety, and those girls from families with a bit more money than the village norm could display it with lace frills around the bodice and on puffed sleeves, a pair of gold earrings from Ghana, imitation-leather shoes from the Bata store in Kpalimé instead of the usual flip-flops. But hair plaiting was forbidden. The general impression that the rows and rows of students gave was egalitarian, uniform, dull. Most girls wore simple blouses or even white T-shirts.

Few collections of Americans this age—about eleven to twenty—could stand scrutiny in the sun, lightly dressed, and come off looking as good as these. Somehow the swarms of village kids with rounded bellies and skinny limbs—the ones who survived childhood—turned into boys with rock-hard stomachs and shapely girls. But the striking thing about them was the variety of sizes. Girls with full bosoms and hips towered over flat-chested prepubescents, boys under five feet stood in line with young men who looked like stevedores. It was hard to guess which line was the youngest class, the *6ème*, and which the oldest, the *3ème*.

Peasants sent their children to begin school as late as the early teens, after years of fieldwork. Once here, they were routinely flunked, even twice or three times a grade. The *doublants* and *triplants* had the bored, slightly mocking looks of the disgraced; they stuck out among their diminutive classmates as if their larger size were the mark of shame. In the older classes, success was visible in the small bodies of a few kids who had started early and whipped through without flunking (at least one-quarter were in the family of Monsieur Amouzou, the government coffee and cacao agent). Technically speaking, there was no such thing as a *quadruplant*: three tries and you were out, back in the fields. But a few students lingered for the fourth time around; they were known by less neutral-sounding names, like *idiot* and *voyou*.

The singing stopped. An expectant murmur stirred among the rows. The students were all looking toward the mango tree, where Aboï, clad in the functionary's synthetic pants and matching short-sleeved jacket, was emerging from the shade. In one hand he held a yard-long whip, two strips of lightly furred goatskin twisting around each other and ending in two tails; in the other, a sheet of paper. He walked out into the center of the field, burly chest upthrust, and addressed the students. It was the same bureaucrat's voice I remembered from the night of my arrival, and the same slightly dull peasant's face, with the front teeth protruding.

It seemed there had been a soccer game in which several of the older boys had gotten into fights. These fights were a blight on the esteemed reputation of the school, he said in his stiff French; they could not be permitted, nor go unpunished. The boys would be persuaded not to repeat them. He read a few names off his paper. From one of the rows, four boys about sixteen years old stepped out. Aboï approached them, grabbed a short, broad-shouldered boy by the collar, and yanked him forward. The boy put up his hands to cover his face, but he didn't shrink away or cry out when Aboï brought the whip down in four hard blows across his shoulders and arms. The snap of goatskin on flesh broke the morning silence and carried over to me, alone next to Aboï's office a hundred feet away. A few students gasped, others tittered. Aboï's face had come alive, it was wild-eyed and furious.

When the boy had taken the blows, he retreated back into line and smiled weakly at his friends. The same punishment was delivered to the other three. A smaller boy cried out and limped back into line holding his thigh and turning an injured glare back at the principal. The others seemed to have a code of stoical silence. In line they shrugged at their classmates, shook their heads, made light of it.

When the offenders had been punished, Aboï went back to the middle of the field. No one made a sound. He read out another list of names, and his face and voice were neutral again, as if the violence of a moment ago had been unreal. These names were the *retardataires*, the latecomers. A sprinkling of students, about eight in all, slunk out from the rows and edged toward Aboï. He met them with his muscled arm raised. Fury had materialized again on his face: it looked real enough.

The goatskin whipped through the air and found flesh. *Snap!* A girl screamed and broke into frantic wails. The others abandoned their stoicism and scattered, and Aboï had to chase them, his whip raining down blows on whatever it could reach—backs, arms, buttocks. One little girl with gold hoops in her ears, who couldn't have been more than eleven, started to plead, "No, *monsieur*—" *Snap!* The goatskin lashed across her arms. Aboï was hoarse with rage. "This will teach you to come on time!" She staggered off in tears. He had wheeled around to find the others, and his last lashes skimmed the khaki skirts of two girls scurrying away like beaten dogs.

He went back to the middle of the field. Within seconds the rubber-stamp voice had returned: assembly dismissed, everyone to class. The lines broke up and the students chatted their way across the field toward their classrooms. The teachers, who had been talking among themselves throughout the beatings, gathered their books and left the shade of the mango tree.

What unnerved me, even more than the hard lashes and the girls' screams, was the way Aboï switched his anger on and off. Every blow packed the force of rage, as if he were avenging the murder of a sister and not three minutes' tardiness. And then, before he'd caught his breath, he was the bureaucrat again. The beatings seemed a ritual, an addendum to the flag raising and anthem singing. The students looking on had treated the spectacle indifferently or as a joke. I wondered if this happened every morning. I wondered, too, if it was part of the curriculum Aboï had studied at the Ecole Normale Supérieure.

He was approaching me, casually trailing the whip down by his calf. "Monsieur Packer," he called out, smiling. "Welcome to CEG Lavié, Monsieur Packer. You permit me to call you Georges? Eh—" The smile broadened uncertainly. "Next time, please, Georges, attention during the national anthem. I noticed you were locking your moped while the children were singing. They might misinterpret you."

The image came before I could block it out: the vengeful shout, the arm raised, the snap of the whip across my shoulders.

My first day was not a success. Peace Corps had armed me, but not for this. In my bedroom I had a cardboard box full of instructor's manuals, model dialogues, word games. I had ten weeks of pedagogy and six weeks of experience teaching practice classes in Atakpamé to a self-selected bunch of town kids, who came for the prizes handed out at summer's end and perhaps the oddity of a new shipment of white teachers—students who, in any case, wanted to be there. After each class, trainers and trainees would huddle and, on a scale of one to five, evaluate the day's lesson for voice, organization, body language, and use of blackboard.

I was well aware of my potential for irrelevance. In 1982 reports of drought and hunger were already trickling through obscure channels of information, and my other impressions of contemporary Africa—repression in South Africa, massacre in Uganda, civil war in Angola—didn't lead me to conclude that the thing the continent needed most was a Renaissance studies major who could teach the relative pronoun. But the Togolese government seemed to consider American English teachers in its national interest and had already persuaded Peace Corps not to cancel the program once. My group would be the last. After us Peace Corps would limit itself to teacher-trainers, according to the philosophy in development circles of not duplicating and displacing local workers.

After a half hour at CEG Lavié I doubted I had the upper-body strength to duplicate or displace anyone. And I had already decided—or rather, I already knew, in my liberal bones—that I would not use corporal punishment in my classes. I clung to the vague idea that I might be able to earn my keep if I brought some of the values of my own education to receptive students in the classroom: independent thinking, self-motivation, love of learning. I hadn't come to spend two years with a whip in one hand and a pen in the other, demanding: "What's this? Repeat: It's a pen!"

And so, smiling and sweating and flushing green, I was led by Aboï into my four classrooms—floors deep in dirt, bamboo rafters exposed under the metal roofs, a charcoal blackboard caked with so much chalk that it was ash gray, the bush just outside one wall and starting to come in through the window openings. In each class a boy slapped his hand on his desk as we entered, and forty or fifty children in khaki, sitting in pairs on benches at crude wooden desks, rose to attention. In each class Aboï informed the wide-eyed, whispering students that they were extremely fortunate at last to have their new American teacher, who was going to teach them correct English and whom they would respect—a tap of the goatskin against his calf—as they did their other teachers. If there was any trouble I should report it to him. In each class I delivered a thirty-minute speech I'd prepared in French on the benefits they would receive from learning English—the international language of commerce, the language of their neighbors, Ghana and Nigeria, the language written on cans of Quaker Oats and boxes of macaroni in the market; they would also have the chance to discover new cultures, a new world, new ways of thinking. . . .

Each class met me with the same blank, puzzled, or amused

stares. My call for questions was answered with the same minute of silence. One boy ventured that he wanted to be a farmer when he grew up, and his classmates laughed and jeered; another, indicating my map, asked what the surface area of the USA was and where my mother lived. My mother lived in California, I remembered that. The surface area of the USA? Was that square kilometers, or square miles? Well—I was an English teacher, not a geography teacher. Did he know the surface area of Togo?

"Fifty-six thousand square kilometers," answered a chorus of voices.

At noon, my button-down shirt wringing wet and my right hand covered with chalk as if I'd dipped it in a jar of flour, I rode the moped home for lunch, reflecting that perhaps I'd been a little too abstract and trying to remember what I'd come here to teach anyway.

"Good morning, Mistah Puckuh!"

"Good morning, class. How are you today?"

"I'm fine, thanks. And YOU?"

"I'm fine. Sit down, please. Who knows the date today?"

Hands shoot up. "I! I! I!"

"Yes? Adjo?"

Adjo, fourteen, the chief's niece, with high cheekbones and side-long glances at her girl friends, slowly stands in the second row.

"Today—ees—Wesday—Novembah—threeth—1982."

"Any mistakes?"

"Oh, I, I!"

"Simkundu?"

Simkundu, an effeminate Kabyé boy with a mole above his lip, gets up confidently. "Novembah *thud.*"

"Adjo?"

"Novembah *thud.*"

Adjo takes my chalk and goes to scratch the date across the blackboard.

For a year, sixteen classes a week started with this routine.

Difficulties surfaced fairly quickly. There was the problem of names. The Togolese teachers called students by their last names, but after a week of stumbling over the Agbodjavous, Amegawovors, and Kpetsus who proliferated in my classes, I broke custom (far from the last time) and went to first names. But here was the rub: among the Ewé your first name is determined by the day of the week you're born on. For example, a boy born on Wednesday is Kokou, a girl Aku; a boy born on Saturday is Kwamé, a girl Ama. So the pool of first names is severely limited, and in every class there were bound to be at least three or four of each name. In one class eight Koffis all sat in the same row. It was hard enough to keep the names straight, another problem altogether to get across which Koffi or Afi I wanted an answer from.

Then there were the copybooks. In the almost complete absence of textbooks, these lined notebooks became the students' lifelines. They also seemed to take the place of thinking. In their copybooks students wrote down with the care of medieval scribes every word their teacher deemed important enough to utter. Enter a mistake in one and it might never get corrected; lose one and a student might as well quit school. I once had to correct a geography teacher's exam. One of Kafui's questions was *"Qu'est-ce que le Nil?"* ("What is the Nile?") In response, every student wrote: *"Le Nil est loin des plus grands fleuves du monde"*—a piece of nonsense translating to "The Nile is far from the biggest rivers in the world." I had marked twenty-five answers wrong before I understood the mistake. The class had thought she said *"loin des plus grands"* instead of *"l'un des plus grands"* ("one of the biggest . . .") and duly inscribed the mistake in their copybooks. The sentence had gone from mouth to copybook to exam like a defective product moving along an automated assembly line. Kafui laughed at the error, at the students' stupidity—but not at the system that wanted mimicry without thought. They should have listened better, she said.

But for two months I forbade copybooks. In training we'd learned to start with just spoken English, and it seemed a good idea. No English copybooks, then; and the kids responded like snails whose shells have been snatched off by a sadistic boy.

Finally, discipline.

One morning in November we were on the present progressive

tense of the verb *to look at*. I walked up and down the columns of
desks. "I'm *looking at* Afi. I'm *looking at* Kodjo. I'm *looking at* the
window."

I had my fingers around my eyes like glasses, widening my eye-
balls like a man possessed as I stared at Afi, Kodjo, the window.
They were in hysterics. Such moments teetered perilously between
good feeling and chaos. Aware of the risks, I still felt I'd gained
enough control over the class to try an experiment in putting on.

Suddenly a young boy on the left, sleepy-eyed and long-necked,
stood and shouted:

"*Yovo, yovo, bonsoir!*"

The laughter didn't die down, it was shut off in a second. The
boy, Kodjo, stood there as the smile dissolved on his face and gave
way to horror and disbelief. He was as stunned as everyone else.
He hadn't spoken the words, they had burst out of him, a memory
from early childhood, village talk, erupting in the classroom; and in
this setting they had the shock effect of profanity. And yet he was
right. I had been acting like a *yovo*, which is to say exotic, bizarre
compared with the other teachers and their harsh or monotonous
lectures—*akla*, Ama would have said. I had broken the rules. Now
anything went, and for an instant Kodjo became a five-year-old again.

He was sinking back onto the bench, his mouth still half open,
his eyes weakly watching me. Gasps and murmurs rippled across
the classroom. I knew I would have to punish him. If I didn't, the
veneer of authority would crack even more and the class might be
lost for good. It had happened to the American woman here before
me. I wasn't going to let softness ruin a year of teaching. Besides,
I was furious, though I tried mightily not to blow up. His name for
me had triggered the vulnerable anger that lay beneath the surface
of even the most placid African days. I ordered him to go outside
and stand in the sun for the rest of the class.

Fifteen minutes later Asamoa, the aging, bespectacled Ghanaian
English teacher, came by, whip in hand. He was *professeur de semaine*
this week, in charge of discipline. From the doorway he motioned
me over.

"Good morning, Mr. Packer. What has that boy over there done?"

He pointed with the whip at the transgressor standing on the grass.

The truth had already embarrassed me enough. "He was talking during the lesson."

"With your permission I would like to beat him."

"I've already punished him."

"But if he has misbehaved it is necessary to beat him. What will he learn otherwise?"

"He'll learn if you do?"

Asamoa stared at me as though I'd suggested his whip was made of Chinese silk. One part of me wanted nothing more than for the goatskin to deal a couple of blows and teach them all the lesson I wasn't willing to give; but with another part I knew it would make nonsense of what I was trying to do, of the way I'd been teaching a moment ago, of the way I wanted them to think of me. It would be cowardly too—yet another sign of my weakness. Asamoa relented and left, shaking his head.

When I went back into the room the students were whispering excitedly. We'd spoken in English, but they grasped the essentials. For most of them it must have been a revelation, the first time in their lives a teacher had intervened on a boy's behalf, and a boy who'd just insulted him too. It was plain that something decisive and irrevocable had happened. From that moment a handful of them probably began to think of me more as a friend than a *gendarme* and to associate the class with pleasure instead of pain. Students began appearing at my house with gifts of bananas or pineapples, and some of them learned English faster than I'd thought possible. But in that moment I knew that others—far more—wrote off me and my class. They would come every day, and even make an effort from time to time, but I had taken away the main incentive to learn. If I wasn't going to beat them, why should they bother?

Aboï came by to see me that night, on what he called a *"visite de courtoisie,"* showing that side of himself I associated with his degree from the Ecole Normale Supérieure and the elaborate words—*"corps professoral," "intervention collégiale"*—that swam to the surface of his conversation like water snakes. But he'd come to discuss something specific. Asamoa had spoken to him about the incident, and Aboï wanted to set me straight.

"Georges," he began with an uneasy smile, "you have an American idea about punishment. With your American students the soft method will work. But Africans are not self-disciplined; they need to be persuaded. Otherwise the students will perform badly in school and then their parents will say we of the teaching body are failing in our work. You see? It is an unpleasant duty. For the African, you need a stick. *Pour l'africain, il faut le baton.*"

I couldn't count the times I heard this argument. It was about the only thing Aboï and the teachers agreed on. *"Pour l'africain, il faut le baton"* should have been the motto of CEG Lavié, posted in bold letters over the doorway of Aboï's office. I only stopped hearing it when I'd exhausted myself asking. Sometimes the sentence came with a hint of sorrow, as if we were talking about a congenital ailment like sickle-cell anemia. Or else with scientific detachment, as an ethnography lesson. Or with a note of triumph: *"You* don't understand Africans; *we* do." Always it was uttered with the conviction of a law of nature. The only counterargument that produced a quiver of doubt was in effect an appeal to the same instinct: that beating students was against state law. The irony that the speaker, an educated adult, had to be included in this crew of lazy Africans seemed lost on everyone but me. We were always talking about someone else—them, the students.

A boy was whipped for correcting his teacher's definition of *archipelago*. Half a class was whipped for doing badly on a math test. Sometimes, as I heard a whipping through the cinder-block wall dividing my class from another, it sounded like a game. Kanyi, a good-looking young math teacher who wore Levi's and the latest shirts from France, seemed to whip girls as a way of flirting; his jokes and the laughter of the class were punctuated by the girls' screams. Nyaku, the soft-bellied music and Ewé teacher, had an unmistakable streak of sadism in him. When his turn to be *professeur de semaine* came around, he would rub his hands and giggle, "I'm going to tap them well this week."

Even when the goatskin wasn't used, it had a way of hanging in the air where a lesson was being taught. Teachers didn't educe, or even lecture; they interrogated and commanded. "What is the penis?" I heard the biology teacher grilling his *6ème* class one morning. "*What—is—the penis?* Yes, you?" A small boyish voice: "The penis . . . is . . . the reproductive organ . . . of males. . . ." The voice trailed off. From the front of the room: "No! No! Who knows? Nobody? The penis is *the reproductive and urinary organ of males which engorges with blood and achieves erection when stimulated!* You had all weekend to learn it. You're going to fail the exams if you go on like this. I'll repeat it." And the teacher repeated three or four times what the penis was, while forty twelve- and thirteen-year-olds frantically scribbled it word for word in their copybooks, next to their careful illustrations in several colors.

The biology teacher was named Koba. A skinny man with angular features and mirthful eyes, he came from a remote village on the northern end of the plateau, had just earned a degree in theory from the Ecole Normale Supérieure, and was now doing his *pratique*. In effect, he was under scrutiny and could be sacked at the end of the year if he didn't measure up. Like me, he was new in Lavié, new at teaching, and we became friends.

One morning after classes Koba invited me over for a lunch of *fufu*. He lived at the other end of the village from me, down a dirt trail that led off into cornfields and yam fields and then bush. His compound was a teachers' ghetto of modest concrete-and-iron buildings. A number of teachers lived there in relative isolation from the rest of the village. None of the teachers at the CEG came from Lavié; all had been assigned here by the government.

Koba's girl friend, an eighteen-year-old from his *3ème* class (officially, like the beatings, this was illegal), pounded *fufu*, while we sat in his cramped living room and drank warm beer fetched from the bistro by a student. Students were always running errands for teachers. One afternoon a week was set aside for TM, *Travail Manuel*, when whole classes had to bring water and firewood to teachers' houses.

"It isn't a good use of their time," Koba was saying, "but there is no alternative. We teachers are here on our own; we have no family in Lavié, and no time to do our own chores. So it's necessary for the children to do them."

"It must be hard, with your family so far away."

"Very hard, very hard! An African relies on his parents, his cousins. It's a nice thing to have a girl friend, but a girl friend isn't a sister. . . ."

His family also relied on him, he said. Of ten siblings he was the only literate one, the only functionary, and his salary had to be divided among a score of relatives back in Kouniohou ("Death Is Better"). He couldn't save a sou. "Things are difficult especially now, with the *crise économique*. Teachers haven't had a raise in three years. And some months I can't touch my salary at all. Since I'm a newcomer, they withhold it, to make sure I don't grab the money and quit the profession." A smile cracked his sharp features; his eyes danced ironically. "But it isn't like *chez vous*. We can't complain; we are silent."

As we dipped our fingers in the bowl of *fufu* the girl friend had brought in, Koba sketched a bleak picture of education in Togo. There was no money, everyone knew that; the national debt was even discussed in the newspaper. Fewer teachers could be hired, and as a result the degrees of those entering the job market meant less and less. Fifteen years ago a CEG degree was all you needed to teach in the CEG; it was all Asamoa had, for example. Ten years ago you needed a *bac*, from the *lycée*. Now it was an ENS degree, and already that was becoming worthless; soon a university degree wouldn't be enough. Koba himself was lucky to have slipped in before the gates closed.

"And the children see what is happening. They see that their older brothers and sisters with *bacs* can't get a job, and they see how hard it is even to get the *bac*. More and more of them flunk because there are fewer and fewer places available. The effect is a general demoralization. Our enrollment at CEG Lavié is declining. The boys go off to Kpalimé to learn carpentry or mechanics, or else they turn into *voyous*. It's a shame. The government tells us to return to the land. You've heard of *la révolution verte*. But who wants to work the fields after he's gone to school? We know what that work is like. It is painful. And today it doesn't pay either."

Then I quizzed him about the beatings. Did those help to make school desirable? He pondered, pinching off a morsel of *fufu*. He had given it a lot of thought, he said. At ENS a French instructor had taught them the new theories of child psychology, that one must treat the student as a person with a mind and a sense of dignity. It all sounded right. But now he was doing the *pratique*, and he'd found that *pratique* and theory had nothing to do with each other.

"When I started I tried to teach that way, and I had nothing but problems. The children don't learn. My effort is a drop in the ocean. I've already begun to change; I don't beat them, but I don't mind if somebody else does. You see, Georges, it is a thing we Africans learn at home. The mother and father teach respect and obedience with the back of their hand. By the time we go to school we are used to this, we couldn't learn any other way. It has to change in the family, where it starts."

I suggested that things never changed at home, that it was school that put new ideas in one's head.

He sighed. "I agree. We are at a crossroads. Many people want to change, but we don't quite know what to do. We can't liberalize now because behind us we have so many years of rigid discipline."

"But if—"

"That's how school began in Africa," he said, heating up. "The same way roads were built. The Europeans beat our fathers and forced them to go to school, just as they forced men to labor on the *route nationale*. We've always gone to school to the whip in Africa. The idea has been with us since colonization. That's why it's so difficult to change. You see?" He began to laugh. "It's your fault! And now the *yovos* come back here to tell us it was all a mistake, we have to start teaching another way!"

We both found this extremely funny. We laughed and laughed, and finished the *fufu*, and sent a student for two more bottles of beer.

I rode home to sleep the last hour of siesta before afternoon classes began. In the yard I found Atsu and Claudie having a play-fight. Atsu was chasing his younger brother, pretending to beat him with a stick. I asked what it was all about. Atsu pointed at Claudie and mocked:

"He doesn't know that six plus six makes twelve!"

. . .

My earliest ancestors in Togo were Protestant and Catholic German missionaries. The German colonizers brought Western education to Togoland for two reasons: the need for skilled workers and the need for Christians. But the underlying agenda, the complicating aims and effects, were barely clearer to them than to the "natives" on whose behalf they were there. From the beginning, missionary-teachers found themselves at cross-purposes with each other and with the German colonial administration from which they had an equivocal independence.

An early issue of conflict was the one that, indirectly, made my presence in the country possible. In the 1880s, with the expansion of British trade along the Slave Coast of West Africa, English became the lingua franca of commerce, clerking, and accounting among the Ewé. Once the Germans had won a foothold in the Bay of Benin, and had begun to penetrate the interior and set up a colonial government, they feared subversion from Britain. In 1894 the local governor, Jesko von Puttkamer, refused to grant the colony's education stipend until the missions eliminated English from upper-level courses. Nearly a century later, with English still the language of African commerce, I was in Lavié to restore what decades of German and French colonialism had obliterated.

Germany wanted education in the colonies, but only education of a certain kind. It did not want English; it did not really even want German beyond the level necessary to meet its requirement for lower-level civil servants and railroad foremen. The colonial government recognized that large numbers of educated natives would not willingly build railroads and work the soil for the big export crops, coffee, cacao, and cotton. So it kept the education budget to a minimum: fifteen thousand marks annually represented a compromise between the need for skilled work and the fear of a population of German-speaking slackers. "A drop of water on a hot stone," one missionary complained.

The North German Mission had its own agenda, phrased with admirable brevity: "Without schoolwork, no mission work." It was difficult to convert the illiterate, more so to run an Ewé church without a body of educated churchmen. Sometimes the missions protected their Togolese pupils from official intrusions insofar as the latter threatened the missionary activity. Yet even among these earliest development workers, internal quarrels exposed a general confusion over what exactly they were doing in the colony: defending the black man against the white man, or vice versa? One clergyman assured the 1902 German Colonial Congress that

> the mission's contribution to the linking of colonial peoples to the motherland is contained in their reconciliation of defeated peoples with their new mistress Germania. They impress upon their pupils the old Christian commandment of subjection, that everyone is a subject of the authority which has the power over him.

The Bible as gun. Perhaps he was only telling his paymasters in Berlin what they wanted to hear—that education would make the natives patriotic. Another Protestant missionary saw things differently.

When Martin Schlunk warned that a universal language in the colony would not guarantee reliable Africans and indeed might unite diverse tribes against their masters, he stumbled across the paradox that lies at the heart of an effort to educate a subject people. The Germans could not exploit the land without bringing changes to its population; but those changes were bound to put new and dangerous ideas in the very minds the Germans were trying to subjugate and convert. Colonial education (and much else in colonialism) could be visualized as a man sawing off somebody else's tree branch for firewood without realizing he is sitting on the wrong end.

Yet in thirty years the missions managed to establish, if not a coherent philosophy of African education, at least a smattering of habits and opinions that might as well have been set in stone. The courses, an English observer wrote, consisted of German history, the lives of the German emperors since 1870, German geography, and German patriotic songs; eight decades and political independence have scarcely budged the curriculum toward something more practical. A certain Father Schönig and Father Kost of the Catholic Mission were astonished to find that Togolese boys had the same intellectual abilities as their German peers; but the director of the mission's teacher-training school qualified the discovery by decreeing that Africans were superior in recollection and imitation, Europeans in logic and analysis. The birth of the copybook. Both Protestant and Catholic missionaries rated Togolese girls below German girls, and only a tiny fraction of the mission pupils were female. This, too, proved a durable model. By 1982 girls still made up no more than 10 percent of *lycée* students, and at CEG Lavié the upper classes had fewer and fewer. During my first year I lost almost half the girls in one of my classes—none older than sixteen—to poor grades, discouragement from school and home, and, above all, pregnancy.

Finally, as Koba pointed out, the goatskin, too, had its origins a century ago. The whip of choice among the earliest colonizers in Togo was a leather rope lash, favored over the rhino whip because it inflicted pain without breaking the victim's skin and thus, through infections, disabling him from further work.

The Germans never had time to work out the contradictions in the colonizing mission. With Germany's defeat in World War I, France and England split German Togoland, and a new colonial administration, with a new education and a new European language, relieved Germany of its old contradictions. It was hard to find evidence that the French in Togo had any more luck resolving them than their predecessors, for by the time I came to teach English in an African country with a French curriculum that had replaced a German one, the contradictions were still firmly in place—had penetrated bone and even marrow.

"You are lazy, you are all lazy! *Pa-res-seux!*"

The speaker is the Subregional Inspector for Education in the Second Degree in the Circumscription of Kloto. A fat, mild-faced man with oversized dentures that make him lisp and slobber a little, he addresses a classroom crammed with two hundred teachers sitting at benches, standing, or squatting on the floor. We have come to this school in Kpalimé for a day-long seminar on pedagogy. The Subregional Inspector is the featured speaker. He parades back and forth at the blackboard, chalk in hand, and without writing much of anything delivers an hour's tirade on the state of secondary education. The children aren't learning, are failing their exams; the teachers shirk their duties, fudge exam results for students who do them favors (a leer lets us know he knows what kind), draw hefty salaries, and live off the sweat of the peasantry. "My dear friends!" he exclaims, catching his breath, then launches into another harangue, punctuated rhetorically with, "And why? Why? Because you are lazy! *Paresseux! Pa-res-seux!*"

Laughter and protest from the teachers. Vigorous assertion from the Subregional Inspector, softened by a hint of a smile. After all, it is a kind of game. This is our pedagogy lesson: excoriation, shame; the lesson is the Subregional Inspector himself. The day's program includes other topics prescribed by the Ministry of Education in the Second Degree—the new oral method of language instruction, developments in child psychology, the latest word from the theoreticians at the Ecole Normale Supérieure—but all that really counts is this performance by the Subregional Inspector. His is the lesson that gets across, the one everyone understands. No matter that it makes nonsense of the rest of the day's seminar.

I was beginning to realize that an unofficial system linked everyone to everyone else in the hierarchy of the education firmament. Shaped like a pyramid, it massed students at the bottom, with teachers above them, then principals, subregional inspectors, inspector generals, education ministers, and at the point of the pyramid, *le grand*, President Eyadema. Teachers whipped students; principals harangued teachers; inspectors insulted teachers and principals, and in turn were called to Lomé for invectives from the minister, who himself was subject to the wrath of *le grand*. Only Eyadema could not be called *pa-res-seux*. The first law of the system specified that you had almost complete authority over anyone under you, which always put you in the right, and at the same time you lived at the whim of anyone over you. A corollary law of gravity and momentum stated that anger traveled downward through the pyramid, never resting in the upper tiers but always descending and gaining speed, so that the students at the bottom received the brunt of its accumulated force. In cynical moods I decided that whenever Aboï or one of the teachers delivered the skin in particularly large numbers, it meant the president had woken up the day before with a headache.

Aboï was a creature of this system, and he applied it with a vengeance. As principal he was not first among equals but *chef hiérarchique*, and he never failed to remind us of it. At the same time he was young, unprepared, neurotically suspicious and defensive, and a northern Kabyé in an Ewé village with an Ewé staff. He isolated himself from both, made a point of not learning the local language, and spoke disdainfully of the all-night wakes that had drums rolling at least once a month in the village. He tried to enlist me as an ally, filling my ear with poisonous tales about the irresponsibility of the other teachers. He was not entirely unjust in this, but I cultivated a careful neutrality, until his petty tyrannies turned even me against him.

Aboï's mixture of authority and insecurity was volatile. The tyrannies bred resentment and long-running feuds that occasionally, in an outburst from him or one of the teachers, came to a head during one of our interminable meetings.

The scene is Aboï's office. The principal has called—as he does at least once a week all year—a *conseil de professeurs*, a teachers' meeting. He sits behind his desk, which takes up about half the floor space in the cramped room filled with stacks of dusty books, two soccer balls, a bulky wooden statue of a woman carrying water, ink pads, and rubber stamps. He is signing and stamping the last of a stack of papers. The dozen teachers, summoned from their classes, sit on hard wooden chairs or lean against the wall, arms folded, chatting in Ewé. In the anteroom the secretary, a tiny bug-eyed man who wears the same clothes every day and is paid fifteen dollars a month, clacks away at the school typewriter under the portrait of General Eyadema. It is midmorning, and the office, with its tiny barred window facing out on the basketball court and the row of banana trees, has filled with heat and choking dust.

Today's topic is *Travail Manuel*. It is late March, the planting season has finally begun, and the teachers have started using students in groups to weed and till their cornfields and yam fields. On TM day a teacher appears at a classroom with a long list of names and announces: "The following will report to Monsieur Nutsua's house at three o'clock with cutlasses and hoes." The system of punishment is used for the same purpose. In a classroom where two boys have a quarrel, the entire class is punished and ordered to report to Monsieur Gbadamassi's house at three-thirty with cutlasses. Classes are routinely half empty or even down to six or eight students. The students are staying home, knowing that in the rainy season school means punishment means unpaid labor. Parents have begun to complain that their children are staying away from school, or are coming home past dark, when it's dangerous, tired and dirty from hoeing.

Aboï opens the meeting cordially. "Welcome, dear colleagues. Thank you for coming. Monsieur Gbadamassi, will you take minutes this morning? Thank you. Today we have before us a most grave situation to consider and resolve. It has come to my attention that . . ." Aboï launches into an elaborate explanation of the TM crisis. He speaks for five minutes uninterrupted, and by the time he finishes, his expression has taken on something of the vigor it has during sessions with the goatskin. "No! Sincerely! It can't go on, it isn't normal, it must stop! You are dirtying the reputation of this school! Well. That's what I had wanted to speak about. Now I welcome your comments."

Rosalynne, besides Kafui the only woman on the staff, speaks up. "*Directeur*, I don't even have a field. It isn't all the teachers who are doing this; and last week you yourself had students in your field planting manioc. If you want to set up a rule against it, do so, but don't make a general case."

Aboï's voice begins to strain. "No, it simply isn't so, I have never abused the system! The children aren't here as slaves. The decent peasantry of Togo has to pay for field hands; you teachers can do the same."

Monsieur Nutsua comes to the defense of child labor. A small man with a pencil-line moustache and acid eyes, he has been coming to school for several weeks now only on days when he has a class that will be eligible for punishment. His real interest is the Peugeot he leases to merchants. *"Jomblé-man"* the teachers call him—"the man with no time to spare."

"Directeur, these are services that the children are happy to provide us. We are keeping them in contact with their authentic origins in the land. The families tell me they're grateful—"

Aboï interrupts. "I thank the colleagues for their interventions, but . . ."

But he vents more rage. The meeting degenerates into accusations and insults hurled back and forth across the big desk. Two or three teachers, bored, rest their foreheads on their knees. Eventually they go outside to sit in the anteroom, where it is cooler. Every few minutes Aboï gets up to order them to come back in. They refuse. Gbadamassi scribbles minutes. The secretary clacks away. A few students are wandering outside between classrooms, keeping a watchful eye on the principal's office.

Aboï is shouting. "I am your hierarchical chief! I am your hierarchical chief!"

From the anteroom, Agbefianou shouts something in Ewé. He knows that Aboï, the Kabyé outsider, can't understand. It is the last transgression, the final blow.

"That's enough!" Aboï barks. "Colleagues, we are at school, speak French only."

More laughing comments in Ewé are exchanged among the teachers. Aboï, suspicious, furious, insists on French and demands an apology from Agbefianou.

"J-J-Je refuse! J-J-Je refuse!"

This refrain catches on as Agbefianou's nickname among his colleagues.

The meeting drags on. At noon a whistle blows and the classrooms empty. Students with copybooks on their heads walk home for the midday meal, glancing curiously through the window at their teachers. Kanyi, the math teacher, complains of hunger and mosquitoes. The sun is at its height, and the heat in the cramped room has become oppressive. Nutsua informs Aboï that he has to leave. Aboï warns him not to go, but Nutsua gets up and walks out, trailed by a stream of half-threatening pleas from Aboï and joshing shouts of *"Jomblé-man!"* from the teachers. Around one o'clock the meeting peters out. Gbadamassi reads the minutes, which suggest that a polite round-table discussion has just taken place. The principal has decreed that TM will henceforth be limited to water and firewood.

In this atmosphere, which worsened over the year, with Aboï snatching us out of class once or twice a week for meetings to inform us of the latest directive from the inspector general in Atakpamé, not much learning got done. But I had already realized that learning was unlikely even in the best circumstances, given the curriculum the government had inherited and continued to insist on. It was imitative, shot through with a French devotion to abstraction and rote learning. Math meant game theory; physics, lists of formulas twenty years out of date; in geography students copied page after page of maps of weather patterns in northern Europe. French, the language of instruction, was taught as a series of increasingly obscure points of grammar. It would have seemed remote enough to a child in the capital; in Lavié, where students went home from school, changed into *pagnes* and shorts and Ewé, and took a bucket down to the stream for the evening's water, the lessons hammered home day after day must have seemed as alien and arbitrary as some indecipherable dead language. School amounted to dressing village kids, children of illiterate peasants, in French khaki and stuffing them like livestock before slaughter with a borrowed, anachronistic subject matter forced down in a language some of them could still barely read or write.

What they spewed up at the end of term was boiled down to a single number, carried to the hundredth decimal place, between one and twenty—the average of a dozen numbers that in turn had been averaged from dozens of others. On this number their future hung. Ten, and they passed; 9.99, and they doubled, or tripled, or quadrupled, or went back to the fields. Most did not pass. This year, out of seventy-five or eighty, the number who would pass the BEPC exam and reach high school was three.

None of this really mattered; or so I was starting to guess. Education wasn't the idea here, not even the stale, secondhand education of an ex-colony. It counted for less than discipline, for less than bureaucratic forms and teachers' meetings and farm labor. The idea of education as a mark of development carried some currency, but as for the thing itself, CEG Lavié went through the motions with a tacit agreement from everyone not to admit the charade.

With the resolution of the TM crisis the classrooms began to fill again, but the year ended badly, in a series of scandals. Gbadamassi, the affable sports teacher, turned out to have knocked up his third student in four years and risked losing his job. The big mistake was that this time he'd impregnated the daughter of a successful hog farmer named Degan, who knew the law and threatened Gbadamassi with all kinds of reprisals until he paid up three months' salary. In the end Gbadamassi stayed at the CEG, but he never crawled out of debt. The Degan girl dropped out of school.

Then Kafui and Rosalynne, the two women on the staff, got into a fight on the school grounds. Rosalynne, who was estranged from her husband and lived alone in Lavié with her two small children, had been in love with a math teacher named Amavi for some time without requital (her domestic situation made her all but unmarriageable). Kafui, younger and more attractive, was Agbefianou's lover, but her friendship with Amavi got under Rosalynne's skin and filled her with jealousy. One morning she confronted Kafui under the mango tree outside the principal's office and taunted her that she was sterile. The only worse thing Rosalynne could have called her was "whore," and when she did, Kafui slapped her across the face. Rosalynne returned the blow, Agbefianou rushed over to protect his lover, and Rosalynne turned on him and started kicking. Koba, Gbadamassi, and other teachers separated the fighters, but the damage was done: the fight had taken place in full view of students.

Aboï wrote a report to the Inspection in which he exculpated himself and blamed just about everyone else. Agbefianou threatened to write a report on Aboï. Meetings began to sound like the floor of the stock exchange, or a weigh-in before a prizefight. And the end-of-year exam results were abysmal, worse than the year before. This led to a rare display of unity among Aboï and the teachers.

One morning during the last week of school, Aboï and the teaching staff went from class to class. Aboï had the goatskin in one hand and a sheet of paper in the other, as he'd had on my first morning at school. On this paper was a list of the final average of every student in the school, the number between one and twenty that summed up his year's work and determined his future. We started with the youngest class, the *6ème*. Aboï read off the names in alphabetical order, while the teachers stood behind him snickering and shaking their heads at the miserable results of their lazy students.

"Amedji!"

"*Monsieur?*" answered a fat girl who looked too old to be in *6ème*.

"Eight point seventy-three. I hope you know how to weave mats, Amedji! Ametowossi, do you like this classroom so much that you want to spend a third year in it?"

The students laughed nervously. The teachers, in a fine mood, seconded Aboï.

"Seven point zero six. A disgusting performance." He read more names. "Dewu. Fourteen point sixty-seven. Why not fifteen, Dewu? If you slip next year I'll come after you with the whip."

"*Oui, monsieur.*"

"Ketekou! Six point twenty-five! *Pa-res-seux!* We don't want you here at CEG Lavié. Understand? You have no right to be alive. Togo doesn't want you! It's better for you to die, and let those of us who want to work eat a little more."

Ketekou, all eleven years and five feet of him, was speechless in his disgrace.

In the final week of school an event took place that almost redeemed the year for me, and perhaps—if it needed redeeming in their eyes—for a handful of my students. With six boys and a girl from my second-year class I staged a production of "The Emperor's New Clothes." Our textbook—this was the only class of mine that had one—included an English version at a level they could manage, and twice a week for a month we gathered in the afternoons at school for rehearsals. They mastered their lines with no trouble (demonstrating that natural African facility for recollection that German educators had noticed), so we focused our energy on nuances, facial expressions, dramatic embellishments. I watched them with growing pleasure, as if something as small as this might vindicate my refusal to use the goatskin and the year of struggle and failure I'd just taught through.

Liberated from education, most of them turned out to be terrific hams. Through their inspiration the play took on an African tone. The Emperor became a village chief, the Chief Minister an elder, the two tailors a pair of swindlers from Kpalimé; and during the procession, as the Emperor shows off his set of invisible clothes, one actor beat a tam-tam and the Emperor's wife did an Ewé dance. But what seemed to absorb them most was the satirical theme: the way the greedy tailors preyed on the Emperor's vanity to rip him off and ridicule him, the idea that the wise are foolish and the foolish wise, the comeuppance of the powerful at the hands of the lowly. The day before the performance, during a scene where the Emperor signs a note giving the two tailors five large bags of gold, I asked the boy playing the part to try pounding the note with an imaginary rubber stamp. The idea of aiming the satire at the school hadn't occurred to me—I was thinking more of the government bureaucrats and postal clerks in Lomé and Kpalimé—but this little piece of subversion clicked with them. They thought it was hysterical. And the next day, when the teachers and students assembled on the same field where Aboï had read off the names of victims on the first morning, the play the students performed had a look and an energy I wasn't ready for.

The boy playing the Chief Minister improvised a long introduction in Ewé, a sort of Shakespearean chorus, setting forth the business of the play. What followed was a burlesque of CEG Lavié. The Emperor unmistakably became Aboï—the same puffed chest, the glower, even the tortured official speech. The Chief Minister was a publicly unctuous, privately mocking subordinate. The tailors lowered their voices to ask for the payoff like a pair of wisecracking *voyous* in 5*ème*. And when the Emperor in his invisible royal clothes affixed his invisible royal rubber stamp to the receipt, he hit it not once but four times. Titters broke out among the audience. From the side I looked across the three hundred students sitting on the grass and the dozen teachers in chairs, at Aboï. He had his arms folded across his chest; his face was unreadable.

At the end of the play, which received a sustained round of cheers and applause, Aboï came over to speak with me.

"Really, Georges," he was saying, "you have made remarkable progress with these children. They all knew their lines by heart and no one forgot a word. You are to be congratulated."

The Emperor and the Chief Minister were fifteen-year-olds, best friends, who lived in a village four kilometers away from Lavié. Kpatcha and Kodjo made the long walk past the hydroelectric plant, past the coffee and cacao nursery, four times every day, once—at noon—on empty stomachs with the sun angrily overhead. When I taught their class at three o'clock, the first afternoon period, the two of them were always at their bench in back, sweat streaming down their faces. Kpatcha walked a few additional kilometers since his thatch hut was at the end of a path cut through high grass well off the road. His family was Kabyé and had immigrated from the north; his father, ancient and nearly blind, had a yam field that Kpatcha and his mother farmed. Kpatcha had the sober, stiff, conscientious manner of an ethnic outsider. He ambled with his shoulders straight, had a deep polite voice, studied hard, and was at the top of his class. In America he would have been an Eagle Scout and a scholarship student, working his way through college and landing a job as an engineer to support his old father. In Togo he had trouble scraping together the two thousand francs—six dollars—for yearly tuition, and was always on the verge of dropping out.

Kodjo was his Sancho Panza: short, potbellied, an Ewé. On the second day of class he raised his hand, answered a question, dragged himself to the blackboard in his ragged, oversized khakis, and gave me a grin that never quite left his face again: wry, knowing, half ashamed. His English was better than anyone else's, and perhaps it gave him confidence to pursue me as a friend. No one else really spoke it beyond gluing together prefabricated phrases. Kodjo's sentences spilled out, accumulating errors and energy, rolling on, startling me with words I hadn't even taught: *cabbage, flat tire.* If Kpatcha would have been an engineering student on a scholarship, the American Kodjo would have edited the irreverent school newspaper. It was his comic intelligence that transformed "The Emperor's New Clothes." But most of his grades were barely average, and math was his downfall. I tried tutoring him in algebra at my house, but he was more interested in my poster of the New York skyline. No number between one and twenty was averaged in for imagination. He was on his way toward tripling *5ème.*

I once asked Kodjo what he wanted to be in life.

"Ambassador," he said immediately. "Or secretary."

He had never been farther than Kpalimé. His father, a local agent for the state coffee and cacao company, was angry at Kodjo's poor report cards. He told me his son was *paresseux* and threatened to pull him out of school and put him to work in his cacao grove. If a boy couldn't make it out of CEG, wasn't his education worthless? Shouldn't he do something useful for the family instead? On these occasions Kodjo's face screwed up with anguished pleas that it was bad luck, illness, math—but not laziness. In class he complained of mysterious headaches and stomachaches and during the lunch hour would appear at my door for aspirins. On one assignment he wrote a letter to his uncle in Ghana that revealed him as pained and misunderstood:

Dear Uncle Ata: First my clean safety to ask your health. As you know, the main-road Togo to Ghana customs are very difficult, I don't know whom to give a letter to post at the post-office. I forgot to tell you when you went back again. Please can you pay a bicycle, but my father hates to buy me it. Please I don't like my father. Why not? Because he can't see my suffering. Always I'm ill and it's too sunny. I'm too tired. Best wishes. See you soon.

At the end of the school year, two weeks after the play, Kpatcha's mother died. Walking out to their yam field, she put her foot on a green mamba. Kodjo asked me to come to the village for the gathering that would follow her burial.

I found them in a room of Kodjo's compound, by the roadside: Kodjo, Kpatcha, Kodjo's father, and a dozen relatives and villagers chatting loudly. The room was dark and cool, bare except for a wooden chair, a table with copybooks and a small kerosene lamp, and a straw mat on the dirt floor. On the wall I recognized pictures from *Newsweek* that I'd clipped and passed out in class—an attractive white couple boating in a cigarette ad, the rubble of the bombed embassy in Beirut: Kodjo's room. Shed of their eternal khaki uniforms, the boys looked incongruously colorful in dead *yovo* pullovers and shorts. But Kpatcha was ashen-faced as he greeted me and led me to a corner of the room where an old man was sitting in the chair.

The old man was staring straight ahead with his hands on his bare knees. He wore nothing but an open shirt and a skimpy cloth around his loins. The flesh hung loose off his ribbed chest; the eyes were glassy and scarred with greenish cataracts. He could have been one of the beggars squatting outside the door of a Lomé bookstore. Kpatcha bent to his ear and said something in Kabyé. A hand rose for mine.

People had gathered around, telling me that this was the dead woman's old blind husband, that now he had no one but Kpatcha and a daughter down from Lama Kara to help him, that it was too good of me, their teacher, a white, to come see him. Kpatcha stood stiffly behind the chair. I asked if it would be appropriate for me to give his father money.

"Oh, yes sir, you can easily."

I pressed a thousand-franc note into the old man's hand. He gripped it, gripped my hand with his callused fingers, moaned *"Merci, merci,"* rocking in the chair, nodding his white head, the eyes large and expressionless. Someone offered me a glass of *sodabi*, which I forced down before escaping outside.

Blind for a moment in the sunlight, I heard a voice behind me. It spoke in English. "Thank you for to come," Kodjo was saying. Africa's small or huge shocks never appeared meaningful all at once. Moments of mental clarity were belated and brief. I was aware most of the time only of the sensations overwhelming my own body, and for weeks the funeral reception made me think of nothing but the blind figure moaning in the chair and the foul taste of *sodabi*. But a deeper feeling had taken root. I'd had my first glimpse of the students' life at home. And to say it seemed remote from the other, school life hardly described the dislocating split they lived with every day, the odds stacked against them. Something about the half-naked old man, and Kpatcha's courtesy, and the *Newsweek* cutouts on the wall struck home and moved me.

As I thought back on this encounter—above all as I remembered Kodjo's parting sentence, with its small error—I began to grasp something essential about school here. The CEG, with its imported, sterile remnants of colonial education, its anger and humiliation, its bureaucracy and its whips, was a place where everyone was bound to fail, where failure was built in. Africans dressed up as dumb blacks imitating whites were made to see their own inadequacy. It had served the old need of the European colonizer to feel his superiority and importance; it served the need of the independent regime to preside over what it called "development" without losing power. Even under a black government, contempt for the black man hadn't been forgotten.

In this light, the four-kilometer walk Kodjo and Kpatcha made four times a day was an act of either extraordinary gullibility or extraordinary faith. It meant holding out hope that they might be among the few dozen to reach *3ème*, and the three or four of those to pass the BEPC and go on to the Lycée Kpodzi in Kpalimé. From there, their chances always slimming, they would stumble over the first year of high school, the second, the *probatoire* exam, the third year, and the *bac*, washing dishes to pay their way; scramble for the available scholarships to the Université du Benin in Lomé; spend three or four years in poverty working toward a bachelor's degree, living in one rented room, cooking on a petrol burner. By then they would be among a tiny fraction of survivors from the first year of CEG. Their education would have become increasingly complicated but, in its essentials, unchanged. If the impulse to question had somehow endured over the years, there were still remedies. Not the goatskin anymore, but new goatskins—a scholarship withheld, an exam result nullified, even a stay in jail. Then, with the university degree, they might finally ferret out a functionary's job. In the best of all possible scenarios, Kodjo and Kpatcha would outlast the odds and end up as teachers in a CEG.

The last time I saw Aboï in Lavié, just before the beginning of the new school year, he was standing in his living room amid a clutter of boxes and books. He had just received word from Lomé that he was being transferred to another school.

He hadn't requested it, I heard, but some figure in the education hierarchy apparently decided that something at CEG Lavié had to give. Aboï was assigned to Patatoukou, a village near Atakpamé that consisted almost entirely of Kabyés transplanted from the north when their village was subsumed by a game reserve. It seemed to me an admission by the government of a failure in its policy of national unity: Kabyé soldiers were stationed in the Ewé capital, the two languages had equal national status, but a young Kabyé principal in an Ewé school was too much. Aboï had hated Lavié, and Lavié had hated Aboï. When news spread through the village, the glee was undisguised and vengeful. "He's going to see now!" Christine exulted. She regarded Aboï not as a fellow outsider but as an ignorant Kabyé imposter. "He's tried to play the big man here, but he's going to see!"

I went to visit Aboï at his house a few days after word reached me. He had seen, but not understood. I read it at once in his face: a terrible injustice had been done him. He couldn't fathom what had happened.

"They have always been against my efforts here. You've seen it, Georges," he exclaimed, clutching my arm. "I devoted three years to make this an exemplary school, but I have received only ingratitude. It's a bad place, a bad people. You don't know because you're a Westerner, but it's futile to work with these people—the teachers, the students. . . ."

I had plenty of replies in mind, but at this moment I didn't feel like arguing with Aboï. I saw him as a creature of the system, a true believer, and, in his way, another victim of it. Now the system rewarded his zeal by shipping him off elsewhere. There was something pathetic in the way he tried to justify himself to me one last time—wounded, baffled, standing among the half-packed boxes and stacks of dusty textbooks. Two days later he left Lavié.

A squalid footnote. Aboï quickly made enemies among the teachers at CEG Patatoukou, a Peace Corps friend who taught agriculture there told me. Even the Kabyé farmers came to dislike him. Charges of corruption were brought against him, as they'd been against the man he'd replaced at Lavié, by the villagers—money pilfered from the school treasury; school gardens, chickens, and goats put to his own use. He was stripped of his title of principal, demoted to ordinary teacher, and sent packing once more. But this time north— home.

CHAPTER 4

Yovos and Other *Fous*

CHRISTMAS 1982—MY FIRST IN AFRICA. I STUFFED A few clothes in my faded army backpack, said good-bye to the Agbelis, went out to the road, and flagged down "Who Knows the Future?" for the eighty-kilometer trip to Atakpamé. In two months I'd hardly left the village. Now the vacation offered a chance to visit my volunteer friend John in Hiheatro and make my first trip to the north.

The van stopped in Adeta, a few miles out of Lavié, to let off passengers and pick up others. Adeta was a Togolese Trenton, an ugly junction town where the Kpalimé-Atakpamé road met the road winding down from the plateau at a Mobil station.

While we waited, a face poked in through the window where I was sitting and planted a moist kiss on my cheek. I shrank back, and found myself staring at a madwoman.

Most village *fous* were emaciated, half-naked ghosts, but this woman was still handsome in middle age, bosomy, dressed in clean, pretty *pagnes*. But her face gave her away. It was daubed with crusty white streaks of greasepaint across the forehead, cheeks, nose, and chin. The paint was peeling off as if from a weather-beaten house; it didn't seem likely she had washed her face in months. The madwoman contemplated me, smiling fondly.

"*Yovo.*"

I'd seen her before, when I'd come to Adeta a month ago to buy yams. She'd been in the taxi station, spotted me, automatically waved as if we were old friends, and come over to speak a few unintelligible words. She'd defied *fou* behavior by not asking for money. This was her first kiss.

Now she was talking to me. A small, neatly dressed man in front of me provided a running translation.

"*Monsieur*, she says that in the land of the blind, the one-eyed man is king. . . . She says if you don't work, you won't eat." The madwoman turned and shouted ridicule at a man passing behind her. "She says he walks there like the *patron* of this station, but if you cared to search him you would not find five francs. . . . *Monsieur*, *excusez*. She says"—the man gave an apologetic little cough—"that with your wealth you could feed all of Kpelé and Danyi and still have some for Agou."

"Oh, she does?" I cursed my poor Ewé. I wanted to hear her wit unvarnished, the glossy veneer of French scraped off.

The madwoman moved on. My interpreter shook his head in wonder. "The authentic wisdom of Africa, really, it is developed—what the woman says is strong!"

The taxi filled, the driver jumped in front and started up. Without looking I knew she was back at my window.

"Bye-bye," the madwoman said. "*Yovo*, bye-bye."

On the way my interpreter filled in the madwoman's story. She had been one of the wealthiest women in the plateau region, traveling in hired taxis from market to market with her goods. She remained unmarried for a long time, contemptuous of African men (like the "*patron*" of the Adeta station), who were all out of pocket and unworthy. Eventually she met and married a Frenchman who'd been living for years up on the plateau with its cool air. And for a while she enjoyed the good life of being married to a white, which was even better than having money of her own. Not long ago the Frenchman left her and went back to France. Rumor had it a wife had been waiting all this time in Lyons or Marseilles. The African wife he left behind went mad, and painted her face.

I couldn't judge the story's veracity, but if the interpreter was making it up for my entertainment, then he had a streak of imaginative genius in him. Fabricated or not, on a deeper level something in it rang true. It hit very near the heart of how I saw the strange relations between black and white in Togo, and it hit with a parable's simplicity and the bluntness of a lunatic.

We raced along northeast toward Atakpamé, keeping the chain of green hills on our left. The land was lush, and innumerable frogs lay squished on the pavement. But the last rain had fallen in late November, and within a month the bush would recede, thin, and yellow under the dry heat.

Unlike most volunteers, my friend John lived unapologetically well in Hiheatro. He didn't bother with the usual pretense of going native and stoically suffering. Midway through our summer training he had switched programs and decided to become the accountant of an Evangelical Church project that sold tractors on favorable terms to enterprising local farmers. This move increased John's standard of living considerably. He had a functionary's house—metal gate, flower beds, glass-louvered windows, tiled bath, flush toilet, electric stove and oven—on a sort of Functionary Row in the village that served as an upscale suburb to Atakpamé. John's neighbors were women from the north who sold fermented millet beer, or *tchook*, Togolese in the upper ranks of the civil service, and many whites— missionary families, volunteers, USAID officials. His house had a dizzying supply of electrical gadgets. After only a few months in Africa, things like televisions, blenders, fans, and ice cream makers struck me as fantastically luxurious. The living room was always cluttered with *Sports Illustrated*s and Doonesbury clippings from home, the liquor cabinet stocked with Scotch and Kahlúa, the refrigerator with canned strawberries, ham, cream, cocoa, all bought at the Lebanese store in the Atakpamé market or on business trips to the capital. Weekends with him were a guilty pleasure, a stolen half step back homeward. After the kerosene lamps and manioc *fufu* of Lavié, I sat in his kitchen eating ham, drinking Scotch, and talking about NCAA basketball like a Catholic breaking fast in the middle of Lent.

On Christmas Eve we took about ten steps homeward. A family

of Baptist missionaries was throwing a little party down the dirt road for the local American community. Festivities were well under way by the time we arrived. The family had decorated their living room in grand Christmas style with red and green crepe paper and Santa cutouts. An artificial tree, frosted and covered with shiny balls and tiny lights and candles, stood in the corner over a pile of wrapped gifts. The stereo was playing, Bing Crosby was dreaming of a white Christmas, and the guests were devouring red- and green-frosted cookies and unspiked eggnog. Several small blond children—beautiful, like their parents, like everyone in the room, beautiful and groomed and cheerful—sat on the floor in pink party dresses and navy blue suits, while the adults sat around in chairs and listened to them take turns reading the story of the Nativity from the Bible in soft Southern accents. Egged on by her parents, the family's teen-aged daughter, in glasses and braces, sang a mildly naughty version of "Twelve Days of Christmas" that she'd learned at the Christian girls' school she attended in the Ivory Coast: football players took the place of turtle doves. The adults laughed; the girl went red. More cookies were passed around. The children were allowed to open a few presents and gasped over electric trains and play makeup sets. The talk among their parents was of home, Jesus, project accounts. We were all white here—the maid had been given Christmas leave—and the noises coming from outside might as well have been their Decatur, Georgia, neighbors playing tag in the red clay before dinnertime.

But Decatur, never my milieu, now looked like Oz. On the road back up to John's house—farmers appearing out of the blackness in the Yamaha's headlight, a million bugs smashing against our helmets—the party was already slipping into hallucination. I wondered if the Baptist family felt this disjunction every time they left their house. To me the party had seemed staged, like the rotating ethnic dioramas in natural history museums where the local artifacts have been laid out so perfectly that the scene loses the look of truth. And yet was my existence in Lavié any more honest? They were leading their lives as they thought right. Why should a change of locale stop them?

The day after Christmas, spirits high at the prospect of adventure,

I headed north alone. It was the first of half a dozen trips to the savanna, and in memory all of them seem about the same.

You are never more white in Africa than when you are traveling. To leave Atakpamé for the north, I hiked uphill to the Texaco station on the road leading out of the market. A dozen drivers' apprentices swarmed on me and grabbed for my bag to steer me toward their taxi before they even knew my destination. "Sokodé Sokodé Sokodé?" one asked. "No, Kara." "Ah, Kara." He dropped my bag and went off in search of someone else. Others came after me—*"Yovo? C'est où?"*—like a line of barkers trying to lure me into a peep show, but I hung on to my bag and scanned the station for the taxi closest to full. That would mean the shortest wait. Otherwise I could be stuck in Atakpamé for hours; I might not leave today. Various vehicles were parked in rows opposite the gas pumps. The least desirable were the *bachés*, the blue Toyota pickups with their beds covered by wood and canvas; a cut above them, the battered white Peugeot 504s with three rows of seats; and best of the lot, newer Mitsubishi vans with separate seats and decent suspension. If I was lucky, I would find one of them ready to leave, and—luckier still—be given the seat next to the driver because I was a *yovo*. Only a soldier could bounce a *yovo* out of that seat.

Today I was unlucky. A *baché* was at the head of the line, ready to leave, and the apprentice, a muscular young guy in shorts and a Bob Marley T-shirt who had probably just dropped out of CEG, was assuring me that there was plenty of room. I climbed over the tailgate and wedged my bottom on the wooden bench between a fat woman with a baby in her lap and a wizened old Moslem lost in the folds of his robe. At a glance I saw that there were fifteen or sixteen others with me, knees together, arms pinned to their sides, on two opposing benches, as well as two or three babies, and a pair of chickens tied at the ankles on the floor. The legal limit was twelve people. Before the *baché* left the apprentice crammed another passenger on my bench and a young crippled man on a tiny stool in the middle of the bed, among an arsenal of knees. This was enough to get the passengers muttering as they shoved over, but no one refused to admit another. The driver, if pushed, would inform them that it was his truck and he would do what he wanted with it, and if they didn't approve then they were free to find another *baché*. Through the rear window of the cab I glimpsed the faded green of a soldier's fatigues in the passenger seat.

The *baché* started up and lurched into motion, but only to go over to the gas pumps. The driver hadn't been able to buy gas until the passengers paid. Finally we were moving toward the road, and the apprentice jogged behind, waiting until the last moment before hopping up onto the tailgate—a ritual among them. He sat facing us on the closed tail, head out, Bob Marley smiling in. We were bound for the savanna.

Togo is a thin slice of land between Ghana and Benin, running north from the coast of the Gulf of Guinea to Burkina Faso (when I was in Africa it was called Upper Volta) in the dry reaches of the Sahel—four hundred miles long but never more than eighty wide. The *route nationale*, built under the French with forced labor—the president's father was killed on a work team—cuts Togo in half from Lomé all the way to the northern border. This year the road was being repaired between Atakpamé and Blitta. A French contractor's signs appeared on the roadside every few miles—JEAN LAFÈVRE WORKS FOR YOU; JEAN LAFÈVRE THANKS YOU—assuring the Africans, as he would not have had to do only twenty-five years before, that Jean Lafèvre was neither exploitative nor ungrateful. In the rainy south the road was cratered with potholes and washed away at the edges, and lack of money left it to devour vehicles for years at a time. Where the road was under repair, we took a long detour on a rocky dirt track through the low hills. The *baché* filled with dust that came over the tailgate, Bob Marley disappeared, people coughed and muffled their faces with cloth. My skin, moist in the rising heat, collected a coat of dirt; dirt ground between my molars. For twenty miles of jolts and dust clouds no one said a word.

The dust was particularly bad now because in December and January the harmattan winds from the Sahara blew south and carried—along with tuberculosis—thick white clouds of desert, like a fogbank rolling in. They partially blocked the sun and with the breezes they eased the heat a little, but dust got into everything and all the pores went dry.

Past Blitta we rejoined the route. Here the rainfall was lighter and the road was smooth. The landscape had changed while we were lost in dust. For miles now the *baché* passed forests of teak—tall, thin-trunked trees with round leaves as large as lily pads, browned, littering the forest floor. This central region was the least populated in the country. Every fifteen or twenty miles a village appeared out of the teak forest—a flash of conical mud huts, a boy trying to sell a bush rat, dangling it by the tail, a couple of girls waving—and was gone in seconds. The driver never bothered to slow down through the villages. In fact, he seemed to accelerate a little, hugged the edge of the road, and leaned on his horn, continuing to honk for no apparent reason over the next few miles, as if the device had just been invented. As we skimmed past them, women with headloads hustled into the grass, children's arms were yanked by parents, and the village livestock scurried in every direction. The pygmy sheep were particularly given to improvident panic, and one ran directly under our *baché*. As I looked back its legs were twitching violently, and an unhappy but helpless villager was approaching it to prepare the evening meal. The driver did, however, slow down for potholes, which posed a more direct threat to his vehicle. Every now and then he misjudged one and hit it at full speed with a terrific crash that raised shouts of protest from his freight in back.

Teak trees rushed by; the sun climbed. The air was changing too. Moisture had vanished, my face and arms were smooth and dusty, my eyes stung. With so many bodies packed in back, the heat was beginning to stifle. I took a sip from the bottle of mineral water I'd brought along. We seemed to be leaving behind one Africa for another, leaving the banana trees and the smell of mud and wet for dry grass, thin air, and blazing sun. Togo's tourist posters called the country *"L'Afrique en Miniature."* During a single *baché* ride one felt Africa's two essences, rain and dry heat, in the nose and skin.

From time to time I noticed eyes staring at me. Each time I caught an old woman's eye she said simply, *"Yovo,"* as if she were

pointing out something interesting and faintly comical. I smiled at
the baby on the lap to my left, and held my finger out for it to grip;
eyes huge, it pulled back into the folds of its mother's *pagne*. I might
have been its first white face. *"Il a peur de vous, monsieur,"* a well-
dressed young man across from me explained. He asked where I
was from and where I was going, said he'd like to be pen pals, tried
to make small talk. I answered him but didn't encourage conversation.

Among the bodies the smell of sweat and pepper sauce was sharp;
women carried bowls of rice to feed their children on the way. The
mother beside me quietly fed her baby from a swollen breast and
droplets of milk dribbled onto her *pagne*. During the journey the
baby might spill food, throw up, piss, shit. The mother would calmly
clean it up with a cloth she'd brought along, and at the end of the
trip mother and child would somehow be as clean as at the start.
And another thing baffled me: none of the infants made any noise.
I could imagine a truckload of American kids on a ride like this.

Eventually the teaks disappeared. Now only an occasional baobab
or mango tree interrupted the monotony of grass and dirt. The huts
were no longer clustered along the road but scattered out in fields,
which a few months ago had had a green fur and been thick with
corn rows and mounds of yams. Now the cornstalks hung limp, the
mounds were a pox erupting over the land.

After three hours the trip began to wear me down. My buttocks
and thighs had gone numb on the wooden bench, and for twenty
miles I'd been waging a covert war with the heavy woman beside
me for leg position. She probably wasn't even aware; she was feeding
her baby again. Men slept with their foreheads on their knees, a
girl's head lolled on the shoulder of the old man next to her. The
babies might have been dead. This patience was beginning to awe
me. My own suppressed fits of pique at a toe on the foot or an elbow
in the side were signs of some moral inferiority. I tried to sleep but
couldn't find a way to hold my head other than on the fat woman's
shoulder, which would have drawn laughs. Anyway, with the heat
and jolts, I knew sleep was impossible. I sighed, and the well-
dressed young man looked at me sympathetically.

"On arrive, monsieur," he assured me. I did not want to be treated specially, I wanted to endure it as they did. But the boredom I'd felt earlier at his attempts to ingratiate himself now turned into childish gratitude.

And one did arrive. Hills with great boulders, the din of an iron bridge, a wide river where women waded and kneaded clothes over rocks, and suddenly we were entering Lama Kara.

Kara was an idea, a man-made graft onto the rugged hills. This was Eyadema country. His home village of Pya was a few miles to the north. Kara had been built up with banks, a luxury hotel with pool and tennis courts, and a vast aluminum indoor market—signs of Kabyé prestige and power that were synonymous with the prestige and power of the Kabyé president. Rumors had even circulated that the capital would be moved up here from Lomé, like Brasília or the prefab capitals being planned for the interior in Nigeria and the Ivory Coast. But the land around Kara, hills of hard red laterite and millet fields, was desolate. The city seemed to have no natural function. The avenues with their metal streetlamps were empty; scores of young men hung out in the taxi station by the new market. The streetlamps and the luxury hotel seemed to be for the likes of me; for them the artificial city offered nothing. Yet they would rather sit in the taxi park smoking, swapping jokes, and making odd change than in the deadly stillness of their villages in the laterite hills.

After a few questions, I learned that the morning taxis for the savanna had left, and though a couple of youths assured me another would go in an hour, I knew they were saying what they thought I wanted to hear. It was high noon, siesta, and no one would travel until two or three. I walked to a bar on the far side of the parking lot, past vehicles, past tall Kabyé women crouched with their mounds of bananas and oranges from the south. I bought a hunk of fried cheese made from the cows of Fulani nomads who wandered the Sahel; in Kpalimé, where there were no Fulani and no cows, it was a delicacy. The women's Kabyé chatter came in staccato bursts from the lips, different from guttural Ewé. The physiognomies, the shallow vertical tribal scars on the cheeks—everything seemed unfamiliar up here. The sun was a thin red disk hanging behind the harmattan dust clouds, giving off impossible amounts of heat like a split atom. You couldn't stay in it for more than five minutes.

The bar was dark and almost empty except for flies. I waved them off the lip of my mercifully cold Coke. I was reconciling myself to the stretch of time ahead and trying to take an interest in the surroundings. A boy with a two-string guitar walked in. His long neck ended in a tiny old man's face, insectlike and wise. He plucked the two strings and sang for me in Kabyé. His voice, monotonous, querulous, and pinched, was strangely pleasing. It spoke of old lore, old suffering. He seemed an apparition of the heat. After two songs I gave him money and he went back out into the sunlight.

Passengers trickled into the station. We didn't get under way until three o'clock. Caught unaware in the bar, I had to run after the *baché* as it trundled out of the lot. This time there was no soldier, and the empty front seat was given to me.

Outside Kara a light blue glass palace appeared on the barren hills, fronted by a vast paved parking lot with streetlamps but not a single car: the northern convention hall of Eyadema's Rassemblement du Peuple Togolais (RPT), the only political party. At Pya, a ten-foot bust of the general forced the road to part, and a hundred yards on, his new villa appeared on a bluff, a half-finished steel frame looming over a grove of newly planted pine trees and an artificial pond. Perched above the village's round huts and conical grass roofs, these seemed like the vision of a lunatic, a Fitzcarraldo come home drunk with power and the need to carve his triumph across the face of his humble origins.

With the villa the political landscape ended, and the monotony of savanna began, and the villages were only villages again.

Dark fell before we reached Mango, where I would stay with a volunteer overnight. The dry air suddenly went chilly. In the front seat I looked out over the sandstone plain with its empty riverbeds and saw the glow of dozens of small fires against the night sky. The farmers were burning their millet fields after the harvest, the land to lie charred for three months until the early rains and planting. After the day's fatigue I was strangely alert, and in the soothing cool I gazed at the orange flares across the savanna, keen to the beauty of the land. Then the fires ended. We were passing through a game park. The driver told me about a giant eland he'd nearly hit here yesterday. It had appeared suddenly at dusk, at a bend in the road, a silhouette the size of a horse with great antlers spiraling upward. The driver swerved, and the eland bounded into the bush with a leap that carried it thirty feet. The driver went on to describe elephants bathing in the shallow rivers, troops of baboons in trees. He was humoring me but I didn't mind. I was grateful for the open African road, the sense of excitement again after the rigors of the day's trip. In Mango I wrote down my address before he even asked for it. He laughed. Perhaps he was amused that these whites got themselves so worked up over animal stories, like children.

I spent several days in the savanna, taking buses or hitchhiking from town to town. I stayed with volunteers—some friends, others just giving me a place to sleep on their concrete floors. Not a place for tourists. During the days there was nothing to do but travel, eat rice at noon, hike craggy hills, and try to hit the market towns on their market days, for cloth and leatherwork. Great birds circled in the sky, and I spotted a few antelope and baboons between the trees around bodies of water. The villages were isolated and poor. Peasants sat for hours drinking watery brown millet beer. Many wore rags; the children looked dirty and underfed. In one village a *fou*, naked, scratching at his testicles, lingered near me and bummed bowls of beer. These tall, gaunt people with their strange languages seemed too remote to be reached.

In a village twenty miles off the main road into the bush, I met two Canadian women, Mennonites. Entering middle age, pale and thin and calm in the hundred-degree heat, they invited me for a lunch of garden salad. The lettuce, carrots, and mushrooms, which they'd bought at a Swiss project in Mango, looked like small miracles. We ate outside their spacious concrete house, in the shade of a mango tree. Fanning themselves with their hands, they explained that they were in the second year of a seven-year mission in this village. Trained linguists, they were translating the Bible into Gam-Gam, a language spoken locally by about ten thousand people. They had nearly finished the first phase, the development of a Gam-Gam grammar and orthography.

As they spoke of the need for these people to know the Word of God in their own tongue, I thought that only a belief as strong as religious faith could keep one from going mad in seven years in this place. Perhaps the notion of futility never occurred to them. Perhaps this meant they were mad. I envied their serenity here anyway. They, too, seemed remote. Midway through the salad the Mennonites and I ran out of things to say, and I left shortly after lunch.

After a week of this vagabond life I was ready to go back south. Harmattan had left my skin and lips cracked and raw, I had dust in my ears and nostrils, the few clothes I had brought were all dirty. My money was running low as well, just enough to get me back to Atakpamé and the bank for my January check. At the taxi station in Kara a Mitsubishi van was almost full. I settled in, thinking of dampness, bougainvillea, and short energetic women in bright cloth.

In Atakpamé I didn't stop at John's, but went straight from the bank to the Kpalimé station and the first car down to the village. A driver demanded 200 francs for my bag. A ridiculous sum, and the trip was short. I refused the *yovo* price. *"Bon."* He shrugged and started the ignition. I offered 125. He knew I wanted to leave with him, and he wouldn't budge from 200. I argued some more but in the end I paid, for by now I had had enough of waiting in taxi stations and hearing wrong information about departure times and eating market rice and finding myself watched everywhere I went. I was about as anonymous on my travels as an eight-foot circus freak let loose in the streets. I wanted to be in the one room in Africa that I'd colonized for myself. I piled in next to a woman with a child on her lap and reached to roll down the window; the handle was broken. The taxi roared off, and as we wound down the hill past banana trees and metal shacks along the road to Kpalimé, I realized I'd been quarreling over twenty cents.

I traveled in Africa poised between exhilaration and ennui, the eland and the flies. Rooted in a village, I found ways to tame Africa's wildness for me and mine for it. Superficially, it became routine much faster than I'd ever expected. But on the road I was naked. Traveling exposed a white to the African elements—not just heat and wind and dust, but price gouging, stares, the sense of dislocation, the beguiling mixture of privilege and squalor Africa offered up to its new missionaries. Unless we were very rich or very poor at home, it was unlikely any of us had ever experienced such privilege and such squalor—least of all at the same time. I had the honor of the front seat—unless a soldier was traveling, in which case I was squeezed along with the others like livestock into the back. It was impossible to forget my white skin, even for a moment. And I began to see more clearly what it is to be white in black Africa.

"One of the most curious and interesting features connected with the annexation of Togoland by Germany, the colonisation of the territory by its Teuton administrators, and its final surrender to the allied British and French forces, is the quietness and decorum that has characterised every incident and phase of the several processes."

A. F. Calvert, a British imperial journalist, began his book *Togoland*, written at the end of World War I, with this paradox: that Togo under the colonial heel was a "smiling and prosperous" place. Nothing else in the book (essentially an assessment of Togo's value to the European victors and a pitch for British rule) is worth the phrase in that first sentence, "quietness and decorum." It captures what has apparently been in the European experience of Togo from the beginning. Calvert went on to enumerate the German misdeeds, the forced labor and rhinoceros whips, the exorbitant taxes, and, worst of all, the arrogance with which Germany believed it could achieve in thirty years what took England two patient centuries in India—and the shoddy, upstart version of empire that resulted. No wonder, he concluded wryly, that in 1914 "the ungrateful Togolanders should have acclaimed the Anglo-French troops not as invaders but deliverers, and have welcomed their triumphant entry into Lomé with every demonstration of enthusiastic joy." These points are true even though a propagandist is making them: the Germans did use indentured railroad labor, floggings, judicial execution, guns, and a primitive version of South Africa's Group Areas Act to bring civilization into Togo and cacao out of it. But Calvert found that they relied less on force than on prestidigitation and the promise of gain. The white presence in this part of Africa, and perhaps elsewhere, began with quietness and decorum, under the illusion of mutual goodwill.

In a ceremony whose centennial was celebrated a few years ago in Togo ("A Hundred Years of Germano-Togolese Friendship," the commemorative stamp proclaimed), the Ewé king's staff carrier and the German Consul Gustav Nachtigal signed a treaty on July 15, 1884, in which "King Mlapa of Togo, prompted by the wish to protect the legitimate trade of Togo, which is chiefly in the hands of German merchants, and by the desire to guarantee German merchants complete security of life and property, asks the protection of His Majesty, the German Emperor."

That needs to be parsed. In exchange for winning the German emperor's protection of German merchants doing business in Togo, the king agreed to sign away land to no other foreign power and levy no new tariffs without the German emperor's prior approval. One historian reassures us that the 1884 treaty wasn't signed in a drunken stupor or by force, but a German gunboat had docked down the coast in Anécho on July 2, and the Germans were anxious to beat out a British district officer named Reginald Firminger, who was pressing agreements on the chiefs in Lomé.

Within two years of the German treaty, chiefs in the villages around Kpalimé were complaining that they had seen no benefits from what they'd signed. The Germans sent James Badahoo, a mulatto factotum of the new colonial government, to pass out flags and money to mollify the chiefs. And so, before the whites had penetrated as far as Atakpamé, a pattern was already in place: European promise; African acquiescence; deception, disappointment; new promise.

Aside from rare uprisings, put down in blood, the pattern was played out for decades. The Ewé became the Togolese Kikuyu, flocking to schools and competing to fill positions in the civil service. But when a group of black elites from Lomé drew up a seven-point petition of grievances on law, punishment, representation, and taxes, the visiting colonial secretary wouldn't give them an audience. Instead, he pronounced himself satisfied with the state of Togo's roads and rest houses. The Germans were spending on education slightly more than on the maintenance of two automobiles, while a million and a half liters of liquor were imported into the colony every year. By 1914 Germany could vaunt Togo as its *Müsterkolonie*, its model colony, the only one whose revenue equaled its cost.

In August of that year World War I broke out, British and French troops moved in from the Gold Coast and Dahomey, and Germano-Togolese friendship collapsed within three weeks. The new masters were apparently received with the same goodwill as the old. Along no particular road or river, they sliced Togo and its Ewé population in two, bickering only over the lush cacao hills around Kpalimé. Lavié, by a whisker, made it into the sliver that was French Togoland. Forty years of colonialism under a League of Nations mandate followed, with no white settlers, no civil war, and a steady decline in French spending on the local population, which continued to build roads, attend schools, and hope for government jobs.

Something had happened to the *Müsterkolonie*. Always small, a historical anomaly in West Africa between the British and French empires, it was now barely two-thirds its original size and sinking into insignificance. An astute German imperial commissioner for Southwest Africa foresaw something like this while Togo was still German: "Togoland, from the first, has obtained the reputation of being our model colony," Paul Rohrbach wrote, "because it succeeded at an early date in paying its way, and no doubt it was spared sets-back [*sic*] by the wisdom of its administrators. In spite of all this we must not deceive ourselves and expect that a small colony that is not as richly endowed by nature as Kamerun and East Africa will make such important strides as those countries. It is therefore comprehensible that, should an opportunity arise, Togoland might be well handed over to a foreign power in exchange for a more satisfactory African possession."

France and Britain had divided up a backwater on the Gulf of Guinea. Maybe it had a balanced budget, maybe the natives were, as Calvert wrote, "smiling and prosperous." But after the scramble between Germans and British, between British and French, after the treaties had been signed, the government put in place, the people sent to school, to work, to war—after all this, Togo began to languish, in quietness and decorum.

. . .

The whites dotting the Togolese landscape today—an assortment of volunteers, technicians, priests, businessmen, diplomats, freelance Africanists, and drifters—live under the historical burden of this long anticlimax. And although they are guests now and free of the responsibility of ruling, few I knew seemed equal to the expectations that had been piling up for over a century.

There was still no shortage of goodwill, on either side—partly because of the accidents of size and climate. Whites never settled in Togo in any numbers because profit was limited by its smallness and the weather was too oppressive, so the deep enmities between blacks and whites in East and southern Africa never took root here. Everyone wanted to see the Togolese—who, seventy years after Calvert, were still smiling though not yet prosperous—become "developed." Visitors came through on two-week tours, fell in love with the place, and went home to publish promotional articles in their local papers about the beautiful little country and its friendly and hospitable people. "A vast chasm of cultures and continents separated us," read one, "yet how easy it was to bridge." Businessmen spoke of Togo's potential for Western investment. Those who stayed longer had to find ways to accept or explain away or ignore the failures. The worst temptation of all was to begin believing what the Togolese themselves seemed to believe of you—that here finally was someone who could make the difference.

In the last century a German named Heinrich Klose recorded an Ewé myth that, he asserted, dates to the arrival of the first missionaries on the coast. God, the myth goes, created blacks and whites, and gave each two baskets, of which they might choose one. The blacks chose a basket with farming tools, the whites one with a book of wisdom; and while the blacks worked the soil and gained physical strength, whites read the book and grew smart. With their superior strength blacks drove the whites into the sea, but God in sympathy saved the whites, who were fruitful across the sea, and eventually came back to Africa. Wiser than the blacks, favored by God, they gained back the land the blacks had forced them from.

As an African myth it strains credulity—just the sort of story a German missionary would concoct to justify to the Ewé their own

subjugation; at best, a way for the Ewé chiefs to blame their ig-
nominious treaties on fate. And yet no white who stays long in black
Africa, and isn't blinded by political principle or simple uneasiness
with his role, can fail to notice the deep sense of inferiority among
many blacks. Christine brought it home to me the day after a great
tree fell across the road outside our house.

Men with chain saws had cut up the massive trunk and hauled
the pieces aside to make the road passable; but one log was left
sticking out over the pavement. I came home from school the next
day to see the wreckage of a taxi in the bushes along our back wall.
It had missed the house by a few feet. Apparently the driver had
glanced off the log, lost control, crashed into the bush, and nearly
killed himself and his passengers. Villagers were hauling off the
culprit section of trunk, but for Christine, shaking her head in the
kitchen, the true culprit was blackness.

"That's the *ameyibo*," she said in disgust, using the word for
"black man." "They take away the tree *after* someone is dead."

I suggested that the same thing could easily happen in America,
but she was unmoved. The Ewé, she said—meaning, I think, Africans—knew nothing compared with whites: whites imitated
Mawu, God, while blacks tried to imitate whites. They knew nothing for themselves.

"And Ahonsu?" I asked, citing the engineer who had designed
Lavié's water system.

Christine laid her trump card. "Can Ahonsu make an airplane?"

"Can I?"

"Yes. You are *yovo*."

Christine admired not just my skill in aeronautical engineering
but my straight hair, my overlong nose, and above all my mottled
skin. Africans, she told me, had dark skin because they worked so
hard in the dirt. When Mawuli started informing me that I was his
father, and I held up my arm to disprove it, he answered, *"Ma klo
asi."*—"I'll go wash my hands."

Along with the beauty of the *yovo*'s pinkish skin came a super-
natural power. I once heard of a soccer game between two small-
town teams in the north in which one team had tied a rabbit's foot

on their own goalpost and managed to hold their opponents scoreless. But when a volunteer asked one of the players whether the Togolese national team ever did this in international competition, the player shook his head. "It wouldn't work. The *grigri* is strong, but not as strong as the whites'." One of the teachers in Lavié, explaining the attitude in economic terms, told me of an old villager who, upon learning that some whites had pensions which were passed on to their wives when they died, announced that a dead white was therefore worth more than a living black.

These were all anecdotes, but I wanted psychology. Did the proclaimed inferiority mask other feelings—anger, envy, distrust? For our benefit, or for theirs? Or were they telling us what they assumed we liked to hear, the way the hangers-on assured whites that a taxi was about to leave? Did the survival instinct, acquired during the years of colonialism and still applicable in a period that some described as neo-colonial, demand a flattery of whites' own self-love? Or was nothing behind it but the simple recognition, like the old man's, that whites were rich and they were poor?

But that was the fact you avoided facing day after day. And resisting it as you lived alongside them produced a constant strain, as if you'd had to alter your breathing slightly. The fact impinged anyway, in privilege and squalor. It was difficult to go on thinking kind thoughts about the Africans' decency amid such poverty when my frigo ran out of kerosene just as I had a rare sack of fresh vegetables from Atakpamé; difficult, too, when the attendant at the Texaco station in Kpalimé came up to me near the end of a long line for kerosene, on a rainy night, and took my *bidon* to fill; and difficult when the Africans in front of me did not call me dirty names but pleaded with me to get their *bidons* filled too. And finally, as I rode home with the full *bidon*, it was difficult not to feel some anger at the attendant and at the people in front of me, and to think that as long as someone like me could get kerosene ahead of the needier mothers and workmen who'd waited longer, the country would never develop, and I might as well go home.

But I had two years here—long enough to give in to temptation. I found myself the object of intense sexual attention. Hard not to cash in! I became a *patron*. Local boys appeared on the doorstep asking to do the laundry, sweep the house, wash the mobylette. Strangers came by, hands together in entreaty, for a loan, for medical advice or pills, for me to take their child to be educated *"chez les blancs."* It moved me to be needed. Life seemed more serious and dramatic than it ever had at home. I could hardly stand to disappoint them—and usually I gave out a few francs, faked my way through a diagnosis (all the while protesting that I wasn't a doctor), and even left them with a shred of hope about having a Western-educated offspring. Assigned the role of Albert Schweitzer, who could resist beginning to play it?

Yet alongside this unprecedented power and importance lay the obvious fact of your own futility. Teaching English grammar on a continent where millions of people were undernourished didn't inspire a flood of self-congratulation, but at least the "host nationals" knew what an English teacher was. An American who came to teach preventive health, or to introduce a high-protein but quite tasteless bean, or to set up a cooperative among seamstresses, spent half a year just finding local people to spread the word. One animal-traction volunteer who went home for a month when his father died returned to discover that "his" farmers had all abandoned their new AID oxen and gone back to the hand plow. And then, after two years, when you were just beginning to make some headway, your end of service came—and the Togolese around you smiled, shook their heads over how kind you'd been, and bade you good-bye, and didn't say what most were thinking: "But we're still poor." The mixture of expectation—and Peace Corps/Togo, like the old German colony, had the dubious label "model program"—with almost certain failure produced an unconfessed sense of guilt and resentment. You were asked to be Schweitzer, but you were feeling more like Kurtz.

In fact, rumors circulated of minor-league Kurtzes springing up among Togo's 120 volunteers. A teacher in the north had taken to beating his students and chasing *"Yovo"*-yelling kids on his mobylette. A cooperatives volunteer in the south pretty much stopped working altogether, accrued a vast collection of beetles, and hoarded his monthly allowance by living off his neighbors until he'd saved half a million francs; on a trip to Benin he was kicked out for taking pictures of women's naked breasts.

More often, though, loneliness and the sense of failure festered, scabbed, and eventually healed into more acceptable emotions— sentimentality, or cynicism, which amounted to the same thing. Either we were corrupting them and they could do fine without us (this approach went with wearing local shirts, speaking in French-African phrases, and counting the bowls of brew you drank with the peasants every day) or it didn't matter what we did, they'd never get it (accompanied by a trace of mockery during the endless greetings and devout readings of *Newsweek*). Both attitudes provided a way to simplify or overlook the messy situation they and we had inherited. Sometimes you held both simultaneously.

Yet these could and did exist alongside intense friendships with individual Togolese, in which both sides managed to transcend the roles set up for them and meet equally and honestly, with the thrill of human connection across barriers. Not the two-week tourist effortlessly bridging cultural chasms in a single bound, but the harder effort over months of going outside yourself, which meant acknowledging difference as well as commonness. It was a huge relief to confess self-doubt to an African who understood that all my money didn't guarantee happiness here, and to begin to see that the ready smile and laugh didn't guarantee happiness in him either.

But the roles were there to be played, and usually they were played.

The strain was partially eased when Peace Corps threw parties for its volunteers in the capital or one of the large towns. I went down to Lomé when I had to, about once every six weeks, for shots or to work on the volunteer newspaper. I still hated the city from the long wait in September. Humid, stinking, strangely big after the village, Lomé concentrated the ills of Africa without any of the peace and companionship I sometimes had in Lavié. But when white people flocked there for lavish fêtes at the ambassador's house, who could stay away?

The residence was a two-story whitewashed wedding cake on a central avenue, bathed in floodlights, with a tennis court to one side of the garden. One steamy evening in November two or three hundred Americans, with a handful of Togolese guests in functionaries' suits, gathered in the garden for the annual Thanksgiving party. Four long tables covered with white cloths were laden with roast turkeys, vast plates of stuffing and cranberry sauce, piles of rolls, tubs of fruit punch. The Peace Corps contingent could easily be distinguished from the embassy personnel, AID types, and businessmen who made up the rest of the American community; we wolfed down the meal as if we'd been on a starvation diet. Loudspeakers were booming swing music, and a few middle-aged white couples danced on the flagstones. When the music changed to African pop, younger Americans and a few Africans took their place. The Togolese help scurried about in white jackets, refilling punch bowls and collecting dirty paper plates.

During a lull, the ambassador appeared with his wife and daughter on the balustraded steps leading up to the house and spoke into the microphone. He was tall, good-looking in middle age, and deeply tanned. He thanked us all for coming, for remembering that his embassy was our embassy, and reminded us that the quickest way to kill the fun would be for the ambassador to give a long speech. But he just wanted to share with us, especially the volunteers among us, a little story he'd heard from Washington. Samuel Doe, the president of Liberia, had recently visited the States on a mission for U.S. aid. The first person Chairman Doe asked to see—before the assistant secretary of state, before anyone in Congress—was the man who, twenty years before, had been a Peace Corps Volunteer and taught him English in a Liberian village. Chairman Doe had insisted on thanking this man personally. And so, in case we had any doubts about the importance of our work here in Togo, he thought we might like to hear this story. And now, back to our eating and dancing, and don't forget that *Shane* would be screened by the tennis court at eight o'clock.

A volunteer friend turned to me, licking turkey grease from his fingers. Behind glasses his eyes shone with the contempt and envy volunteers felt toward the Americans who weren't making the doomed effort to live on African terms—who spoke feelingly of the local people's gentleness and avoided leaving Lomé. "Yes, maybe one of *your* students will grow up to disembowel a president and line up ministers on the beach to be shot."

But the partial deceptions and self-deceptions of white and black in Africa always seemed to drop away in the presence of *fous*. The madwoman of Adeta kept coming back; but she wasn't the only *fou* drawn by the sight of me. Mad Togolese seemed piqued by whites like mosquitoes by the heat and light of kerosene lamps. An old gray hag wrapped in shreds approached me at the taxi station in Kpalimé, put out her hand to shake mine, dropped my hand for my crotch, and rubbed it vigorously. When I told her to get away, she flew into a rage and shouted insults that made the cabmen laugh. One Friday in the Lavié market I felt my hand grabbed from behind and found myself face-to-face with a man in sunglasses flashing a toothy smile and pumping my hand. His overalls, shirt, and leather tie were splattered with paint of a dozen colors.

"Hale and hardy, hale and hardy!" he exclaimed in lightning-quick English, as if he'd run into a long-lost friend. "Brother, how are you? I'm fine, I'm so excellent, my name is Christopher yes but now that there's no more Christianity names in Togo I am Kokou, I did my school in Ghana first secondary then technic then woo-niversity, I went to the Kwame Nkrumah Ideological School then to Russia. Oh, yes, I did Russia, Jees Christ! So good to know you. Then to Germany that was in 1959 and then to California 1960. Jees Christ! You from California! Oh brother that is beautiful, yes, I was in California, I went to paint school, the Mitchigan Wooniversity in California. What? Yes, Mitchigan Wooniversity. That's right, Which City, come let's sit us down here for some rice. Oh Jees Christ dammit! this bench isn't properly good. I do paint and decorativation in Kpalimé, very happy with my talents that God gave me, yes He is merciful! Well, I must be off, yes write your address here, hale and hardy, God bless you! May you be happy and successful in your business, oh Jees Christ, Jees Christ, I am so joyous to meet you in your village here!"

I met Christopher-Kokou again in Kpalimé, in the same motley garb, at which point he tried to sell me marijuana—he called it "leaf." I later heard that he was known throughout the region as the madman from Ghana—driven over by the *yovo*'s cigarettes.

Encounters with *yovos* seemed to touch some chord in *fous*, of delight, anger, desire, humor, or sorrow—something so deep and troubling that in sane Africans years of social formality kept it hidden. A flash of recognition, a wound or hope too tender to be laid open by anyone who wasn't out of his senses. It was difficult to know what Europe would have to do before Africa would finally say, "Enough, you have gone too far, now get out." A century of promise and exploitation, the treaties and forced labor of early colonialism, the long, slow submergence that led to independence, the new promise of development and the new whites who came to help, the disillusionment of even the best-intentioned, continued dominance of the economy by foreigners, continued poverty—all of this, and the white was still welcomed, still admired.

The madwoman of Adeta greeted me many times; I saw her greeting other whites who stopped in the taxi station. It was as if she were searching with her white-painted face into the white face of each of us for the husband who'd betrayed her, to smile and forgive him and have him back, or bring vengeance on his head with a lethal kiss.

CHAPTER 5

Authenticity

I WAS BACK IN LAVIÉ WHEN 1982 GAVE WAY TO 1983. The villagers celebrated with a heavy flow of palm wine, libations to the ancestors, and dancing on the road throughout New Year's Day. Aboï had marked the holiday by having greeting cards printed up in a florid script and distributing a dozen copies each to his staff:

LE DIRECTEUR CEG LAVIÉ
ET SON PERSONNEL

VOUS SOUHAITENT UNE BONNE
ET HEUREUSE ANNÉE NOUVELLE

Agbefianou pointed out that a *du* belonged before *CEG*, and objected to being reduced to *"Personnel"* for the sake of a rhyme. But he said the card was elegant and would please his mother back in the village.

We were entering the political season.

January 13 and 24 were the supreme days on the Togolese calendar, eclipsing even April 27, Independence Day. But neither of them marked anything an American would associate with a national holiday—no famous birth, no document signed, no victory in war. They commemorated, respectively, a murder and a plane crash.

By 1963 Sylvanus Olympio, the Ewé from Anécho who led Togo to independence and became its first president, had lost a good deal of his popular support. Economic austerity, growing repression of opposition parties, and a "pan-Ewé" vision that put reunification of the Ghanaian and Togolese Ewé ahead of national unity, had alienated various sectors of society, from the rich market women in Lomé to the mainly non-Ewé army. Olympio's contempt for the *"petits nordistes"* became clear when a detachment of Togolese officers and soldiers—most of them Kabyé, and among them a young sergeant named Etienne Gnassingbé Eyadema—returned to Lomé from service with the French in the Algerian War and applied for admission into the Togolese army. Olympio, an African nationalist, like most of the first generation of rulers, replied in effect that he would never allow into his army a contingent of troops who had let themselves be used by an imperial power in a war against African liberation. No doubt the soldiers heard the word *Kabyé* before *troops*. And so Olympio had several hundred unemployed, spurned, and armed soldiers of a minority tribe loose in his capital.

Twenty-five years and dozens of bloody coups later, an African leader would recognize such a state of affairs as a signature on his own death warrant. But in the early sixties, between the long colonial silence and the sometimes harsher silence that has now settled over most of independent Africa, there was a moment's opening of free politics and enormously high hopes. The early leaders, as "fathers" of independence—Senghor in Senegal, Kenyatta in Kenya, Nyerere in Tanzania, Nkrumah in Ghana, Touré in Guinea—seemed invulnerable giants. Olympio, by becoming the first victim of a coup d'état on the continent, became the lesson, the most important one in African politics, that every subsequent ruler has had to learn in order to survive: that is, to put survival before anything, to count on force, to take nothing for granted.

A good deal of legend and murkiness surround the night of January 13, 1963. Eyadema has never taken credit for firing the shot that killed Olympio as he was scrambling over the wall from his residence onto the grounds of the American embassy, but he has allowed credit to devolve on himself. In the official version, Olympio broke free of the handful of soldiers who had stormed his house, and—the cowardice is one more blow against his battered legacy—ran for refuge to a foreign embassy. A friend once showed me an article written by an exiled Togolese member of the dissident Mouvement Togolais pour la Démocratie. My friend's copy, smuggled in from Ghana, was kept hidden under his mattress. In this version, which purported to tell the true story, Eyadema and his henchmen shot Olympio while he was kneeling captive at their feet, and Eyadema himself delivered a couple of gratuitous stabs to the corpse with his bayonet. "This was how we made sure they were dead in Algeria," a passing taximan supposedly heard him sneer. The author had taken the pseudonym "Kesedufia" ("The Monkey Shall Be King"). All of this left me skeptical that the dissident account was any truer than the government's. Eyadema had allowed the story to take shape in a way that consecrated him simultaneously as killer and hero. That seemed more significant than who had really pulled the trigger, and whether it had been done in cold blood.

Although the rest of Africa and the West reacted with horror, inside Togo Olympio's murder seems to have been generally taken with relief or indifference. The soldiers set up a civilian government, with a half-Polish, half-Togolese from Atakpamé named Nicholas Grunitzky as president. He lasted exactly four ineffectual years amid riotous demonstrations in Lomé. By November 1966 he had lost control, but Eyadema (now a lieutenant colonel) waited for the symbolic date of January 13, the fourth anniversary of Olympio's murder, to remove him—this time without a shot. Eyadema assumed temporary power "at the insistence of the people," suspended the April elections and the constitution, dissolved parliament and political parties, and devoted the next five years to consolidating his power within a new single party, the Rassemblement du Peuple Togolais (RPT). Each time he announced he was going to hand the presidency over to civilians, "spontaneous" public outcries forced him to stay. By 1972 this man of no political ambitions had consolidated enough power to win 99 percent approval in a referendum in which soldiers guarded the voting booths and voters held up a card of one color for "yes" or another for "no." By 1979 the one percentage point of skeptics had been won over. Gbadamassi, the sports teacher, wore a T-shirt that proclaimed: "Elections 1979: Victoire 100%!" And January 13 became National Liberation Day.

The coal-black face staring out of the early official portraits—to me so strikingly like Aboï's—does not look like that of a head of state. In military uniform, with powerful shoulders and neck, and a hand ceremoniously placed on a stack of heavy tomes, Eyadema has a dull expression, a complete lack of sophistication that is also lack of fear—the thick, blunt face of a peasant soldier who has been gutsy and unimaginative enough to commit a murder and grab power. The face has a bull's resolve, suggesting that power won't pass on until someone just as gutsy and unimaginative takes aim at it.

On January 24, 1974, Eyadema became a statesman and a semi-divine. The date has been transfigured into a nearly religious event, a sort of national Easter; and yet it sprang from the banality of a dispute over mining rights. For some weeks the Togolese had been tussling with the French company that owned the Kpemé phosphate mine near Anécho. On a wind of anti-imperialism that had blown in from Zaire, where Mobutu Sese Seko was in the process of Africanizing the country, Eyadema announced that Togo would nullify a 1957 agreement and demand 51 percent interest in its leading mineral export, as well as control over prices and trade. The Compagnie Togolaise des Mines du Benin tried to buy out the Togolese for billions of African francs, then to bribe Eyadema, according to his French biographer, with a deposit of thirty million French francs in a Swiss bank account. Eyadema apparently dug in his heels. On January 24 he was flying in his private plane from Lomé to his mother's home in Pya, when, on descent, and in full view of the officials lined up to receive him, it crashed near the village of Sarakawa. The two French pilots died, but Eyadema survived almost unscathed.

Immediately the crash dissolved in mythic mists. The French, in order to thwart the national will, had sabotaged the plane; Eyadema had defied the white man and survived; and his survival was testimony to a magical power. Shooting Olympio, he had proved his human strength. Walking out of the Sarakawa crash, he became partly divine.

Two years later a French journalist wrote a biography of Eyadema that amounted to a lubricious apology. Any book beginning with "This book is in no manner that of a hagiographer" can hardly hold out for long, and by page two we are well on our way toward a saint's life: "Athletic build, glowing smile, frank, direct expression, he's a force of nature who has leapt to the highest peaks through courage and decisiveness." A photograph shows Eyadema, the day after the crash, standing at a microphone on an outdoor stage before a sea of worshiping faces that shine in the brilliant sun. Enveloped in a traditional white robe, hands spread, he has been brought to them as a sovereign cleansed through an ordeal by fire, a savior returned from death. On his nine-day descent from Kara to Lomé he was always dressed in the white of purity and sovereignty and received everywhere along the "itinerary of victory" by joyous crowds. The book quotes a contemporary publication describing his arrival in one northern town:

> A beneficent rain, herald, according to ancestral tradition, of the goodwill of the gods toward humans, and gauge of the presence of the shades of the ancestors alongside the living during the events that would follow—a rain, then, had fallen the night before on the happy town of Bafilo, whose inhabitants were going to have the honor of the disciples of Emmaüs. . . . They led out a goat and burned it as tradition demands on solemn occasions. The horsemen brought out their harnessed coursers as on the greatest feast days, and the cannon fired twenty-one times when General Eyadema arrived at the Place de l'Indépendance.

Triumphantly entering Lomé on February 2, Eyadema appeared on the steps of the party building and addressed ecstatic throngs. A Togolese journalist reported, "After he had submitted to different rites prescribed by tradition to dispel bad luck, we gave him such an ovation that for several minutes it wasn't possible to hear the loudspeakers which were asking for silence. We felt that the forces of evil had been overcome at Sarakawa." When the speech finally began, it was sprinkled with proverbial testaments to his own virility in surviving the crash: "When you hunt in the bush, never try to fire on a buffalo if you're not sure of killing it on the spot." At the climax Eyadema announced the nationalization of the phosphate mine.

January 24 was canonized as Economic Liberation Day. New luxury hotels were named Sarakawa and 2 Février. A museum was built on the crash site, a road paved to it through the local farms, and the shell of the plane preserved for pilgrims and tourists. The village of Sarakawa turned into a somnolent Mecca, a holy shrine among the millet fields.

And what came of all this was Authenticity. Eyadema had already decreed it on the eve of the crash. "In celebrating liberation," he had said, "we must not only think of political liberation but must also have in mind the other liberations which are not yet complete and which remain for us to conquer. We mean cultural and economic liberation. . . . To free our spirits is to return to the African sources; it is to free ourselves from foreign ideologies and examples, which are adapted neither to our means nor to our soul and which, finally, chain our growth, block our development." The next day Sarakawa became a divine sign for this too.

Christian names were forbidden in public. This explained the piece of tape affixed to portraits of Eyadema in shops, bars, and schools all over Togo, blocking out "Etienne" in the name. Now he was, authentically, just "Son Excellence le Général Gnassingbé [blank] Eyadema." It also explained the names of the Agbeli children: Lucien, Claudie, Markie, and Emma—all with French names—were born before 1974; Dové, Mawuli, and Aku came after the Authenticity decree (Atsu, the one exception, kept an African name in customary memory of his twin, who had died in infancy). When she went to school, where her spirit was not returned to the African sources, but instead to learning French, Emma was called

Abra; back in her mother's thatched kitchen and speaking Ewé, she became Emma again.

With Authenticity, tribal festivities began to draw dignitaries in sunglasses, and sometimes even *le grand* himself would helicopter into the interior for a Kabyé wrestling tournament or the Feast of the New Yam, while the official daily in Lomé ran headlines on it for a week.

But the touchstone of Authenticity was *animation*. Hordes of young men and women, the *militants animateurs* of the RPT's youth wing, assembled wherever the president appeared. Rows of them—muscular young men, young women resplendent in *pagnes* patterned with the president's face—danced to drums in synchronized gestures, sinuous and jerky, soft and fierce, now political cheerleaders, now fanatics at an African Nuremberg rally, singing the praises, chanting the name of the Father of the Country. Every village, every school, trained its own corps of *animateurs*.

Authenticity, however, did not spring from the native soil of Togo. Eyadema lifted almost the whole of it from his good friend Mobutu Sese Seko, president of Zaire, who was busy formulating his philosophy of Mobutism at the time Eyadema was surviving the crash.

"When we speak of Authenticity, we don't pretend we never laid eyes on Europeans," a Togolese friend of mine said one day at the school where we were training, explaining the banners—*"Vive la Culture Africaine," "Vive le Recours à l'Authentique"*—strung from trees above the streets of Atakpamé for the Feast of the New Yam. My friend had laid eyes on more Europeans than most Togolese. A French teacher with Peace Corps and the son of the director of the American Cultural Center, he had spent a summer as an international counselor at a camp in Pennsylvania and was about to receive his degree in statistical economics from the Université du Benin. He was as intellectually privileged as anyone I knew in Togo, and that same day spoke of the alienation he and others like him felt when they came back home from the Western dreamworld. Privileged enough to be able to put Authenticity in terms I could understand, yet "authentic" enough to believe what he was telling me.

"We know it is both undesirable and impossible to return to a precolonial state. A return to the authentic means taking stock of what Togo has and is before moving ahead. We don't want to be in such a hurry that what we have, what holds us together, is destroyed in our haste. This has happened in Nigeria and in the Ivory Coast. We are moving forward, but with a policy of slowness."

While we were chatting a cry rang out from the teak trees in back of our school, and a crowd of sixty or seventy kids went running and screaming down the hill past us, carrying the green leaves of yam stalks like Birnam Wood rushing toward Dunsinane. The Feast of the New Yam had begun. And I wondered, was this authenticity?

Or when an old village *griot* on the plateau with a wad of tobacco in one cheek sang his repertoire of songs, half of them parables of hard work and tales of war, half hymns of thanks to Eyadema the "liberator"—was I hearing authenticity, or the new state religion with a capital *A*? Were they the same thing?

The problem, as I began to puzzle over Authenticity, was that no one who ever used the term seemed terribly "authentic." The Nigerian writer and Nobel Prize winner Wole Soyinka wrote with disdain about Negritude, an older cousin of Authenticity: "A tiger does not speak of its Tigritude." A tourist might hear of Authenticity from his hotel guide during an excursion to one of the villages near Lomé for a staged fetish dance, but farmers (whose vocabulary included *development* and *economic crisis*) didn't seem inclined to refer to their own authenticity in my presence. Instead, I was more likely to hear of it from a man like Monsieur Ati Dadjo.

During our training the cross-culture specialists at the Peace Corps office decided that the new arrivals should have firsthand exposure to traditional life in a Togolese household. I was given money, the name Ati Dadjo, and a rough map to the village of Atchakpo in the flat humid grassland north of the coast.

A Peugeot 404 was parked with its hood up in the driveway next to a glass-louvered window. A concrete wall with an iron gate ringed the yard, and around the base of the elegant brick house frangipani and other tropical flowers grew in a bed of chocolate-brown soil that looked deliciously rich amid the yellow sands of the region. Beside the front steps an arrangement of neatly trimmed green shrubs announced "DADJO." The house was separated from the rest of Atchakpo, with its mud and grass huts, by a cornfield, rather like a feudal manor standing apart from the hovels of serfs.

Monsieur Dadjo, the principal of CEG Atchakpo, lean and weasel-faced in his forties, did not seem to understand who I was or why I'd come, but he invited me in anyway. The interior of the house was spacious and dark, like most houses built for functionaries, as if anything smaller would be unworthy. But a shortage of possessions left it eerily bare: a few mahogany chairs arranged on the concrete floor, a couch, a buffet with glass doors, a dining table. On the walls—this, too, was typical of functionary housing—framed aphorisms dispensed bits of optimistic wisdom in French: "A Man Who Follows His Heart Can Have No Fear." But what caught and held my eye was a small television next to the couch. It was on, with the volume off, and a pair of jumper cables led like feeding tubes from the back of the set out the open window to the engine of the Peugeot under its raised hood. They were hooked up to the battery. Atchakpo lacked electricity and running water, but Monsieur Dadjo had managed to improvise modern life even here among the huts and cornstalks.

The television was on through most of the two days I spent in Monsieur Dadjo's house, volume on or off—and a good thing it was, since we didn't have much to say even after I'd reminded him why I was spending the weekend here. For the first few hours we sat before the TV and endured long stretches of silence, punctuated by sudden questions from him: "Monsieur Reagan, he is too old. Will Kennedy defeat him?" My answers got a nod or a laugh—and then he had a way of covering his face with his hand and groaning.

He seemed excruciatingly bored. A beautiful and utterly wordless younger sister did the cooking and sat with us at meals. Other than her and a handful of children whose origin I couldn't quite establish, Monsieur Dadjo lived alone in the big house. It occurred to me that Togolese saw nothing rude in silence, and at the same time privacy held no value for them. Monsieur Dadjo considered it an obligation to sit with me or accompany me on every walk though the village, where funeral drums were rumbling through most of the weekend. And so we spent hours on end together, saying nothing.

In the long intervals I had my first look at Togolese TV.

The evening's program starts with *animation*, and continues with more *animation*, at the airport, on the steps of the RPT palace in Lomé, under a baobab tree in a northern village. The music and singing don't change, the gestures don't change—only the backdrop, as if a kaleidoscope of locations is being projected on a screen behind the same group of *animateurs*. Authenticity is Authenticity, it suggests, in Lomé or the bush. The *animation* has been a warm-up for the evening news. In tonight's clips an emissary arrives at the president's office, smilingly shakes hands across the vast desk, sits humbly while the president dons glasses and reads the bearer's letter from some head of state, then stands, is thanked, shakes hands again, goes out. This is repeated four or five times—emissaries in suits and ties and emissaries in robes and turbans, black emissaries and white emissaries—so that in these vignettes the set, including the president behind his desk, remains, while the other character changes, each new one going through the same routine, as in silent comedy. The news in French ends, and the same program is repeated in Kabyé by a man in a dyed cotton *bubu* shirt, and in Ewé by a heavy woman in expensive Dutch Wax *pagnes*. By this time the president has received at least twelve emissaries. An ad for Rothman's cigarettes follows, elegant, attractive black couples smoking in a plush bar. A video act comes on; an Ivorian reggae singer in a rugby shirt dances under a palm tree, mouthing the words to the music. Then, in a solicitous celebrity interview, the same singer is in a studio telling us why Lomé is a good place for recording artists. With this the evening's programming ends and an attractive African woman in Parisian fashions bids us good-night; but the channel doesn't go off the air for another half hour. Unintroduced, the long filler coda is a sun-washed scene in a field where women are dancing to Ewé drums. They wear simple cloths and dance with great energy, but they seem to be outside the context of any village, in the middle of nowhere. No one is watching. The film goes on and on. And then, without closure, it's cut off, and the tube shows static.

By this time I had the impression that Africa is two distinct worlds in which the African viewer feels equally at home: the modern and the authentic, reggae dancer and Ewé dancers, *animation* at the airport and *animation* under the baobab. Africans move between these as easily as the segments change. They left me a little dizzy, these collages of Africa as it saw itself or wanted itself to be seen— at any rate by whites and the few blacks who could afford a TV. I had to blink and look over at Monsieur Dadjo on his couch to remember that the images had been a hallucination.

Lying on the couch after dinner the second night, the only light the fluorescent glow of a rerun soccer game, Monsieur Dadjo suddenly opened up. He said his wife, who worked for the post, lived with their children in Lomé, and since his assignment to CEG Atchakpo he could only visit them on weekends and holidays. He enjoyed Lomé; he never found himself bored there.

"The man of the city," he said, "is not as happy as the peasant, you know. He owns so many things, and he has so many worries. For the peasant, authentic life is work, work, work, very hard—but at least he is in peace."

"And you?"

He passed his hand over his face. "This place is not my home. What is there for me in Atchakpo? Could you live here?"

What was enough for the farmers in the huts across the cornfield was not enough for him. The Peugeot, the flowers, the functionary's house, elegant but barely furnished, the TV that was never turned off but had to run on a car battery, were barriers thrown up against the sun-drenched village and the monotony of the grassland. Monsieur Dadjo seemed to see this as his own loss. For all I knew he'd grown up in a village just like Atchakpo, and he still spoke the local Watché with his sister; but his focus on the peasants across the cornfield was already distanced and softened. He knew their lives were hard, but he envied them anyway. They were "authentic"; he was not. Monsieur Dadjo's world was nothing like the seamless fantasy on the screen that he stared at every night. His had elements of both TV worlds; but the mixture—neither glamorous nor pastoral—made him uneasy. It was a corruption, full of impurities.

In the silence that returned after his brief confession, beneath the frenzied play-by-play of the soccer announcer, the drumming from the village was just audible. I asked Monsieur Dadjo about the funeral, about the fetishism common in this region. He gave a contemptuous wave of the hand.

"That doesn't concern me. It is not interesting."

By the time I arrived in Togo, Authenticity was almost ten years old. And in that decade Togo, with the rest of Africa, had slid close to economic ruin. As world phosphate prices crashed, the mine at Kpemé went bankrupt and Togo's foreign debt exceeded the GNP. Ironically, the nationalization of the mining industry happened just before the world mineral market collapsed. And so the plane crash, the itinerary of victory, the speech in Lomé, the slogans of economic independence had to do with acquiring a mine that was about to become almost worthless.

It was hard, in 1983, to see how much more "liberated" from France Togo's economy was than it had been in 1974. The cash crops were still controlled by France, at French prices; the currency was tied to the French franc; the luxury hotels in Lomé, named after the glorious event, were designed with their French haute cuisine and their casinos to attract scarce European currency. And the smaller concerns, the shops along the ocean road stocked with radios, bottles of liquor, and kitchen appliances, were owned by Lebanese. Now intellectuals at the Université du Benin were talking about the need for a "neo-colonialism" to salvage a country in which everything seemed to be grinding to a halt. Invite the whites back in, give them the run of industries, open tax-free investment zones. The government had begun to do just this: it was selling off the fifty-eight state companies as fast as foreign investors could be found to buy them. And the state was trying to persuade its surplus functionaries to go back to the village and farm.

The idea of Authenticity was the luxury of a fatter time. Persisting in the austere eighties, as the threat of losing their privileges drew close to educated Africans, Authenticity now seemed perfunctory and without conviction. At the All-Africa Trade Fair in the Togo 2000 Park—erected like a Disney World on the airport road outside

Lomé to celebrate African productivity and cooperation—among the pavilions of Algerian cosmetics, Italian mechanized threshers, and Japanese minibuses, one stall had displays of millet and local cloth. Except for the lovely bored women sitting behind the displays, the "authentic" stall was empty. The Africans who arrived by the busload—hordes of schoolchildren, functionaries in leisure suits—lingered by the rows of gleaming Nissans, as if they knew that Togo would not make it to 2000 on millet and local cloth. They weren't gulled by shiny chrome and bucket seats; it was just that most of them knew poverty well enough to know that the alternative to Nissans was not Authenticity but sweat.

Imported from Mobutu's Zaire, Authenticity existed only for the Westernized Togolese in Lomé who adapted it. It was a nostalgic dream, a false answer to a real need. The need would not disappear under the whitewash of any slogan: the psychic problem of alienation and loss was authentic enough. But state-sponsored Authenticity, I began to think, was a contradiction, authenticity turned on its head. As soon as the regime blessed the Feast of the New Yam, the Feast of the New Yam ceased to be a rite and became a tourist attraction, a fantasy for intellectuals, a ready excuse for underdevelopment, a part of the leader's cult. Anything authentic remained in spite of Authenticity.

On the morning of January 13, 1983, the twentieth anniversary of the bloody coup, while President Mitterrand, visiting from France, was being hailed alongside President Eyadema on their parade route past the new grandstands in Lomé, I woke up in Lavié to the sound of drums. After fried eggs and coffee I went out with my tape recorder into the yard, where Christine, alone except for Aku tied to her back, was slitting dried palm fronds into strips for matting. Wasn't she going to watch the celebration of National Liberation Day? She gave me her sad smile, tilted her head, and murmured, *"J'aime pas ça."*

She was about the only one missing. The patchy yellow grass between the road and the primary school in front of the CEG was thronged with villagers. The elders sat in a row of plain wood chairs, frail shoulders exposed toga-style by traditional robes. Cushioned armchairs were reserved for a man in an olive-green functionary's suit and for the chief, who sat in the dead-middle, erect, nostrils flared, in his most brilliant *kente* cloth, all royal blues and oranges and reds and greens. On his balding head he wore the cardboard crown with imitation jewels that was brought out for special occasions. Behind these dignitaries a few teachers were standing a bit uneasily, among them Aboï. His powerful arms were folded across a traditional *bubu* with a pattern that looked like an infrared image of his rib cage; on the shirtfront a small gold badge gleamed, the Eyadema badge. He surveyed the crowd like a security man sent to make sure the Ewé village went through the proper rituals of homage to the Kabyé president.

Facing the VIPs, hundreds of villagers milled about in a rough semicircle around the grass: farmers in work clothes; women in *pagnes* (a few printed with Eyadema's portrait) and head scarves, babies clinging to their backs; old men passing bowls of palm wine; old women munching tobacco; barefoot children dashing among the legs of the grown-ups, the smallest cross-legged on the grass in front. A few CEG boys had climbed two baobab trees and were lounging in the limbs. I found my way to the front of the crowd and crept out a few yards toward the VIPs, started my tape recorder, left it, and retreated to kneel by the children. I noticed one of the elders seated across the grass staring at me, perhaps unsure what the machine was for or what a *yovo* was doing crawling out among the hoi polloi.

The noise of laughing, shouting, and quarreling was raucous. Children pushed each other and bumped into adults, who wheeled on them in exasperation and raised a hand before the kids went squealing off. Heavy with the smell of cloth and sweat and baby, it could have been a market, or a taxi station, or a ticket line at the airport, or a funeral dance, or even the pictures I later saw of the refugees filling buses out of Nigeria—loaded with energy that could explode any moment, in fury, panic, or euphoria, there was no telling which.

Someone was giving a speech: the functionary, hands clasped over his olive-green belly. A teacher later told me that he was a local party chief. He made a halfhearted speech in Ewé on behalf of the government's planned parenthood campaign. Apparently this pitch was a yearly event; every year the village elders nodded their approval, and every year nothing was done about it. The farmers wanted babies, their wives feared sterility. While he was talking, the crowd's noise didn't diminish a decibel; his back to us, the functionary was addressing the VIPs, and none of the commoners listened.

After ten minutes he sat down, and my landlord, the chief, stood, arranging his royal *kente*. He gave a mercifully brief speech—again in Ewé and again to the VIPs. The boisterousness kept up. As soon as he sat down the crowd let out a tremendous cheer. Immediately a group of young men under one of the baobabs lit into their drums, another roar went up, and a line of boys and girls came dancing out from behind the VIPs onto the grass. They were my students—the younger CEG kids who had been out of class rehearsing all week. It was time for *animation*. The crowd had been gearing up for this; now all its energy was directed at the kids, who danced in rows with their backs to the VIPs.

A skinny, anxious boy and a heavy girl with mare's thighs led them from the front. The first song was a welcome:

"*Soyez, soyez, les bienvenus! Soyez, soyez, les bienvenus!*"

The drums were beating up-tempo, bodies of all sizes were making rapid-fire synchronized moves, absurdly unlike anything from traditional dance—a twirl of the index finger, a clawing at the air on one side, then the other, touching a toe, pointing to the sky, like background vocalists of a Motown group. The drums stopped with a thump, the students shouted "Hey!" and froze in place. Their two leaders tossed out questions.

"Are you ready to work the land?"

The answer came back in a chant:

"Yes, and of course yes! Eating to one's fill must be the enterprise of Africans in general and of Togolese in particular, by the harvest of our own garden!"

More questions, more answers. Long-winded French phrases about "economic independence" and "authentic culture"; a local proverb I couldn't quite make out that ended, "It is the hunter who dies!" Then a chanted tribute to Eyadema: "Thanks to him the spirit of the new Togo has been born. *Merci, merci, merci.*" Before the crowd could get restless with these abstractions the drums started up, the same hollow rolling beat. They were singing of Eyadema again:

"Eyadema eh! Eyadema eh! E-ya-de-ma!"

It had a catchy pop tune. By luck or genius the tribal drumbeat and the radio melody interlaced perfectly. These jingles could be hard to dislodge from the brain. I watched the crowd around me, absorbed, swaying and dancing in place, some still talking, some shouting approval and delight: *"Enyo, enyo! Bien dansé!"* Children drummed their hands on the grass, a mother bent forward with her baby on her back and rolled her buttocks. The VIPs looked on approvingly. Even Aboï had uncrossed his arms.

The drums stopped, another "Hey!" another round of slogans. A question was flung out by the anxious boy, and the students were ready with their reply:

"Yes, yes! Every conscientious Togolese must add something to humanity by planting a tree every June first!"

A man who lived in our quarter shouted "Bravo!" and others took it up. Drums, dancing, singing, another infectious melody:

"Happy, happy the people!
 Happy the Togolese people!"
"Be Togolese!" the boy commanded.
"Take up your axes!"
"Be Togolese!" the girl commanded.
"Take up your hoes!"

My pants pocket was being tugged. I looked down. Dové, Christine's five-year-old, was at my hip beaming. She giggled and jiggled her shoulders, mouthing her own mangled version of the French slogans.

Something had happened. Without a word or sign from the VIPs, without any change in the songs, the occasion had ceased to be political. "Eyadema" was repeated mesmerically, but the name had given way to an older spell—the pounding of leather drums. The VIP section sat silent, the RPT man was forgotten. The hoi polloi had taken over. Peasants and children were enjoying themselves as they would at an all-night funeral. No one laughed when students got the French slogans wrong, because these had ceased to matter. They were words—even less, sounds; the rhythm and the energy they awoke obliterated their sense and the even weaker echo of the day's speeches. And the students—the *militants animateurs*, members of the RPT youth wing—were now village children, intent on the movements they'd been rehearsing all week. The command may have been "Go back to the land"; the chants may have been "Eyadema, Eyadema"; but the voices of children and farmers and women with babies gyrating on their backs said, "We are here, together, dancing the dance of the village, of the ancestors, for we belong to them, to each other!"

As the dance came to an end I retrieved my tape recorder, turned it off, and squeezed through the crowd. Already people were heading home. If a closing speech had been planned they would miss it. I went home, too, marveling at the method the government had hit upon to infect with its propaganda even this remote, self-contained village of peasants. Roll the words out with drums, sugar them with pop melodies, turn it into a fête. State Authenticity had insinuated itself into something truly authentic, and its success was fatal. Eyadema presided over the whole morning. By the end he was irrelevant.

That afternoon I had lunch at the chief's. He was not in a good mood. He had changed out of the ceremonial *kente* into Bermuda shorts and a fishnet T-shirt, and he received me in his living room, at a desk stacked with papers beneath the framed black-and-white photos of himself enthroned, his predecessors, and his mother. A radio was crackling on the desk. We went outside to sit at a small table under palm fronds in his concrete yard, where one of his wives served us fermented corn mush and sauce; the other wife and an older daughter were picking through a pile of dried cacao beans and throwing out the bad ones. The cacao harvest was just in; it had been sparse. As he pinched fingerfuls off his ball of sour mush, the chief's forehead was creased. Suddenly he said: "He has become a *voyou*."

"Who?"

"Lucien! Benjamin's oldest, my nephew. Does he come to class anymore? Does he do your chores?"

"Well, I don't see him in class these days. But he still does my wash even if he forgets to sweep sometimes. Last week he wanted four weeks' pay in advance to buy a pair of shoes."

"A pair of shoes!" the chief snorted. "What does he need with that? He wastes his time in Kpalimé, or out on that rock."

There was a rock between the chief's compound and the road opposite the bistro, where the village *voyous* hung out making comments at passersby. Some of them tossed out a friendly *"Yovo!"* at me, but in my presence Lucien was polite and diffident and never failed to use *monsieur*; after all, I was his *patron*.

"No, no"—the chief smacked his lips—"he isn't good. And now the dry season is with us, and my cacao harvest has come to nothing."

I was reminded of the chief and his burdens some months after I left Togo when, safely in Boston, I opened the *Globe* one morning to an article about Pope John Paul II's trip to Africa. I'd been carefully following the news of his trip, since his first stop was Togo. Apparently the authorities there knew about photo opportunities, and every morning for a week a new picture greeted me in the paper, each a variation on the same exotic, comical theme: the pope blesses a woman with a basket of pineapples on her head, the pope drinks water (bottled, I hoped) from a calabash, the pope shakes the hands that protrude from a flock of tribal chiefs. That last one stayed in mind the whole day after it appeared, and when I looked again in the evening, I saw why. The hand in the middle belonged to my landlord, my Scrabble partner, the chief himself. He was wearing the same *kente* cloth and paper crown he'd worn the morning of January 13. He was reaching out for the pope's hand, about to clasp it.

And I thought of the first time he reached for my hand. The

pope's reception in the capital outdid mine in Lavié (President Eyadema didn't turn out for me), but the expression on the chief's face was just the same: the expectation, the delight. "Things are going to change now," he had assured me as I was unloading the boxes and wicker baskets. "With a Peace Corps here—ah, *c'est bien*."

During the dry season, when the village men had nothing to do but argue and drink *sodabi*, the chief and I sat in my living room and played Scrabble on a French board. The game fascinated him— another stroke of Western cleverness, like the radio he never turned off. I knew the rules better, but he would beat me with words like *kora* and *fufu*. "That's not in the dictionary!" "It's an Africanism," he would reply with pious finality.

In the evenings we drank lagers inside Kodjo's bistro, or had a boy bring them across the road into the chief's compound (public drinking would have been unseemly for him). He always wore the Bermuda shorts and fishnet T-shirt, and always had his radio tuned to the European football results—not just because he bet on them in the Togolese national lottery (and had his hopes of an insider's line wrecked when I had to tell him I knew nothing of the subject) but, it seemed to me, because they belonged to the same elusive world as Scrabble and bottled lager.

Evening was the time to tell me of his troubles. The paltry rains of 1982 had withered his cacao fields, which would mean several poor harvests. Every one of his children and his nephews and nieces had flunked school. Lucien was turning *voyou*. And always there were his own money problems. The government owed him a year's back rent for my tenancy, and he waited for it like the rain. Whenever the chiefs were summoned to the capital for a conference, he would lodge a complaint at the Service de Matériel, the bureau that had kept me dangling in Lomé for six weeks. These excursions were signaled by his appearance out on the village road in the *kente* cloth and the paper crown: for the benefit of National Liberation Day, his fellow chiefs, the international photographers, or the pope, the chief had to become authentic. As soon as he got back to the village he changed into the Bermuda shorts and fishnet T-shirt again. And when I asked him what response he'd received from Service de Matériel, he would simply shake his head and smack his lips.

"Without development," he said one night, sipping beer, "life is too difficult for us Africans. Consider me. My wives have given me twelve children. Too many! How can I support them with the economic crisis? I advise you to stop at six, you'll never be able to afford more."

The pope had something to say to Africans on the same subject, after he'd left Togo and arrived in Cameroon. "Birth control programs carry a powerful antilife mentality," he announced at a rainy mass. And, in his own gloss on Authenticity: "They suppress the African people's healthy love of children. You must beware of the streak of crass Western materialism in development."

But the chief's idea of *le développement*, a word that echoed in Togo like a mysterious fetish incantation, was already crass and materialistic before either the pope or I met him. He had two schemes for the wealth and well-being of the village. The first was to bring electricity to Lavié, in order to make way for a bar and perhaps even a gas station. Shortly before I left, he informed me that the village would commemorate me for all posterity with a plaque on a stone in the center of the market if I arranged the funds for electrification.

That done, he would install one flush toilet in a hut for all the villagers' use. Most people defecated in the woods, and brought back dysentery and cholera; a flush toilet was a modern luxury and status symbol that the chief could justify on grounds of health. My counterproposal of latrines struck him as rather underdeveloped, but he was a practical man with a real desire to improve life in his village, and eventually he agreed. Today, by the CEG, there are a few concrete slabs over holes in the ground. I'm sure the twin dreams burn in his imagination all the same. The pope may have been about to discuss traditional religion or polygamy, but electric lights and a flush toilet seemed to animate the chief's face in the photo as he waited for the hand of the man in white.

Westerners passed through the chief's life like white birds flying just overhead, signs of a land his dinghy never quite reached. A month before my arrival, Jeane Kirkpatrick, Elizabeth Dole, and

Ursula Meese had stopped by the village with the American ambassador to inspect the water project and smile at the primary school children. I can see the chief's expression as he came out, *kente* and crown, to greet them. They stayed an hour, and left behind a piece of hope that ripened and rotted, and a promise of soccer balls, which arrived periodically from Washington—white birds flying around the village.

I stayed longer than most, but by the time I left there was a perceptible disappointment, a look in the chief's eye that said somehow things hadn't come out as he'd thought they would. A few concrete slabs, a couple of fuel-saving clay stoves, children who could speak some English—those were my soccer balls.

After their handshake the pope went on to half a dozen other African countries to celebrate mass with millions of people. The chief—perhaps after looking in at Service de Matériel—took a bush taxi back to the village. Since it was August, he would inspect his yam field to see what the earth had coughed up, and calculate the cost of twelve school tuitions, and wonder if this time, this bird might bring *le développement*, electricity, a flush toilet.

After lunch with the chief I went home to take a nap. As soon as I walked into the bedroom I knew something was wrong. A pair of pants that I'd left on the bed now lay on the floor. I opened the desk drawer where I'd stashed the money from my January paycheck. The wad looked thinner. I counted it twice: ten thousand francs, a seventh of my monthly allowance, was missing. It wasn't the first time I'd been stolen from, and it wouldn't be the last.

CHAPTER 6

Footprints

OMEONE WAS GETTING INTO MY HOUSE. COMING IN and stealing, leaving small things out of place. My wallet was in the wrong pants pocket, with a bill or two gone. Change disappeared from my desktop. Mints my aunt sent at Christmas vanished from my frigo one afternoon; the thief left me three to nibble on. A Bob Dylan tape—*Blonde on Blonde.* Then a packet of Peace Corps–issue condoms. I got back from another volunteer's village one December night to find the frigo door open, an empty bottle of Coke and a half grapefruit on the floor. The thief found my wallet where I'd hidden it in my desk drawer, and again under mosquito netting in the spare room during the trip north. Sometimes he took no longer than the half hour I spent at dawn running to the next village up the road and back. He had the house staked out.

It had been going on sporadically since November. I had ignored it, at times even tried to pretend it wasn't happening, that my own carelessness accounted for the losses. I didn't want it to be happening—not because of the losses (they never amounted to more than a couple of dollars; and if he needed the food, Christ, let him take it) but because the invasions were a humiliation that reminded me of my vulnerability; therefore, they weren't taking place. Then,

with the new year, the thefts became regular. When it was too plain
that someone was coming in to steal and the losses started to add
up, I made sure I always latched my windows and locked the bedroom door as well as the front door. But the thefts didn't stop.

The afternoon I came home from lunch at the chief's marked a
turning point. I blew up. Ten thousand francs, twenty-five dollars—
that was balls, that was brazen. I had a little under fifteen bucks
left to get me through the last eighteen days of January; I would
have to borrow, or take a trip all the way to Atakpamé and the bank.

When I'd finished slamming my fists against the plaster and cursing loud enough for the Agbeli kids to start murmuring on the other
side of the wall, I went back to the chief's. He was out. I left a
message with the first wife: I wanted to see him immediately. No
answer came that day, or the day after. The next evening I button-
holed him outside the bistro. I wanted his carpenter to install a new
lock on the outside door. Someone was getting into the house—his
house—even with the place secure; the thief must have a key.

The chief smacked his lips. "No, no, that's not good. The carpenter will come to do the work tomorrow."

Three days after I bought the lock in Kpalimé it was on the front
door. And the next day, as if to mock me, five hundred of the two
thousand francs I'd borrowed from a teacher disappeared from the
bedroom. So his entry was the kitchen. I put a latch on the door
between my bedroom and kitchen, so angry I could hardly turn the
screwdriver. Now at least the bedroom, with my valuables, was
secure.

I went to the chief again.

"Someone is still getting in, I don't know how. I want you to
catch this thief. I want you to *gong-gong* the village, tell everyone
there's a thief in the Agbeli quarter, put them on the lookout."

Koba had advised me that this was traditional procedure: have
the chief assemble the village with a cowbell and alert everyone to
the thefts. The chief was responsible, not just as my landlord but
as the highest official in the village, the traditional arbiter of disputes.
A goat thief had been caught in the village a few weeks back and
carried by an angry crowd to the chief's house, and if the chief

hadn't been home they might have gone ahead and torn the thief to pieces. In Lomé you took a man's life into your hands if you ran after him shouting, *"Voleur! Voleur!"* Unless the police materialized right away, a crowd would chase him down and execute its own justice. A thief was reviled, lost to the village, his family, himself, hardly human.

The chief promised that his *gong-gongeur* would ring tomorrow; but tomorrow came and went, and more days, and the village was never called.

I'd ignored my thief for weeks while he had his way with me; now I became obsessed. I wanted to catch him, and not just catch him but scare him, taunt him as he was taunting me. I fantasized lying in wait in the spare room, knife in hand, and when I heard the noise in the kitchen I would leap out, eyes wild, knife brandished, and watch him fall to his knees in terror at the avenging *yovo* Fury.

But I had no suspects. Everyone was a suspect. One morning in December, while I was teaching, a visiting Peace Corps friend had been awakened on the floor of my living room by a small boy squeezing between the bars of a window; wedged there, spotted, he stared in terror before diving back out. My friend thought he looked like Claudie. With misgiving I mentioned it to Christine. Heating water for Aku's bath, sweating over the wood fire, she burst into tears and cried that she would never send her children into my house to steal, she would die first. That night I heard her beating Claudie while he wailed what sounded like howls of innocence.

Was he innocent? Who knew? But I regretted mightily having told her. After that we were uneasy around each other—as if she were in fact guilty, or I in fact thought her guilty. And sometimes I did. Sometimes the whole family was guilty. After that episode, every primary school boy in Lavié, all four hundred–odd of them, was my thief. And then, for a time, the *voyous* on their rock, Lucien—who hadn't come to class in weeks—and his pals. One of them shouted *"Yovo!"* as I walked up the hill toward school. I didn't stop, and was well past him by the time I'd silently articulated my answer: "Who the hell do you think you are? My name isn't *yovo*.

I'm a teacher here and you'll call me *monsieur*—is that clear, you little bastard?"

Another time I arranged for a student to stay in the locked house while I spent the day in Kpalimé. I made elaborate preparations for departure, packed a bag as if I were going away for a few days, said loud good-byes to all the Agbelis. If someone was watching the house I wanted to tip him off. But when I returned in the afternoon, the student said that no one had tried to get in. I looked him in the eye. How could I know that he wasn't in on it too? He read my look; he fell into vigorous denials. I believed him, and disbelieved him.

I confided my obsession to no one. Whom could I trust? Eventually I found myself thinking that everyone who greeted me at school or in the market, even the teachers, was conspiring against me, laughing behind my back because it was taking me so long to figure out what they'd known all along. Expressions of sympathy became stabs in the back. I went out less and less, spending evenings in my living room with a book by lamplight, sleeping badly.

One evening in early February, Benjamin, who had shown a minimum of interest in the case and was hardly at home anyway, came into my kitchen at my request to inspect the ceiling. There was an opening in the panels above the sink, where the two barrels of water lay on the joists. It had been there from the beginning, it was part of the scenery, I hadn't given it a thought. Now, remembering, I had a theory. Someone was scaling the drainpipe on the outside wall, slipping under the eaves of the metal roof onto the ceiling, and crawling down through that hole. The bushes and banana tree between the wall and the road would hide him from view on his way up and down. Benjamin heard me out, and then announced that no one could manage it. But as his flashlight danced around the shadows of the opening and glinted off the barrels, it caught something on the wall.

"What's that?" I said.

"What?"

I grabbed the light. Just below the ceiling, over the sink, there was a footprint. Several. A trail of muddy footprints, leading up the wall and out the hole. Brown smudges on the pale blue plaster, blurred like a series of superimposed images, but unmistakably footprints. Large ones—not Claudie's, not a schoolboy's, but those of someone grown. Now I knew: my thief lowered himself from the ceiling by putting his feet on the sink, went about his work, and then hoisted himself back up by hanging on the top of the toilet door next to the sink, braced himself against the wall, and pushed off with his dirty bare feet.

Benjamin made a noise of insight. "Eh-*heh*. Like that. Like that. He's coming down there. Those are his feet. This means," he concluded, "that it's someone from outside the village."

There was no logic; it wasn't an explanation, only an excuse.

I said, "It doesn't mean that at all."

He would have the ceiling fixed—he would have the ceiling fixed this week, he promised me. For several days Christine badgered him about it, and privately urged me to put boards over the hole. It wasn't my job, I answered; it was for the chief or her husband to do. I wasn't going to let them slight me anymore. And the ceiling remained unfixed.

Now my thief was with me all the time. The footprints were his presence on the kitchen wall. At night, cooking spaghetti or potatoes, I held up my lamp and caught the footprints in its swaying light. I imagined him dropping down with a thud, hunting about, smiling over my possessions, licking his lips by the frigo, swinging back up. Acrobatic sonofabitch. I dreamed of chasing a faceless youth down an arcade, my thoughts bent on murder. In the mornings the feet were palpable, clear, an outline of dirt and treachery. And at times they became those of Sakpaté, the forest god who brought the pox and made night travelers lose their way. The one whose name wasn't spoken at night—the darkness at the edge of the village that lay in wait for anyone who strayed.

I isolated myself in these days. Writing letters home became impossible. From the outside, to the villagers, I must have seemed unchanged. We went through the greetings, I flirted in the market. But even if there was no conspiracy (which, in my more lucid moments, I knew was so), what would they understand of this? For them it was a case of stealing—shameful, reprehensible, they said, their anger genuine, a blight on the good name of the village. But for me it had become something more.

It was hard not to feel this presence in the house as my double, the shadow of my own strangeness here, the footprints my own feet.

A week after Benjamin's light flashed on them, Claudie was helping me clean the kitchen floor. We were on our knees, sponges in hand, scrubbing years-old dirt out of the concrete. I was going to pay him well to make up for the beating he'd gotten. Suddenly he looked up at the wall, pointed to the footprints overhead, and announced simply:

"That's Lucien."

I gripped his shoulder and asked him to repeat it. The smile died on his face as he told me again who my thief was.

That night Atsu and Claudie showed me the hole in the ceiling in their part of the house where Lucien climbed up to crawl across and down into my rooms. It was there for anyone to see, and everyone had seen. The boys informed me that the entire family and the chief had known for at least two weeks that Lucien was the thief; they couldn't explain why no one had thought to tell me.

The Agbelis were suddenly as incomprehensible to me as their thick, guttural Ewé. They were the family I'd trusted, in the end the only friends I could really count in Lavié. Now my most paranoid conspiracy theories had been borne out by the people closest to me. Lying in bed that night, I weighed the possibility of leaving.

It took me three days to get hold of the chief. He was always out, and never returned the messages that his wives received from me with stunned nods. Then, one afternoon, he wandered over. Did I want something? I told him I wanted nothing, only that I was going to leave the village. I followed this with an incoherent stream of abuse the likes of which the village chief could not have heard often in his adult life. Taken aback, he muttered that he'd wanted to wait to see if I reported another theft. I cut him off.

"You were responsible for me here. I'm very angry."

Then he bowed his head. "Yes, you are angry. You are angry."

I calmed down, and after some pleading on his part I agreed not
to pack my bags. Afterward I realized I'd been bluffing. When I
confronted Benjamin, he quickly asserted that he was a good man
and no one in the village could say he was bad, and he had given
his son a whipping besides—on his head, even. Such whippings
were not the work of the cowardly or wicked. Christine looked
stricken, the color of wet ashes. My reproaches dissolved before
they were out when she cried, "Oh *monsieur*, it's bad enough for
me, not you too!" And then: "I'm a woman, I'm there." Later we
even had a laugh together when she tried to explain the piece of
evidence that had tipped the family off. *"Carnet de voyage,"* she kept
saying, but I didn't know what it meant until she showed me the
condom that Atsu had found Dové and Emma trying to blow up.
He'd gone to his mother with it, and she'd gone straight to the
menfolk. The cover-up was theirs. I accepted the chief's apology,
but I didn't easily forgive him: his authority was supreme in Lavié.
In my eyes his was the real betrayal.

He and I agreed to have a traditional trial in his house rather than
go the more involved route of the police in Kpalimé. I knew that
the stakes for Lucien and his family, the disgrace, money, and
punishment, would be greatly raised if I brought in the authorities;
it was my trump card. I would play it if Lucien stole again, or if the
chief kept dragging his heels. But I had the chief's attention now,
and the trial was held within three days. I spent them avoiding the
Agbelis. When I needed to leave the house, I peered out the window
and waited until Christine was in her kitchen. There was some relief
in finally knowing, but I felt sick at heart, too, as if the idea of
coming here had been a mistake from the start.

The day before the trial I motored to Kpalimé, to the room on
the edge of town rented by my friend Mensah. He was a twenty-
eight-year-old primary school teacher who'd trained in health education with Peace Corps and helped us build the latrines at the
CEG. He sat on his bed and listened in silence to my long story.
It was the first time I'd told it to anyone. Feeling anger and self-
pity well up, I tried to put it as coldly and clearly as possible, as if
I'd heard it secondhand. When I'd finished, he shook his head for

a long time, and then agreed to act as my "lawyer" at the trial, in order to interpret the Ewé and explain procedures I was ignorant of. I had done well to arrange for a village trial, he said. The police were a last resort in Africa. But he didn't like my idea of the punishment. I had thought of obliging Lucien to do my work unpaid until he'd reimbursed me, or else sack him and forget the money.

"That would be a mistake. To you it might seem tolerant to forgive like that, but to the village you would only seem weak and make yourself more vulnerable. Let him be punished according to custom. And demand reimbursement from the family. It's better."

I put the affair in his hands. We would do things the African way, by shame and retribution.

The chief and the Agbeli elders were sitting around his living room when Mensah and I arrived on Sunday afternoon. It was mid-February and stifling hot. The harmattan dust had blown away and the sun had been burning naked for days. The shutters were closed, and in the darkened room the old men were fanning themselves. Benjamin wasn't present, nor, of course, was Christine—"a woman, there." The Agbeli family patriarch, an octogenarian who'd been chief for decades before retiring, stood to greet us—a tough, grizzled man with no teeth and sunken gums. Formal introductions of the uncles and brothers followed, then the presentation of Mensah, who was greeted with respect as an educated young man from town. He and I sat in our assigned chairs, facing the elders against the opposite wall. The chief sat immobile behind his desk; beside his papers was a ceremonial cane that he rolled from time to time with his fingertips. Whenever he spoke it seemed a huge effort, and he never looked me in the eye.

Lucien was hustled in by Erasmus, the chief's long-faced "secretary," a factotum with hardly anything to do. The detainee stood barefoot and pigeon-toed in the middle of the room, wearing what he always wore: black stretch biking shorts and a sky-blue V-neck velour shirt. He looked sullen and scared. Absently he chewed on a stick that he'd taken from behind his ear.

Mensah stood and began questioning him in Ewé. Had Lucien stolen the money? He denied it. The old men sat forward, attentive.

I struggled to follow. Not even a few hundred francs? No, nothing. And the footprints? They were not his. Lucien's jaws slowed, the stick was starting to disintegrate in his mouth. Mensah prodded on, and Lucien fell into a contradiction, then another: he was never in my house alone; he was in my house alone, but only to sweep; he had eaten a grapefruit once, being hungry. His voice got higher as he felt himself cornered. Mensah tossed off a few proverbs I couldn't catch—he was something of an expert on them—and exhorted Lucien to tell the truth. It would be easier for him later if he spoke up now. Still Lucien denied everything.

It was time for the coup de grâce. Mensah reached in his pocket and took out the orange condom wrapper the children had found among their older brother's clothes. Where had Lucien gotten this? Had he bought it in the market? The elders snickered. Nothing of the sort could be found outside Lomé. I stood and held aloft a chain of half a dozen wrappers of the same sort. The elders gasped, leaned back, and murmured to each other. Lucien was running out of rope. Yes, he had taken it when he was sweeping, but he thought it was a toy his brothers and sisters might enjoy. So he had taken things? Yes, but . . .

It was no use. Rather paternally, Mensah told him it would be better to confess now; if he held out, he would receive harsher treatment at the hands of the police. Besides, the police could easily identify the footprints on the wall as his—they had such machines.

A clever courtroom move. The word *police* cast a pall over Lucien. Barely whispering, he admitted he was the thief—so quietly I didn't realize a confession had taken place until he was on his knees signing a piece of paper Mensah put before him. It was an admission of guilt and an IOU. But when I informed him of the sum—21,200 francs—he started protesting again. The elders couldn't believe it either—enough to feed a family for two months! What could this boy have done with so much money—gambled at the market, gone to Kpalimé, spent the night in hotel rooms? Whored? Their anger was building and closing in, and Lucien had lost his credibility. When he said he knew nothing of any Bob Dylan I was ready to call him a liar then too.

Mensah laughed. "The snake never counts the eggs it steals."

Lucien signed. While he was signing, the old chief came up behind him and grabbed his ear. The mashed chew stick, which he'd put back there, fell to the floor. The old man's eyes were on fire.

"The Agbelis are an honest family!" he shouted in Ewé. "We work for our food like honest people! You are a disgrace to us, a disgrace! Better not to have been born!" The others were on their feet now. Their old hoarse voices bellowed curses from all sides: "Quitting school to gamble in the market! Going to bed with *ashawo! Bandit! Voyou! Voleur! Fiafi!*"

The terrible names rained down on his head, and as they did a memory rushed back to me. The first night I met Benjamin he'd said that his oldest son was a *bandit*. And over lunch the chief had said, "He has become a *voyou*." Now my stupidity seemed immense. I'd been blind to what was in front of my nose. And in this moment I also understood why. I'd blinded myself, I hadn't wanted to know. Lucien was my neighbor, an Agbeli. He worked for me and I paid him well. For him to be ripping me off—it would have meant that I'd been too soft, been taken for a fool with my Western ways, that Aboï and the others were right: *pour l'africain, il faut le baton.* I hadn't wanted to believe that. Now I saw they'd been warning me all along.

There wasn't time to pursue the thought. The elders were forcing Lucien belly-down on the floor, like a goat being prepared for slaughter. I stood to go; I'd had enough. But the old chief looked at me in surprise: *"Miakpo?"*—"You will watch?" Mensah motioned for me to sit.

The old man slapped Lucien about the head and neck and boxed his ears. The others joined in. The chief stood up from his desk and came over with his ceremonial cane raised. While the others held Lucien down, kicking and hollering, the chief delivered swift heavy blows to the buttocks and thighs. His face had lost its sickliness. He wasn't holding back; none of them was. They laid into Lucien with a fury that was scary, their biceps flexing with the strength of years in the fields, veins bulging in their temples. It was like watching a dog being whipped. I was happy no one offered me the cane; I couldn't have managed more than a few weak licks. Lucien on the floor was no longer the shadow-stranger who'd tormented me for weeks—he could have no idea how much power he'd had—but a *voyou* boy, cursed, fallen from grace in his family's eyes. His wails were wrenched out of him like the cry of a life ruined at sixteen.

It ended, after an eternity. Still slapping and cursing, the old men picked him up and dragged him toward the door. I noticed for the first time that a crowd, mostly boys and girls, had materialized in the courtyard. As the elders hauled Lucien out, the children began yelling—horrible high-pitched shrieks of delight—and Lucien struggled far more than when he was beaten. Better the blows than the ridicule. But he was pushed out the door into the crowd, which received him with fierce jeers.

The old chief, panting, turned to me and bowed. He was asking my pardon. I was only too glad to give it, just to end the trial. I begged him to stand up. I'd had a stomachful of the African way. They thanked me profusely, and we agreed that we would forget the whole affair and resume normal life in Lavié. I pocketed the IOU. The chief was back behind his desk, looking more tired than ever.

And for days, weeks, after the trial, when I saw him and made a point of greeting him, his smile was faint, his reply brief, he hurried off. Lucien didn't appear at home often after that. Christine told me he was staying with cousins in the village, and occasionally I saw him sitting on the *voyou* rock. Irène, the neighbor woman across the cornstalks, thanked me again and again for my pardon. The old chief and I became friends. Christine lost more weight, and her smiles thinned. Benjamin was home less than ever.

The Lucien affair wasn't quite over. One evening two weeks after the trial, I was sitting in my living room with a volunteer visiting from Mango. Angry shouts rang out from the yard, as they always did when Benjamin came in; but quickly Christine's turned into childlike wails. Then she ran into my living room in tears, and without a pause cried out in a confusion of French and Ewé that

Lucien had stolen the thousand francs she'd earned gathering and selling firewood, he'd pushed her, Benjamin had said nothing, had turned away to go drinking, the scar from her Caesarean operation when she had Aku was oozing pus, she had no reason to be here, none, only the children, if not for them she would be gone, she would go back to Lomé, now one of her own was stealing from her . . .

The next day I met Lucien on the road outside the bistro. At the sight of him I went temporarily insane. Steal from his mother now that he couldn't steal from me! The affair had taught him nothing, he was nothing, he was less than nothing! In full view of his rock friends I delivered a clumsy blow to the chest that surprised me at least as much as him. *Pour l'africain, il faut le baton.* He stumbled backward. The *voyous* stirred. Oh, I shouted, if Christine ever reported another theft to me, maybe his father wouldn't lift a finger but I would make sure he ended up in a cell in Kpalimé where the *gendarmes* would give him a worse beating than his uncles ever had, where they had machines to hurt, where the food would be rat and black water . . .

He looked stunned; his falsetto voice denied it all. I grabbed the velour shirt and made him follow me back to the house. Christine was under the bougainvillea with the children. Would he deny it to his mother's face? He did. She began taunting him and encouraged the children to join in. It was a terrible thing to see, Lucien standing there in his own yard, jeered by his mother and brothers and sisters. Mawuli was dancing around in circles, imitating the older ones, chanting the strange word, *"Vo-leur! Vo-leur!"*

Lucien's disgrace was complete.

After the trial of Lucien, as emotions subsided, I began to experience in a new way certain trivia of daily life in the village, like a baby who has noticed for the first time the individual features of the people around it and begins to look for them. One day I was riding in a *baché* from Lavié up to John's in Hiheatro. That day the front seat was taken by a soldier, so I was stuffed in back with fifteen or sixteen passengers. Halfway, the driver parked along the roadside at a cluster of mud huts, got out, and entered one. I waited for a passenger to descend, but no one else moved. We sat in the back and waited. And waited. The steamy heat became intense. Still the driver didn't return. Some of the women began to make the little clucking sound that signals displeasure. Soon nearly all the passengers were clucking like chickens in a coop and mumbling in Ewé, but no one got out to investigate. Mothers nursed their infants, men slept with their heads on their knees. After half an hour the driver came back and started up again. I had no idea what had happened, and asked the man next to me.

"Oh, the driver has a wife in this village and he went to have supper." A woman smiled mischievously and added that he might have stayed for a little dessert too. There was laughter in that cramped, stifling taxi, and the irritation vanished.

On another occasion, one of the teachers told me about a friend who had recently become head of a technical school in Lomé. The man had given an entrance exam that, like all exams in Togo, was almost impossible to pass because of the scarcity of openings. When the exam had been corrected, he posted a list of those who had passed. A week later he received a summons to the Ministry of Education—and there he was docked a full month's pay, a loss that could mean financial disaster to an African. What had he done wrong? I learned that any entrance-exam results have to be sent to the minister of education before they are made public. The minister crosses out a few names that don't suit him, pencils in a few others, then sends the list back to the school to be posted. The unlucky students are almost always from a different tribe and region from the minister's; the substitutes come from his part of the country, perhaps even his village. The teacher smiled at my shock and slapped the back of one hand against the other palm, meaning, "What can you do?"

In America, of course, no Greyhound driver would put his wife and his stomach before his job, keeping his busload waiting halfway between New York and Boston while he stopped at home in New Haven for steak and potatoes. And a Westerner would be quick to see both of these incidents as evidence of corruption, however minor: the corruption that infects all of Africa, where a president like Mobutu of Zaire can make himself a billionaire while his countrymen go hungry, or where a Nigerian policeman won't lift a finger to help you until it touches the proper banknote. The more I had heard of this kind of moral bankruptcy, the more depressed I had felt for Africa's future, clogged and reeking as its present was with bribery and favoritism.

But now it occurred to me that the Togolese driver wouldn't make a distinction between on-the-job and after work, between his public and private selves. Charged with neglecting his duty, he might say, "And what of my responsibility to my wife? How could I pass through the village without seeing her? What would my brothers-in-law say? That their sister has a monkey for a husband!" Similarly, the minister might respond, "What would you have me do? Let the exam results stand, and then go back to my village in shame because I did nothing to help the village students? I owe it to the people who raised me to try to repay them as best I can. I couldn't go home again if I didn't."

I was beginning to see that this kind of thing, this confusion between two realms—one public, official, abstract; the other private and personal—happened all the time in Togo, at every level of life. It happened when a peasant pulled his child out of school to have him till the field for planting, or when a teacher punished a student simply to put him to work in his own field at harvest time. It happened when the Kabyé president sent a Kabyé student to Canada on a scholarship won by an Ewé, or when a principal allowed his younger brother to pass to the next grade even though he'd flunked. It happened when a policeman told me to take a woman with her baby and goat in my car to the next checkpoint, where her husband was on duty, or when a woman at the market gave me an extra couple of onions for my money when she learned I taught in the village where her sister lived. It was the way things worked, it was the system. You could no more go about rooting out corruption in Africa than you could root out capitalism in America. The women in the taxi merely clucked; the teacher smiled and slapped his hand.

A community like Lavié was made up, above all, of personal ties.

And what we call corruption the Africans saw as a kind of duty. It was duty based on a web of relations that was not apparent to the casual visitor but that still held together (and also, tribally, divided) a country like Togo. They were personal, not official, relations. They dictated that you give a job to your nephew before a more deserving subordinate; that you lower prices in the market for friends and relatives; that you give half your monthly earnings, if you are on salary, to the twenty or thirty members of your extended family, and thus never save a thing; that, if there is money left over from a government project, you use it to build a house for your second or third wife; that you don't turn in your kin.

My missing money and the aftermath struck close to home; and with the experience I began to learn how things worked in an African community. I came to realize that the chief and the family had not enjoyed deceiving me, or felt any less affection for me than I had imagined. They had not deceived me for money, or even to protect themselves from anger and punishment, but mainly because I was an outsider, a white—a *yovo*. I had been sent to Lavié by my government and the Togolese to teach English; in a year I would leave and, for all the villagers knew, never come back. The people of Lavié appreciated my work and went to great lengths to make me feel at home, and their kindness was not hypocrisy. But in a jam, my interest had to be sacrificed. Yes, Christine was close to me—but she was Lucien's mother, and everyone called her by that name, *Lucien no*. The chief was the chief and my landlord—but he was Lucien's uncle, too, the head of the Agbeli family. Those duties made duty to me irrelevant. They had to protect a boy who, though the family thought him a rotten papaya and cursed his birth, could not be thrown out, for he was flesh and blood. And I? A stranger, an ill-cut patch sewn temporarily onto the tight fabric of relations in the village. I had been naïve enough to think that a few months and a few words of Ewé had made me truly the brother, the *fo*, they called me. I would be gone in a year, while they would have to farm and eat and live with each other until death.

My volunteer friend Isaiah in Patatoukou once said, "If you feel alienated because you don't understand how things work in Togo, just wait until you do understand." The truth of that began to dawn on me after the trial, when, feeling wiser about myself and the village, I felt further from it than ever. Before, I would easily have condemned the minister as nepotistic, the driver as inefficient, the chief as unjust. When I saw that to the Togolese these were all instances of a different kind of fairness, efficiency, and justice, a kind necessary to the cohesion of their society, far from finding my own values shored up, I felt them challenged, even threatened.

This happened, of course, unconsciously, over weeks and months. Lingering anger blocked out connections and conclusions. My friend in statistical economics at the university had explained Authenticity by saying Togo didn't want to be in such a hurry that the country lost what held it together. I'd been analyzing Authenticity like a lab chemist; now it was served up to me in a nearly lethal dose and at first I had no idea what I'd swallowed—only that it tasted bitter.

The image of the chief at the trial stayed in my mind—sitting at his desk beneath the formal portrait of himself crowned and enthroned, listening to the elders and Mensah, glancing away with narrowed eyes and frowning mouth, the noble brow furrowed. He seemed to have abdicated his power over the proceedings that day. Now that the truth was out, his older brothers spat the family venom at Lucien and begged pardon of me; but the chief himself was passive and remote, as if he no longer knew, or had been robbed of, his authority there in his own house. Something seemed to have drained it from him, like a bout of malaria sapping his strength.

He was still too much of a village chief not to protect his family; but he knew his obligations to me and to the state, and his failure to fulfill them seemed to consume him with confusion and guilt. Even in a small village like Lavié, two worlds had converged and got in each other's way: the traditional world, which clearly defined the chief's role in Lavié and his responsibility to his family, and the world of "development" that had brought Western ideas of duty, and me, to the village. A sense of public duty separable from personal ties had reached even this steamy cluster of dwellings in the mountainous bush, and like the dusty sky when the harmattan blew south from the Sahara, nothing was quite clear anymore.

As the tide of Westernization washed over Africa, one change it brought was the weakening of personal ties in the village, under a different, Western code that demanded loyalty of an individual to his public role, his country, to people he didn't know, to a tribe he perhaps despised. The civil service, the military, schools, and commercial enterprises were becoming the focus of life, even in the villages, where every boy and girl wanted nothing more than to quit the backbreaking labor of the fields, get away, and find work in the capital—or France, or America.

These public institutions were forced upon Africans by the colonizers, as a rebellious boy might be dressed by his stern mother for church. And for many years African countries wore their institutions a bit awkwardly, whenever possible loosening the tie and unbuttoning the collar. As they grew older and more used to their formal clothes, they were beginning to take pride in them, even to rely on them—but not without conflicts. The personal relations still dominated; even the minister of education didn't forget his village. Nonetheless, he was the national minister of education, and proud of it, and perhaps when he crossed out the Ewé names and wrote in the Kabyé, he felt a pang of the same compunction that ate at the chief during the trial. Morality for both men had turned an uneasy shade of gray.

A tragic case of ambiguous morality made the news not long after I left Togo. A fellow Peace Corps Volunteer, Jennifer Rubin, was murdered in her house near Kara by three men hired by a girl who had been stealing from her. The story, minus its horrible ending, was similar to mine: her landlord's child, trusted with the housework, had been stealing money and jewelry until Jenny caught her. What differed, besides the conclusion, was that when Jenny informed the girl's father, he took his daughter to the police, who beat a confession out of her. The father, unlike the chief, chose to take the unpleasant path to the public authorities instead of protecting his daughter by settling in private, and this fact was almost as incredible as the girl's violent revenge. The revenge itself may have become thinkable to the girl because her father had gone beyond the pale of the village, and because the victim was a *yovo* woman: connection had been violated on the one hand, was missing on the other. The father's decision struck me as a sign of the changes I had begun to notice. I wondered whether he turned in his daughter with any less ambivalence than the chief shielding his nephew.

Americans value national fairness and efficiency, and we privilege the broader, more impersonal and abstract relations. We have, at least in principle, the virtues of equal opportunity, efficiency, justice before the law. The Ewé student who lost his scholarship wins our sympathy and outrage: a scholarship won by a student from New York goes to him and not to one from Los Angeles, even though the president happens to be from southern California. And if a Greyhound driver were to stop at home, the passengers would do more than cluck. We like to keep public life free from personal taint—even to the point of not selling a used car to a friend.

An African, if he had a used car, would sell it to no one but a friend. Africans privilege the personal relations, but these ties don't make the news or grab our fleeting attention like coups, tribal massacres, and famines. An American tourist in Togo is not likely to remark, "Isn't it nice how they seem to take care of one another?"— or even to notice it. Instead, he might wish that the damned electricity would stay on. It took me months and painful experience to see that corruption could be reciprocity and inefficiency care, that in an African village people did look after one another, often at great sacrifice. Once I saw this, even a poor, hot, dull, oppressive backwater became deeply attractive. Indignation gave way to envy.

While writing this, I came across a story in a San Francisco paper about a young South African refugee who'd turned up in Oakland. It was a fantastic tale, out of Voltaire at his most picaresque and bitter: an escape from Natal to the Ivory Coast, arrests in Abidjan, stowing away on a freighter, discovery and lockup, a leap into the Atlantic off Gibraltar and rescue by another freighter, arrival in the Bay Area and another leap into another ocean, refuge under a pier for seven hours, imprisonment again in an Oakland city jail—and then instant celebrity, standing ovations in churches, promises such as "We're all behind you, we'll take care of you." What struck me about his story was the picture of Africa that emerged: oppression and poverty in South Africa, and then again in Abidjan, where, without a passport, he found no work and was constantly ending up in jail, and where the whites were no better than in South Africa, only less powerful. And yet, alongside this, the fish of the sea, oranges and pineapples and bananas to be plucked for free, and the kindness of strangers who took him in. He was shocked at the homelessness in San Francisco, and only the Oaklanders' political interest in him kept him from the same fate. In the U.S. he was not Patrick Mtoto but a victim of apartheid, whereas what he'd found in Africa was public tyranny and private decency. Something in this contradictory Africa rang true.

Things official didn't work very well in Togo. From the education of children to my toilet that never flushed, development seemed to fail at every turn—foreign, misunderstood, abused, like the Toyota taxis that were driven to ruin on the bush roads. But things personal somehow survived and muddled through, against the grimmest odds. Even after the cruel dry season we were enduring and then the paltry rains, when a family had to spread its food thinnest— even then, neighbors invited me over for corn mush and pepper sauce. By then I belonged with them, and it didn't matter that I had more money than they would ever see. If I fell sick and a neighbor failed to check up on me, he was castigated by another neighbor, and so was I if I showed the same negligence. And when I finally left Lavié, it was the villagers' turn to feel betrayed by me.

These thoughts came later. Some had to wait until I was back in the U.S., standing in front of an automatic teller machine and feeling a new nostalgia. In the aftermath of the stealing and the trial, down with dysentery that felt like the belated release of a river of ill feeling, I lacked this clarity. It seemed I was starting over again.

CHAPTER 7

You Get Up, You Work, You Sleep

"I T'S BEGINNING TO BOTHER US AFRICANS TOO," Erasmus moaned. The chief's secretary emerged from the bistro smelling of *sodabi*. In the pure sunlight he winced, wiped his mouth, and moved across the road to the shelter of his compound. He was talking about the heat.

By late February it hadn't rained in almost four months. The dust collecting in the village was weeks old; it had blown in with the harmattan winds from the Sahara and been left behind when those blew away and the sun came out. A reddish film coated the trees, and the lower walls of concrete houses were stained as if orange paint had been thrown on them. Dust lay on your skin and got in your eyes, it ground between your teeth and filled the cracks between your toes. I swept my floors and shook out the sheets every day, but whenever a rare breeze stirred, an ocher cloud lifted and settled on everything again. Dust moved between earth and walls and nostrils and throat, always the same dust. Nothing was clean.

In the motionless air swarms of flies appeared, flies the size of black olives. They landed on sores, rubbed their bristle legs, and wouldn't move if you waved them off. You had to swat at them, and even then they only flew a few feet away before circling back.

The dry season, I noticed by mid-February, was less dry than hot: the Togolese called it *la saison chaleureuse*. Once harmattan ended and the sun was free of dust clouds, the heat rose and with it an oppressive humidity. The humidity hinted at rain but rain was still weeks away. To the dryness, which had been creeping over the village since November, wearing people down with its layer of grit, parching them until food and river water and resistance ran low, was suddenly added humid heat (it seemed the temperature was turned up to 105 degrees one particular February morning) without the relief of rain. Humidity did nothing to get rid of the dust. It only added another layer of weight.

The village sagged. My students, fanning themselves with their copybooks, looked half asleep. In answer to my ritual morning question, "How are you today?" I began to get, "I'm hot, thanks." Once Aboï stopped by the classroom and called me over. "Georges, you let the boy there in the last row sit with his shirt all unbuttoned?" I turned to look. The boy's chest gleamed with sweat. "He's hot," I answered and turned away. By noon my cotton shirt was matted and chafed against my back; by noon the feet of students shuffling across the floor to the blackboard had raised a small dust storm, which hovered and drifted in the sunlight pouring through the windows.

During the evil hours, ten to three, movement out in the village was at a minimum. Figures hurried through the white light from shade to shade. Girls spent hours indoors plaiting each other's hair. The old men on the rocks and logs outside the bistro drank palm wine and waved at the flies that had materialized out of the heat, and quarreled or slept through the worst hours. Their greetings to me shriveled to hoarse grunts. Their fields were hard and cracked, like their old skin, and vegetation on the plateau had thinned to the point where I could see its rocky contours for the first time. Nobody ventured out there, except Faustus and his pals to tap palm trunks and bring back the cure-all; nothing was out there now, just the dead earth and the withered stalks of last year's corn. The farmers had nothing to do but wait.

Their wives worked. The chores didn't stop for lack of rain, but the women moved more slowly, talked less, and kept to their houses.

The one who sold beans next to Ama's rice every morning in the public place was pregnant, her belly swollen under layers of *pagne*. It was about the only thing growing in the village. One morning I asked her when the baby was due. Normally cheerful, she dropped her ladle and stared. "Why? Are you the father?" It wasn't a question to ask a married woman—not in this heat, with the rains delayed. By mid-March they were two weeks late and no sign of them on the horizon.

The danger was that the rivers were running low. Every morning and evening women and children from our quarter had to line up at the stream that ran in the bush near our house. It took an hour to get water now, between waiting in line and holding the basin against the rocks while a trickle slowly filled it. Claudie smiled to hide his displeasure when I asked him to fetch me a bucketful; he seemed to be saying, "I wonder if you know how hard it is to get water these days." I had an idea, and though my body craved an endless flow of water, I tried to squeeze two showers (three if I wasn't washing my hair) out of one bucket with a sponge. I caught the runoff in a basin at my feet and washed my dishes in it; the dishwater flushed the toilet. The water coming back from the river was murky gray with brown sediment at the bucket's bottom.

When it grew scarce, I saw that water was the blood of the village. It became an inconvenience, and then a hardship; but no one went without. Lavié was lucky. Up in Atakpamé the reservoir had gone dry and the taps of people wealthy enough to have running water only ran two hours every third day. The enterprising ones, my friend John among them, filled barrels when the taps were on and then sold water by rations for ten francs a bucket to villagers who had only the dried-up streams. This sounds like exploitation, but the intention was charity and John knew that if he gave it away he would have been mobbed; the profits went to his tractor project. Even Atakpamé wasn't as bad off as the north. Stories trickled down of villagers going days without bathing and of women spending most of a morning walking miles to the last wet streams.

One problem caused another, then another. Drought by itself (for this was a drought, all over Africa, the worst in years) was bad, but what made it intolerable was the chain of its effects. At this low level the river was full of guinea worm. If not for the murk their bodies would have been visible, filmy masses shimmering at the surface. The guinea worm was a particularly horrible parasite: it grew inches and inches in the stomach or limbs, and one day when it was big enough it popped its head through the skin. At that point it could be taken out by allowing it to wrap itself around a stick, but this had to happen over a period of days. If you weren't patient and tried to pull, the worm would snap and the other half would be trapped inside the body for months, reproducing, bloating the belly. Children seemed to get it most often. Mawuli's belly had the telltale swelling; Markie, at eight, was so thin that I wondered if he had a permanent colony of worms ravaging him from the inside. I boiled my water religiously; but when I suggested to Christine that she do the same, she stared blankly at this piece of Western *grigri*. Preventive health lagged well behind television and airplanes in the village's idea of development.

Everything became difficult. Children sick with diarrhea couldn't be rehydrated properly, and the worms and parasites in their food and water weakened them for other diseases—diphtheria, measles. In the best of times they rarely ate the eggs and beans that might have given them a fraction of the proper protein in their diet—these were considered luxuries, hence for grown-ups—but now protein disappeared completely. This, too, left them open to disease. Adults, already listless, ate less because their stock of corn, manioc, and yams from last year was almost gone. Most, including the Agbelis, did without manioc and yams completely and had to live off stiff dry corn mush three times a day, with an occasional meal of rice. When she was down to her seed grain, which had to be saved for the rains, if they ever came, Christine bought her corn at the market. With the scarcity and demand, the price soared in three months from 125 francs a bowl to 500.

Every Friday she came home from market with a basin on her head and set it down with a disgusted laugh. "No, no. Five hundred francs—for this? Where is the money? Ah, no, no." Some Fridays there was no corn in Lavié at all, and she gave me money to buy

it in Kpalimé, with strict instructions about what price to pay. I
began subsidizing their food budget. The children's clothes got
ragged and dirty, the same clothes I'd seen them wear every day
all year, but rarely washed now because water was too valuable.

At night my sweaty forearms smeared the papers I was correcting—by candlelight, since the kerosene lamp gave off too much
heat. Outside, the Agbelis slept on mats under a dense black sky.
I heard Aku's muffled cries, and Christine singing to quiet her, then
snapping at Claudie, whose answer was lost between yard and window. Fear of snakes and parasites kept me from joining them in the
cooler air. In bed even a mosquito net stifled, so I lit perfumed
Chinese mosquito coils. By morning the room was full of hot sweet
smoke.

Heat was the constant thing in life here. Dust clouds blocked it
in December and January, rain eased it from March to June and
again in October, but these were only holes in the blanket that lay
on the village, holes just big enough to make life possible. Make
them a little smaller, delay the rain a month, and the village was
smothered. And the holes had been closing every year. This year's
drought came after three years of poor rains, which meant less corn
at higher prices to spread even thinner. The suffering was an ac-
cumulation of suffering, like the dry weather that gradually wore
the villagers down until the hot weather struck.

The brush fires ignited at the end of February. A few farmers,
heedless of warnings from the government and the chief, had set
the usual fires to clear the bush in anticipation of rain and planting.
But the bush had become a tinderbox, and the fires quickly spread
across the fields outside Lavié and the plateau.

One morning at dawn I saw women racing down the road past
my house, basins of water slopping on their erect heads. They ran
shouting toward the fields that crackled on the far side of the stream.
There the men were already trying to drown or stamp out the fires
some of them had set. No Forestry Service existed; helicopters with
computerized infrared mapping devices were not yet available in
this part of the world; I didn't know if Kpalimé even had a fire
department. The fires consumed brush, blackened soil, and left tree

trunks charred and smoldering over a bed of soft ash. Precious coffee and cacao groves, the only source of income for most village farmers, were ravaged. Vast areas across the hills smoked like primeval swamps, and farther up, where the farmers couldn't reach, the flames glowed on the ridge against the night sky.

The chief led the fire brigades every day for a week, from dawn till after dark. The men were organized into teams, while the women ran out with water from the maddeningly slow rivers. In the evenings farmers wandered back into the village, muttering and shaking their heads. This was not the way they returned from their fields after a day's work; they looked like a badly beaten army, cutlasses instead of bayonets burdening their shoulders.

One old man said to me, "I lost my entire coffee field—the work of half my life. It would take me five years to grow any back, and by then I'll be dead. I've never seen anything like this." He wasn't assigning blame to anyone, though unlike the drought this disaster was partly man-made. I never heard of any punishment or even reprimand connected with the brush fires. Villagers accepted them as part of a string of natural calamities and didn't look for villains in the destruction of a good part of Lavié's wealth. These weeks had an atmosphere of inevitability.

The fire fighting was generally futile and in the end the fires simply burned themselves out.

Just when it seemed things couldn't get worse, a new disaster struck. It rained. A ragged sprinkle fell in the third week of March, and the next day it rained harder—not the torrential release everyone had been dreaming of for weeks, but a rain good enough to muddy the dust. It wasn't naïve enthusiasm but seasoned fear that drove some farmers out to clear and plant their withered fields. They knew that if they waited a few more weeks the midsummer dry spell could abort whatever they'd planted and the harvest would be meager. Corn and yams needed at least three months in the shallow, undernourished tropical topsoil.

Then, after two days of showers, it stopped. Days went by with no more rain. The men who'd planted waited from day to day, now anxious instead of listless, but nothing came. They'd gambled on false rains and lost, and half their seed grain died in the earth. Who wouldn't believe in a divinity and its wrath? But what had they done to earn it? The doldrums came back, heavier than before, and the men went back to their shady perches and took solace in *sodabi*.

Benjamin and I were sitting under the bougainvillea; without blossoms and leaves it looked like a gnarled hand grasping at the sky. Two weeks had passed since the false rains. There wasn't a trace of moisture in the yard's reddish dust. His taxi was in service now, he was explaining, but no one in Lavié could escape the drought. Business was bad on his route, since farmers on the plateau didn't have enough coffee and cacao, or even grain and fruit, to make it worth their money to take the trip down to Adeta and sell in the villages along the road to Kpalimé. It was a Saturday, and somewhere in the village women's voices were raising shouts that sounded like the cheers of spectators at a football game. I asked what was going on. "They are dancing for rain," he said. Then he held up his arm against the sun and squinted into the cloudless sky like a Kansas farmer. His drink-sodden face took on a momentary dignity.

"If it doesn't rain in the next"—he considered, as if the sky held the answer as well as the rain—"the next two weeks, there will be the famine in October. People will go hungry in October, because what we plant now will be killed in August. The dry season will come too soon, the rain won't last long enough."

It all sounded melodramatic. Famine in Togo! Here, where Mawuli was throwing a tantrum, and Aboï and the teachers were still at each other's throats, and the girls in the market were asking me to marry them—what did famine have to do with Lavié? Famine happened in newspapers, in wartime, in Ethiopia or Bangladesh.

I tried to picture my *6ème* kids coming to school bleary-eyed, stick-limbed, bellies distended, flies feeding on their eyes and lips as we struggled through the past tense. Maybe an International Red Cross center in Adeta; Christine, holding Aku (skin and bone), in line for milk and high-protein biscuits out of tins marked "Gift of the People of the USA." "John Kennedy food," it was called. I couldn't believe it. But I didn't disbelieve Benjamin either; I didn't know what to think. On the BBC I heard a list of twenty-two African countries that the United Nations had classified as "affected," whatever that meant. Togo was on the list. Well, of course Togo was affected—anyone with eyes in his head saw that. But famine?

Togo didn't see famine in 1983. The drought wasn't as bad as elsewhere, and the country had a margin of safety in the surplus that had been bought by the government every year and stocked in Togograin granaries. But in Ghana next door, with the mix of drought, fires that destroyed a third of the cacao plantations, and a quarter century of economic waste that had left the currency worthless and essential goods scarce, patches of starvation broke out. Volunteers escaping to Togo for their holiday brought tales of empty shop shelves, functionaries in the capital carrying briefcases full of cash to buy a sack of corn flour, peasants in the rural north eating seed grain and going hungry. The apocalypse grumbled. In Mali, Niger, Chad, the countryside was already beginning to empty with the advance of the desert. In the drought desertification went from its normal fifty miles a year to two hundred in some places. And the first pictures came in from Ethiopia—not much different from the pictures that woke up the world on "NBC News" in October 1984, a year and a half too late to save a million lives.

The chief crossed himself when I showed him a magazine photo of a baby's wasted body. "No, no, may the good God keep that from Togo."

Apocalypses didn't happen in Togo. The bush thinned, the water browned, the price of corn soared; but women lined up at the river and life went on, bringing no exaltation or catastrophe, only a dull ache.

Dové, the five-year-old, was in the yard washing the evening pots in two inches of water. She was mumbling to herself and giggling at some private joke. "Oh!" Christine, grinding palm nuts for oil, exclaimed in annoyance. I was squatting on a stool watching them.

"What is she saying, Christine?"

"She says foolish things. She says: 'You get up, you work, you sleep, you get up, you work, you sleep . . .' "

Dové, aware that our French concerned her, covered her face with the rag and burst into giggles.

She'd hit on such an obvious fact—*the* fact of their lives—that to Christine it was merely irritating, like laughing at carrying water on the head. But Dové was only five—old enough to see the fate that lay in store for her, young enough to find it funny. She was always full of beans, dancing across the yard while the older kids were in school, mouthing French *animation* songs and the songs I'd taught them in English: "Row, Row, Row Your Boat," "Shortening Bread," "Sugar Pie, Honey Bunch." Emma, three years older and in school, was already past the carefree state, and at dawn she swept the yard with a look in her dark eyes that reminded me of Christine's. She already knew in her bones what drudgery her life was going to be.

A friend once told me of a ceremony performed a few weeks after the birth of a baby—its "outdooring." The baby was brought outside for the first time and displayed to members of the extended family. As arranged, one of them—an uncle, an aunt—"bought" it from its parents in exchange for a nominal fee. Then a calabash of water was poured on the roof so that the runoff from the eaves splashed the baby and made it cry. My friend told me that the purpose of these symbols—the selling, the water—was to show the child that its life was not going to be free and easy, that it would consist of work and hardship.

An African childhood lasted about three years, between Mawuli's fears and Emma's chores. Dové was living in the interval—the only one who could laugh at the absurdity she'd just discovered.

For men, without field work, the drought stripped life down to five things: corn mush, *sodabi*, chatter, sleep, and *kala*. This last was a game I never understood played on a piece of wood with twelve hollows in it and a handful of beans—played for hours, by knots of quiet or raucous men under a tree at the roadside, idling away days at a time the way only bums and the very rich in America do. For women there was less *sodabi* and no *kala*, and idleness was never a danger, since cooking, washing, wood gathering, and the ceaseless demands of their babies more than filled the gap. No married woman ever had "official" free time. Instead, she prepared the same food for the same bellies, washed the same galvanized tin pots and the same worn school clothes, collected the same dry wood for the next meal, and sold the same Gauloise cigarettes and Lux soap from the same flowered enamel tray, for money to buy the same corn flour for the meal after next.

Day after day, men under trees, women in yards. When you took away the modest distractions of a funeral or an excursion to relatives in another village (and with the drying-up of money these seemed to have vanished), of harvest and planting, which were repetitions too, but less stupefying, being on the cycle of the year, not the day—take these away and there lay Dové's joke. Babies were born squalling, the old shrank up and died; time wasn't going forward, it rehearsed the same small circle. This was living closer to nature and the life cycle than most environmentalists ever get or would care to. When it didn't rain there were no crops; when night fell there was no light but the moon; when people got very sick they usually died.

No reward came at the end of this endurance, no Jesus or Nirvana or revolution or lottery ticket. No one spoke much about the future at all. My plans weren't questioned, and at times the feeling crept over me that the villagers expected me to stay on forever, and that it might somehow happen. Their time didn't include plane tickets and grad school applications. *Etso*, the Ewé word for "tomorrow," also means "yesterday"; schoolkids always mixed up *demain* and *hier*. To them, I suppose they meant the same thing—"not today." Even the only sure thing to come, death, was a part of the past, bringing a return to the ancestors. Their endurance seemed unearthly, but endurance did not mean waiting for the blessing of the future to redeem their suffering. Instead, it meant accepting that there would be no blessing, no future. The people of Lavié put up with drought, bad food, no money, and a litany of disease; but what awed and intimidated a Westerner more than this was the feat of doing the same thing, or nothing, day after day, without the hope of anything ever changing.

And a Westerner began to cast about for reasons, or at least some descriptive tag to hang on this "character trait" and thereby mitigate its capacity to unsettle. Words like *patient* and *fatalistic* offered themselves. David Lamb, a reporter with four years' experience in Africa, wrote in a universal singular person about "the African," his "deepening mystery" and his "resilience," which "extends beyond any logical human limits; his crops can fail, his children can die, his government can treat him grievously and the African still carries on, uttering no protest, sharing no complaints."

It was hard not to get a little mystical. The idea that "the African" was innately superior, that his quiet suffering ennobled him while our neurotic hedonism made us less human, insinuated its way into my brain on particularly hot afternoons in my living room. But the thought never lasted long. Noble savage–ism made me as suspicious as the other kind of racism; ultimately it left the savage with his same hard lot. Given the choice, everyone I knew in the village would opt for neurotic hedonism if that meant irrigation and an end to malaria. But of course, the choice wasn't given.

Outside in the yard, Christine was not acting like the universal singular African. After the thefts and the trial of her oldest child, with the drought dragging on and money drying up, her mysterious endurance showed itself in thinning shoulders, underslept eyes, increased roughness with her children, and loud quarrels on nights when Benjamin came home.

When I had nothing to do in the afternoon, I would sit out on the stool and talk while she went through her round of chores, or lend an inept hand at chopping wood. "Christine, *nuka edzo?*" I would pry—"What's wrong?"

For an answer I usually got the sad smile and an indeterminate shake of the head. Or else, pointing to her temple: "I think too much. Since Lucien—ah, no. I don't sleep, always I'm thinking." And, once, with a saving laugh: "I'm going to die. I'm here for the children, if not I do what Benjamin wants and go home to Agou or Lomé."

I tried to talk her out of gloom by discussing, as *yovos* do, the future, the kids' schooling, her prospects in commerce. We came up with income-generating schemes: using my freezer to make frozen yogurt, sharpening knives on a grindstone, selling cakes baked in a Quaker Oats can converted into a sand oven. We tried them all, but for one reason or another each of these failed. And efforts to cheer her were hampered by language, my ignorance about her life, and the sense that at bottom she was right.

In spite of or because of all the hard work, her health deteriorated. One week in February she spilled on her foot the water she was heating for Aku's bath, and for days the skin was a raw yellow burn that I tried to salve with calamine lotion. There were mysterious fevers and headaches. The Actifed tablets I gave her out of my medical kit helped her to sleep and "to forget," and she asked for more. I refused; I'd already breached some code of Peace Corps ethics and didn't want to turn her into an addict. I begged her not to "think" too much—not to blame herself for Lucien, who, after all, was only taking after a lousy father. One child had gone bad; she had seven others who were all good.

One day she showed me the Caesarean scars left by the delivery of Dové and then Aku. She was worried. The recent one had begun oozing; maybe she should go to the doctor. When she untucked the sleeveless blue top out of her *pagne* and lifted it, she exposed a part of her private darkness I had only guessed at: a village woman thought nothing of showing her naked breasts, but the belly and legs were taboo. A faded scar ran vertically up her abdomen to her navel, and another fresh one, the thread still in, leaked green pus. It wasn't the belly of a lithe thirty-five-year-old but of a hag twice her age, the wreckage of nine children—horribly stretched, a mass of loose concentric wrinkles, like an aerial view of a bombed city in the middle of soft brown fields. She pointed as if she were identifying her children in a photograph.

"This is Dové. This is Aku. Mawuli I made normal." She waved her youngest boy out of her body. I tried not to stare or flinch, but she must have seen.

"My stomach is ruined."

This time I didn't try to talk her out of it.

That night, through the wall dividing me from the Agbelis, I heard the sound of a terrific slap, and then a furious wail that was

Christine's. The next day she would say nothing and I had to get an explanation from Atsu, who recounted his parents' fight with the studied neutrality of a child caught in between. Christine had left Aku unattended for a few minutes, and Benjamin had happened to come home and find his daughter alone in the room crying. When his wife appeared he had struck her for neglecting the baby whose birth scar was now an infection in her stomach. In the morning Christine wore the face of a mourner.

I was beginning to think that looking for an answer to the Mystery of the Resilient African was pointless. If a Westerner heard no complaints, perhaps he didn't know how to listen. And if there were no complaints, perhaps that was the sound not of quiet resilience but of quiet defeat. Christine's endurance, I thought, was neither a saint's nor an animal's. Her life did not present her with alternatives.

It was my own endurance that preoccupied me. I was working by the government's calendar, not nature's, and school stumbled on through the drought, driven by Aboï's love of bureaucratic detail and interminable meetings. But the CEG was hardly enough to break up the monotony that had Lavié in its maw. For hours every day I was left to my own devices in the village, in my house, no telephone about to ring, no TV to switch on, no chipper American voices in the next room, no distracting noises but the crow of roosters or a baby waking up in the heat.

In the afternoons the bistro's shutters were latched and the paved road was empty except for a rare taxi rushing out of one silence into another. The Agbelis were asleep under the bougainvillea, Mawuli and Aku curled up on a mat next to Christine. Going to Kpalimé to shop or buy stamps was pointless, since nothing was open there either.

I was one of the roosters and babies. I never learned to sleep at midday, and I started taking walks through the back paths between houses, keeping to the shade of an overhanging tin roof. Goats pushed and licked at the black pots left in yards from the noon meal; scrawny chickens strutted about, pecking at corn kernels. On one walk past a courtyard I startled an old man dozing in a hard-backed chair. He stared at me: a white ghost. Only ghosts, thieves, whores, and madmen walked in the dead hours. He scolded me, then offered a calabash from the palm-wine gourd at his feet, heedless of the flies dancing on the lip and floating in the froth.

Decent villagers began making sounds around two-fifteen. A mother yelled at her son to get water, and in a few minutes children were gathering by the grove of banana trees at the river with metal buckets and enamel basins. Boys and girls in khaki formed a straggling line out on the road for afternoon classes. Dové's joke resumed.

I set up schedules. I arranged my books in alphabetical order, and wrote out a reading list: Naipaul, Kierkegaard, "Doonesbury," Jung. Entries like this appeared in my journal:

> Projects for the coming year:
> Athletic—run each morning, work on basketball, maybe take
>   up soccer
> Musical—build up a tape collection and listen to music, learn
>   an instrument like harmonica
> Manual—cooking, carpentry, a craft (pottery, sculpture,
>   etc. . . .)
> Intellectual—read books (lit., phil. and hist., African studies),
>   work on Latin, Ewé, and French

I reread *King Lear* over two afternoons. I'd spent a good part of my senior year in college writing about it, but now I understood the words for the first time:

> Is man no more than this? Consider him well. Thou owest the
> worm no silk, the beast no hide, the sheep no wool, the cat no
> perfume. Ha! Here's three on's are sophisticated. Thou art the
> thing itself. Unaccommodated man is no more but such a poor,
> bare, forked animal as thou art. Off, off, you lendings!

The villagers owed the stalks their corn and the market women their cloth, but not much more. And my lendings—the books, running shoes, tape player, the wealth (as the madwoman of Adeta reminded me) that could feed all of Kpelé and Danyi and still have some left for Agou—struck me as ridiculous. In a minute it could all disappear and there I would be, getting up, working, sleeping. I had an image of the things in my house melting away with the heat and leaving me naked on a cushionless chair. A seductive thought in certain moods. I would sit back, book facedown in my lap, shut my eyes, and yield to Africa with its sun and roosters. I half dozed. Then a fly settled on my elbow. I opened my eyes and shook it away, and turned over the book, and made another try at the productive life—Conrad's station-house accountant making correct entries of perfectly correct transactions in a room where an African was dying.

I had a shortwave radio, a Sony 5900W. It was about ten inches square, a wonderfully sleek thing with an elaborate bunch of dials, needles, and switches that made it look vaguely military. And it was a magic box. In the village where nothing aspired toward completeness or perfection, where there were no straight lines, its tight complexity was miraculous. I sat up nights at the desk in my bedroom, a kerosene lamp burning, and moved the knobs between Paris and Sydney, London, Hanoi. Through the static an exotic array of tongues filled my room—French, Dutch, Swahili. A flick to the left and Radio Moscow came on: the precise, belabored tones of a propagandist well trained in English, indistinguishable from the Voice of America announcer unless you listened to what they were saying. I carried on abusive dialogues with both. A flick to the right and it was the pop African guitars and horns of Africa Number One in Gabon, images of fat hipsters in wild local shirts on a nightclub stage. Another flick to the right brought a babble of Vietnamese or Slavic. Every evening at six—the ritual became sacrosanct—I tuned to the BBC just in time to hear a familiar voice declare, "This is London." Then the absurd jingle, brassy imperial trumpets. The time signal: five short beeps, one long. "Eighteen hours Greenwich Mean Time. The news, read by John Sloane." And then the crisp, reassuring proof that the world outside Lavié still existed.

I was addicted to the BBC. I heard a reading of *Hedda Gabler* one night, *Hamlet* a week later. The meaningless lists of cricket test-match results—what was a "test match"? I didn't care, it sounded

English and civilized. Game shows in which a contestant had to speak continuously for two minutes on an impromptu topic such as man-made lakes—when he hesitated or stumbled, the host broke in, "I'm terribly sorry," and the next contestant started, until the two minutes were up and whoever was left speaking won. A classical music hour called "The Pleasure Is Yours," hosted by a smooth Brit named Gordon Clyde, who took requests from all over the ex-empire. Half the hour was message reading: "Now, from Mrs. Colin Henley, in Freetown, Sierra Leone, birthday greetings to her daughter Miffy in Bristol, and much love to her son Neville in Delhi, and all the Henleys and Chatworths back home in dear England. Happy twenty-fifth, Miffy, we do miss you. Now, Mrs. Henley would like to hear . . ." And then the trite request, Handel's "Water Music" or something from Gilbert and Sullivan. The program reeked of nostalgia—these ex-colonials isolated around the dead empire, desperately trying to stay connected to England and culture. I listened avidly.

At nine every evening a woman's voice suddenly announced, "We now continue our World Service in Portuguese." Portuguese, which sounded like Serbo-Croatian, meant bedtime. I flicked off the power switch, the radio went dead, and I found myself alone in my room again, the mosquito coil smoking, the round flame of the lamp almost burned out, and Christine's voice in the yard reminding me to shut the door before I went to sleep.

The Agbeli family owed me 21,200 francs. The ugliness of the episode was fading, but its residue lingered in the form of the debt. I had no urgent need for the money. My monthly allowance kept arriving at the Banque Internationale de l'Afrique de l'Ouest in Atakpamé, drought or no drought, a trickle out of Washington's ocean of cash. But I'd grown wary of being a creditor and of the potential for manipulation on both sides of that equation. Mensah had told me to do things the village way, and that meant collecting. Otherwise I would invite more trouble.

With Lucien's IOU in my shorts pocket I went to the chief's one evening in mid-March. I found him not, as usual, behind his desk, but out in the courtyard, on the bottom step—an undignified place for a chief to sit. He looked exhausted. His eyes were glazed, a growth of grayish beard stubbled his jaw, and next to a pair of charred, worn-out work boots his feet were cracked and blackened. *"Bonne arrivée, Monsieur Georges."* He raised a weak hand. There was no need to ask where he'd been all day.

"No, no, twenty years I've been chief, and nothing like this. I was out there since this morning at five o'clock. We bring water, we throw water—nothing. The fires burn. Half my cacao fields—" He slashed his throat with a finger.

"I'm sorry," I said. "It's too dry."

"Too dry! That's it!" he said, as if my grasp of the situation were remarkable. "It's too dry. We can do nothing with this. Some peasants have gone ahead with the planting, and we're deceived again." He shook his head slowly. "God is unkind. Too dry."

It was our first real conversation since the trial. He hadn't looked me straight in the eye since then, and he didn't now. The futility of saying anything was plain, so I watched him in silence. The lips were tight, as if to control a trembling; he seemed almost broken. One of his wives and two daughters were at the far end of the court, pounding yams in a common mortar, the eternal work of women who were never broken, could never be broken or everything would collapse: *thwap-thwap-THWAP, thwap-thwap-THWAP.*

Suddenly the chief said, "You will have *fufu?*"

"I can't. Christine is making corn mush tonight."

He nodded. "But you wanted to see me about something?"

I stood. Noticing me across the court, the wife and daughters stopped their pounding to wave. "Just to say *bonsoir.*"

The next day Claudie and a group of boys clapped outside my door. They were out of breath. The brush fires had revealed a work of God up on the mountain—a *hoëkpe*, a rock house! I had to come see.

We walked twenty minutes along the Atakpamé road, then another half hour up the plateau. For the first time I saw the effects of drought and fire up close—close enough to smell. As recently as November the mountainside had looked like my image of the

Congo, vines wrapping lush green branches. Now it was an unearthly landscape of blackened trees with no leaves, some with no branches, dead thickets of brush, the ground a soft white ash that reeked of woodsmoke. This was where half the villagers had their farms. We passed an old yam field whose mounds looked lunar under the drifts of ash. The whole way up Claudie and his friends were in a lather of excitement.

The *hoëkpe* turned out to be an enormous flat rock jutting out of the hillside. Twenty feet across, wildly colored in horizontal striations of brown, red, pink, orange, it formed a kind of cave or grotto with the smaller rocks it leaned out over; a stone mouth gaped open to reveal a narrow slanted chamber. Fires had pruned back the trees that buried it for years. It seemed less than a work of God—a little absurd, even, among the smoky ruins, with a dozen villagers sitting on the lower rocks enjoying what appeared to be a Togolese picnic: people of all ages with bowls of corn mush and sauce and jugs of palm wine. A CEG boy greeted me like a tour guide assigned to the rock. "Welcome, sir!" he started in English, then went on in French: "You see what God has made for the people of Lavié? Perhaps when your white friends come here we will take them to see it, it might attract people to visit our village. It is very interesting. The old ones think this is where the Ewé hid themselves during the Ashanti war. It is of historical interest. God is kind."

Led by a beaming Claudie, I climbed up the rocks and ducked into the opening. For a minute we crawled about on our bellies, his flashlight catching the dirty underside of the *hoëkpe*, bats hanging upside down, bits of bone in the dirt. There was not much of historical interest. There was not much of anything in this work of God besides dirt. And by the time I emerged on my hands and knees I was filthy. The villagers sitting on the rocks below laughed and applauded. *"Fo Georgie!"* a woman shouted. *"Wonye ameyibo!"*— "You are a black man!" And laughter rang out across the charred hillside.

Looking out over their heads, from three hundred feet up I could see the entire village: the shaggy grass roofs, the corrugated tin roofs gleaming in the sun, clay walls, green banana trees and the spreading fronds of palm trees. The afternoon light was softer than it had been recently and the village shimmered. The smoke of the first evening fires rose between the roofs. Beyond the village and the plain, toward the southern coast, a bank of grayish rain clouds was gathering. God's recent work had been unkind—so unkind that a dank cave became a cause for celebration, most of all for the children, who, though they didn't know it, would suffer first when God's harvest was scraped up in August and the cycle started over. But just now, for the first time in weeks, Lavié struck me as beautiful.

In Christine's kitchen that night, Claudie was full of our adventure. He was a born raconteur as well as a truant and potential *voyou*: when Christine wasn't slapping him for eating the manioc she was laughing at his stories. Christine and I squatted on stools and the five other kids sat on the dirt, while Aku slept. Claudie stood with the firelight at his feet and threw wild shadows against the bamboo and thatch as he acted out the battle between the Ashanti and the Ewé, embellished the cave with a few panthers and boas, and ended with my heroic belly crawl and transformation into an African man. Christine and the kids clapped their hands and shouted with laughter. Mawuli, feeling left out, began to cry.

"Old man," Christine said to quiet his sobs, "old man, shh, Fo Georgie won't bring you bread from Kpalimé if you cry."

"Old man," said Atsu, "Sakpaté is going to hear you and come get you!"

Everyone fell silent and pretended to listen for the telltale clopping across the paved road.

"I hear him!" Claudie whispered, finger to his lips. "Clop-clop, clop-clop!"

Emma got up and peered out between the bamboo wall and the grass roof. "Sakpaté can hear you, old man!"

Mawuli's crying had died to a whimper. Christine waved her hand. "He's gone." Within two minutes Mawuli was asleep on her knee.

Markie, Emma's twin brother, had been eyeing me for some time. Finally he got up his nerve and challenged me. "Fo Georgie, when are we going to the stars?"

On a moonless night a few weeks earlier I had told him and Emma about the stars. They were so far away from the sun that they were frozen solid, but the sweetest thing in the world to eat. I had taken a few ice cubes from my kerosene-run freezer, which was in one of its rare periods of operation, and dipped them in a bag of sugar. The kids crunched into the cubes and shrieked at the cold. Ice, even an orange that had spent a couple of days in the lukewarm frigo, was a marvel—sugared ice, another work of God. Well, this was what the stars were like. The edible proof had begun to win Emma over. I promised that the next time there was no moon—in the moonlight Sakpaté's spirit cousins would see us and come after us, since man wasn't supposed to travel at night, least of all in the sky—we would all get on my mobylette, fill up at the Texaco in Kpalimé, take a trip up to a star with forks, and eat a few mouthfuls.

"Ten days, *professeur*," I told Markie, whose grades in primary school were always high. "When the moon goes away. Also, the Texaco has no gas now so we'll have to wait for that."

"You lie!"

"I'm not lying. Emma, didn't you eat some?"

Emma put her tongue in the gap between her teeth and hesitated, afraid of being thought a fool by one or the other of us. "*Oui,*" she finally said.

"I'm a magician," I went on to Markie. "In *Amérique* I'm one of the biggest fetish priests. I can do *yovo grigri*. I've been to the stars!"

"Woo-ee!" Christine laughed.

I leaned over to look out under the thatch. The night glittered with millions of stars, but a damp breeze was blowing and milky clouds had moved in over the trees. The air smelled like rain. Suddenly a meteor shot out: it seemed to slip and fall as if a string had been cut. Christine saw too.

"That means," she said, "that somebody dies. Every man has a star there. When he dies it falls from the sky. Because we see it, it is someone in the village."

Smoke hung in the hut, over the black urn of drinking water, the horseshoe-shaped clay stove, and the rags and bowls strewn about the dirt floor. The log had stopped burning and become a thick glowing coal. Someone, I thought, was a magician here, in the yard, in the village—not me. I was halfway under the spell. Sakpaté the forest spirit, sweet frozen stars, the Ewé warriors in the *hoëkpe* among snakes and panthers, my blackness—things of a magician's night that almost held me in their grasp. Or perhaps love for the Agbelis was coming over me, which did not blot out but finally existed alongside the knowledge that they and I would always be strangers to each other. It was enough to sit here, by the fire, for an hour or so, and still know that no matter how long I sat up with them, in the end I would go back to my room and they would go to theirs. Already it was time.

Christine moved her knee and tapped Mawuli's shoulder. *"Ezado."*

It begins with the wind. Around four o'clock in the afternoon leaves kick up and shutters bang open against the walls and then slam shut. The light fails quickly; in minutes the sky is almost dark. Voices call out on the road, and Emma comes running into the yard, a basin on her head. I go to my door and shout, "The water is coming!" She grins—"Eh!"—and runs under the thatch. The woman across the hedge is yelling for her children to hurry up and get inside. Christine walks by my window, firewood on her head. Our eyes meet, she smiles, then shouts to Dové and Emma to take the clothes down. For a moment the wind dies. With the shutters closed my house is dark. Then the wind blows harder than before, and a papaya branch cracks and falls. I grab a bucket and run to put it on the back step to catch the good water off the roof. I can hear the rain sweeping across the plain from the south. When it reaches the village it comes in heavy drops, falling one by one on the iron roof like stones. The stones get bigger and fall thicker. Then a torrent comes loose. So fast that Emma, who is taking clothes off the line, gets drenched before she can run fifteen feet into the kitchen, her blue dress matted to the small strong body. I stand in my doorway, sprinkled, and watch the yard turn into a muddy delta of rivers rushing down past my two-thirds of the house to the Agbelis' third. The pallid brown dirt is transfigured into brilliant oranges and reds. The noise on the roof drowns out everything else. Through

the sheet of water I can make out the Agbelis across the yard hud-
dling under the thatch. For a few seconds the rain lets up; the
silence is strange. Then the downpour starts again, even harder than
before. Spray rises up and clouds the yard. I light a lamp and pick
up my book, and don't realize the rain has stopped until I hear the
Agbelis wandering out into the mud. The yard breathes and steams
in the aftermath, water drips off the leaves and the roof. My bucket
is almost full.

A ferociously swift change came over the village. At the end of a
solid week of rainstorms the stunted elephant grass alongside the
road was two feet high. The trees behind our house were suddenly
thick with leaves that pushed against the outside wall; the banana
tree had long green tongues hanging out of its center like some
hothouse mutant. The meager stream swelled its banks, and at night
we could hear it crashing through the underbrush beyond the house.
A million frogs seemed to invade it in the space of five days. On
the plateau the great trees and vines were sprouting leaves again
and smothering the signs of drought and fire. Nothing came gently
in the tropics. Life returned to Lavié not amid robins chirping and
crocuses nudging through soil, but with the strength of a baby elephant kicking its way out of its mother's womb.

Everything had been dusty; now everything was damp. My towels
smelled cheesy, my leather sandals began to rot. The frigo was
running well enough, but food molded more quickly than I could
eat it. One morning I saw a greenish liquid puddling underneath
the frigo and opened it to discover hundreds of tiny yellow maggots
squirming and leaping out of a head of cabbage that had spoiled
overnight and was leaking out the door.

Farmers, like columns of ants after a rain, emerged from shade
and torpor and began going to the fields every day. There were no
histrionics, no celebrations, not even a state-sanctioned thanksgiving
ceremony. I saw the men on the road through my WC window when
I was barely awake at five o'clock, or passed them on my dawn jog
to Akata. A long, straggling line of figures, each separated by twenty
or thirty yards, walked along the edge of the pavement in the misty

half darkness, in their crazy assortment of dead *yovo* clothes: baggy
green trousers or grease-stained shorts, neon-orange shirts left unbuttoned, a sweater worn against the new morning chill looped with
holes and stretched out of shape, a girl's smock pulled over worn-
out corduroys, a floppy felt hat, plastic flip-flops or straps of rubber
fashioned into sandals or nothing at all on their feet; some with
bottles to bring back *sodabi*, all dragging cutlasses—the two feet of
sharpened metal that was, along with a crude hoe, their only tool
in turning dense, tangled bush into a cultivatable field. They spent
twelve hours in the fields; they drank and ate at midday, then worked
past dark, through rainstorms.

At first the work—the clearing, plowing, and digging with their
hand-tools—was brutally difficult. To know how hard African peasants work, and under what conditions, you had only to glance at
their feet: hard, cracked and desiccated like mud bricks, misshapen
as ginger, full of cuts and scabs, the toes little stumps with the nails
torn off. Even five-year-olds had ugly feet. A lot of men went barefoot—on hot pavement, over sharp rocks, and through the worst
brambles—to labor the day away on the muddy hillside. But their
bodies were splendid from the years of work—flat bellies ridged
with muscle, narrow waists, and powerful arms and thighs. For
months they had looked like slack, stupefied drunks; now they
performed backbreaking work for hours in the humidity, and you
saw there hadn't been an ounce of fat on them.

A farmer owned land by tradition or found a patch in the trees
where brush wasn't too thick. It remained for him to cut through a
thousand or so square feet of thickets, branches, and grass and to
clear rocks and roots with nothing but the cutlass before he could
even plow and get his seeds in the soil. All this had to be done
quickly now because of the late rains. At dawn, on a bowlful of
porridge, they walked four or five kilometers uphill and went to
work. On their way back in the evening they carried loads of firewood, rodents killed in the bush, jugs of liquor. Between rains the
sun was only slightly less fierce than at the peak of the hot season.
There are not many jobs left in the United States where men's
bodies are put through this kind of labor; for the most part, such

tasks are left to machines or illegal aliens. Togolese peasants did their life's work, fed and clothed a family, and raised their children with two hand-tools that could have been lifted from an archeological display case. Most finished the clearing in a week and spent another week plowing with the eighteen-inch hoe that kept their backs always parallel to the ground. After this came the comparatively easy work: digging two-foot yam mounds and planting seed corn. Then, until harvest and the second planting, most of their labor went toward weeding the jungle that grew and grew and tried to choke off the vital air.

One Saturday morning I hiked with Christine, Claudie, Markie, and Mawuli three kilometers up a steep rise of the plateau. Christine kept her field separate from Benjamin's because, she said, hers would produce more since she tended it better. She gave the children and me a handful of seeds each. We all bent over and shuffled along the slope, scooping out small holes a few feet apart with one hand and tossing in a couple of seeds with the other. Christine worked with Aku on her back. It seemed easy enough at first, but after two hours my back and legs ached from crouching and my hands were filthy with mud. Standing up to stretch, I noticed that Christine had covered twice as much soil as I; even eight-year-old Markie had done more. The next day my entire body was sore from having done this fraction of the work they did week after week.

I would watch the farmers wandering back at night, drinking, singing in their pleasantly gravelly voices, and wonder how many millions or billions of people were doing the same work all over the world, and had been doing it, in ways that couldn't have been much different from this, throughout human history. It has been the lot for all but a tiny portion of humanity until very recently, and still is for the majority. Yet to that privileged minority, the work and the workers are invisible, don't exist. I would have never given them a real thought if I hadn't been living in their midst.

With ubiquitous dust turned to ubiquitous mud, the rains had broken the mood of strain and depression in the village. School, market, public place became scenes of earnest talk, gossip, and gibes; the quarrels and jokes took on their old savor. Christine said she was sleeping better and seemed to put on weight. April came and went, and then May, a delicious month, abundant with mangoes and pineapples, fragrant with rain and bougainvillea. The school year mercifully ended before it could detonate or disintegrate, and the teachers scattered to Lomé and their home villages.

June closed out the circle of my first year in Africa. In all this time I hadn't left Togo once and hadn't received a visit. For the past two months I'd hardly left the village. Now the long hours of solitude in Lavié, the immobility of time and place, were about to be broken. Summer brought visitors from home and travels that took me across the continent.

CHAPTER 8

Three Africas

Ouagadougou

HE ROAD TO OUAGADOUGOU IS LONG FROM ANY DI-
rection, and flat and empty. As far as you can see the
earth stretches out, cracked and dry, like a vast, brown-
ing jigsaw puzzle. Coming up from the south in a bush
taxi, as I did, you reach a fork in the road: one sign points left,
Ouagadougou 140, and the other right, Niamey 560. Though the
distance is in kilometers, not miles, the thought of attempting Niamey makes the head float.

The "rainy" season had begun to spit, and every few miles we
passed a water hole where a farmer leaned on a stick while his cows
drank. Sometimes it was no more than a mud flat. A donkey, or a
woman shrunk like a raisin, hauled firewood across an empty stretch
of land. Here and there a village—half a dozen tan blocks with
window niches—seemed cut out of a bump in the earth. And under
every baobab tree a soldier sat on a motorcycle, his beret a brilliant
flash of red. Eight hours, eleven baobabs, eleven soldiers, eleven
passport checks.

A sickly little Voltaic in a woolen cap who was sleeping and sweating on my shoulder during the ride had an expired identity card.
We waited at the first baobab for half an hour while the soldier and
the man, suddenly come to life, argued over bribe money and finally

cut a deal. The next few soldiers grew bored and stopped checking just before they got to him. As the taxi roared off he would allow a wry grin amid the congratulations of the other passengers. Between stops he seemed about to die on me again; and I remembered a story of a man who died on a bus that had to carry the corpse a hundred miles to the next town. The fifth or sixth soldier under the fifth or sixth baobab wanted more money than the man was willing to pay. Eventually we left him there, and as we drove off I looked out the back of the truck. They were standing by the motorcycle under the tree, the big soldier with the red beret and the little man with the woolen cap, not looking at each other, miles from anything, growing tiny. I doubted he would ever get to Ouagadougou and I wondered which would kill him first: fever, corruption, or sheer distance.

The Sahel used to be the cultivatable underbelly of the Sahara, its water and soil capable of supporting village life. Years of erosion and desertification and the three-year drought had begun to make life here untenable; the desert was moving south. But the peasants who hadn't migrated to Ouagadougou, the Ivory Coast, or France continued to scratch at the ground and draw their jug of water, their jar of millet. Every year the women had to go farther out to scavenge the night's fuel wood. It seemed bleaker than desert, where nothing was expected to grow and the Tuaregs lived as nomadic herdsmen. Here the farming villages were immobile and the exhausted earth was reclaiming them; the figures on the landscape looked like sun-blackened skeletons.

We didn't reach Ouagadougou until after dark. We could see its gas and low-voltage neon lights on the horizon from fifty miles away, a yellow glow in the middle of so much desolation.

In the Grand Marché, famous all over West Africa, merchants opened their stalls at 6:00 A.M., before the sun blazed. The dirt alleys, filled with yesterday's trash and the smell of stray goats, burst into color. A Moslem trader stood to display his stall for me: dyed camel-hair blankets from Mali and hand-sewn quilts of black, red, and white squares. I lifted my camera: *"Foto?"* *"Cent francs,"* he said at once, as if I were the tenth tourist who had asked for his picture this morning. He placed his enormous body, spreading out like a pear under the cream robe, on a stool: in sunglasses and turban, shawls around his neck, he sat with his hands splayed on a pile of cloth and posed with the solemnity of a sultan.

My arm was grabbed from behind. A boy of ten with a scar across his cheek was trying to drag me toward his stall—*"Moins cher, moins cher!"* The sultan lost his dignity and started bellowing at the boy in their language, Moré. "Don't touch him!" he seemed to be saying. "I saw him first, he's mine!"

You could gormandize here, if you had money. In the middle of the maze of leather stalls and used auto-parts stalls, the indoor food pavilion hoarded mounds of fruits and vegetables: cabbages, apples, breadfruit, mangoes, heads of purple lettuce and green lettuce—a mirage of abundance. They came in from the big plantations of French and Swiss projects. The customers were Europeans and Voltaic men carrying motorcycle helmets. Shouts of *"Anasara!"* (from *Nazareth*: "Christian": "white") from the women vendors whistled about the pavilion like parrot calls. On a long central table, the rotten core of so much ripeness, butchers hacked at pieces of cattle, pig, and goat. Bloody haunches, tails, cleft feet, and innards hung from a beam like the dyed cloth in the sultan's stall. Flies swarmed to the stench; overhead, perched on rafters, a gang of vultures kept watch over the Grand Marché and slowly beat their wings.

Ringed by a wall, the market was a small city within the capital. Outside, on Avenue Yemmenary, the colors dulled into the faded brown of Ouagadougou—the color of earth. A hundred feet from the fruit bazaar, beggars lay on mats on the sidewalk in front of the great mosque and prayed or slept, it was hard to know which. Their rags were the same ocher as the mosque's mud walls and the street's dirt, and a glimpse of black arm or ankle wasn't enough to distinguish a man from a woman. Their worldly possessions were scattered around them: a leather sack, a tin cup, a few strings of prayer beads. One or two had set up tattered umbrellas against the sun, and this was the only sign of a mind at work under the rags. Others lay in the sun like animals waiting to die.

I walked by the row of beggars and was free to stare. But near the corner, by a traffic light, I heard a noise at my feet like a goat's squeal. A bundle was squinting up at me and holding out a palm that ended abruptly in finger stumps. The beggar might have been forty, or eighty; from the shape of the arm, the dried face, and the long, filthy knots of hair, I saw it was a woman. I fumbled in my pocket for a coin and dropped it from six inches up on the swollen, yellow hand, aware that I was flinching—but not from the touch of leprous skin. It was the upturned face, the gesture of begging that betrayed her as human.

When it rained in the evening the entire city—only a few blocks of it paved—was transfigured into orange mud. But by late the next afternoon the Sahelian sun had done its work and the streets and the people were again the color of dust.

Ouagadougou was a city built on foreign aid, and it seemed to exist in order to maintain foreign aid. Crossing dirt lots where animals foraged in garbage and sore-eyed children asked for francs, I came upon five-story banks, hotels with swimming pools, international offices of Swiss, French, or American relief organizations. At one end of the city, near the presidential palace, the Europeans lived in a handsome ghetto. Here the streets were shaded by pine trees and the air was purged of the smell of rot and urine. The houses had driveways, high gates, and Voltaic watchmen asleep on chairs outside.

Across the street from the U.S. embassy, the American community gathered at the Rec Center to sunbathe or swim in the brilliant turquoise pool and down cheeseburgers and drafts at tables under beach umbrellas. Every Wednesday at one they crossed the street to watch a videotape of Dan Rather with the "CBS News"; swimmers sat on folding chairs with embassy personnel and watched fragments from home flicker across the screen.

At the Rec Center the man from the World Bank sipped his beer and licked at a moustache that needed trimming. "Ouaga's one of the better jobs, believe it or not. Good pay, and living here costs nothing. 'Course, you get plenty of WAWA anywhere." The acronym, a common usage among old hands in the region, which was intended to sound plucky but came off a little snide, meant, "West Africa Wins Again."

But Ouagadougou was only a way station for the embassy and development people; they paid their dues and awaited release into the embrace of Paris or Geneva. In the interval, their lives moved between the offices and the pool, the banks, the restaurants on Avenue Yemmenary, the Nouvelle Pâtisserie and the movie theater across the street. This constituted, like the market, a city within the city; the nearness of the vendors and beggars whom they had come to develop seemed incidental, as if they had no connection with each other. Ouagadougou went on all around the Westerners and allowed them to pretend it didn't exist.

I was having a cup of French coffee with a young man in the Nouvelle Pâtisserie. On the other side of the plate-glass window a table with imitation Mossi wood carvings was set up next to two dozen Yamaha mopeds, a metallic orange almost the color of the mud, parked in a row. Ouagadougou was full of the mopeds of Voltaics—for someone had to staff the banks, the embassies, the aid offices—and all of them seemed to be orange Yamahas. Beyond, Avenue Yemmenary, the mosque, and the beggars were lost in the glare.

Inside the *pâtisserie* black and white men, and an occasional African woman in European dress, were downing their morning coffee and rolls over *Le Monde*. In the air conditioning white-coated waiters moved at twice the speed of people on the street.

"I need to go to France," André said, coughed, and fiddled with his black beret. I'd met him outside the movie theater the night before; after a moment of chat he had said he wanted to talk to me, and I'd told him to meet me for coffee this morning. He was from the northern part of Upper Volta, tall and very black like the people there, with quiet eyes and a smile that never left his face but only changed nuance. His unease with the waiter and the cloth napkin suggested that he was more used to drinking Nescafé out of goblets at long tables on the street, where big Moslem men spooned in two inches of condensed milk and poured the hot water they had boiled eggs in; this might have been his first cup of French roast in

his first *pâtisserie.* "I have some cousins there. In your opinion," he ventured in precise French, "could I get a job in Paris if
I went?"

I explained that jobs were scarce and there were now restrictions
on immigration from Africa.

"But I've finished my *bac.* I took the degree."

"Are you at the university now?"

The smile tightened. "I was at the university; I failed my exams.
I've been selling sunglasses since then. It would not matter if I
passed them—there are no jobs here. I need to go to France."

We had slipped into the familiar roles Africa always stood ready
to furnish—black suppliant, white provider. Having nothing to provide, I suggested that he give his exams another try, keep looking
for a job in the bureaucracy. He glanced away as if to conceal an
embarrassment for my ignorance: he knew better. "But anyway,"
I found myself saying, "here's the address of somebody I know in
Paris. You can write him."

It was a false hope, but not one I wanted to withhold. He thanked
me as though I'd personally arranged papers, ticket, and a sponsor,
and carefully folded the scrap of paper with the name of an unknown
anasara scribbled on it. I thought of the friend in Paris who would
get a courteous, desperate letter in a few weeks, with an exotic
postmark and wood-mask stamp on the envelope and several spelling
errors inside. He would save the stamp, and be troubled by the
letter for a couple of days before writing a sympathetic reply saying
there was really nothing he could do.

In one way André's reaction to me was not much different from
the merchant sultan's or the beggar woman's: some unfathomable
hope erupted at the sight of a white, expressing itself variously as
a pull on the arm, a request for advice, a squeal. André was a minor
casualty of a city that was crawling with his kind: students, vendors,
skill-less villagers fleeing drought or river blindness, whose expectations dried up as the truth became clear—*pas de travail, pas d'ar-
gent.* But there was this difference. When André was in his village,
Ouagadougou must have held out the promise that had now been
displaced onto Paris. His *bac,* an extraordinary achievement in Africa,

had gotten him here; and he had found it to be worth nothing. He had less place in the city than the sultan or the beggar woman; less than the white foreigners who came from cities like Paris on development business. He had staked out a spot on the Avenue Yemmenary where he sold sunglasses, looking stylish in his beret. He was aware that Ouagadougou had become a trap, maybe even aware that France would inevitably hand him defeats, but mostly aware that there was no choice but France, since his own country had nothing.

When I went back to Upper Volta in December, we were three months into the dry season and the harmattan winds had already blown down from the Sahara and filled the sky with dust. Every meal ground between my teeth. From the highway, villages could hardly be distinguished from the land; the desert seemed to have moved a few more miles south; and in Ouagadougou, where refugees from famine were beginning to collect in camps on the outskirts, even the paved roads were coated with a fine ocher dust.

But change had come over the city. A bloody coup had been staged by Captain Thomas Sankara, and Ouagadougou showed signs of turning into a revolutionary capital. Soldiers paraded on motorcycles with AK-47 rifles strapped to their backs; T-shirts with Sankara's picture, arms raised in victory, were sold by the cloth vendors in the market; banners stretched from trees across the Avenue Yemmenary, proclaiming in vivid red letters: "Long Live Economic Independence!" and "For an Authentic, Nonimperialist Cinema!" Sankara had ordered the closing of nightclubs frequented by Europeans and an end to what he called on the radio "reactionary songs with problems of women and money." Soon the country would even have a new name, a hybrid of two local languages: Burkina Faso, "Land of the Brave." Sankara would cut the salaries of the Yamaha Voltaics, his wife would drop the title "Madame President," and his children would be sent to their grandparents' village every weekend. He would demand justice and self-sufficiency for the skeletons out on the land, and say, "With each grain of millet brought into our country a bit of us dies." And there would be talk among his revolutionary committees of turning Ouagadougou's several cities into one.

But the movie playing at the theater across from the Nouvelle Pâtisserie was French, a spy thriller with luscious blondes and rococo interiors. Vultures still watched over the fruit market, and the pool behind the pine trees remained an oasis for Americans. On the sidewalk outside the mosque, the beggars lay in their rags as if they hadn't moved in six months.

A Boulangerie *in Lagos*

In the courtyard of the Nigerian embassy a barefoot old man was cutting up the carcass of a goat. He had already wrapped the head and legs in newspaper, to be sold on the street, and was carefully sawing at the flank with a kitchen knife. He was the day watchman, and as I walked by he looked up from his work. His face hardened into an official challenge. "Who do you want to see?" "I've come for a visa to Nigeria." "The woman eats her lunch," he said in village French. "Come back in two hours." Guessing his tribe, I said good-bye in Ewé; at once his face relaxed into a toothless smile, and he gave me a sort of salute. *"Yo! Merci, chef."* He wiped his hands on baggy trousers and bent back over the upturned flank.

I was in Lomé again, with its mosquitoes and bureaucracy. I was making plans for a trip to Cameroon, to the east. In my dreams it appeared as rolling green hills with highland breezes and clean hotel rooms and French chocolate.

But Lagos, with its five million, lay in my way. By the logic of official Africa—borders that stayed closed, embassies that didn't exist—I could get a visa to Cameroon only in the most desired, least livable city on the continent. I'd heard of four-hour traffic "go-slows," of bodies left on the streets to be run over repeatedly for days, of casual murder. "Nigerians—they are wicked men," the farmers in Lavié warned me, and any village boy lucky enough to get to Lagos and find work was considered a lost soul.

When I went back to the Nigerian embassy, I met a Frenchman in the waiting room—small, soft, about thirty, with a moustache that curled over his lip. He had also come for a visa.

"Do you know Lagos?" I asked in French.

"I've lived there for six years."

"Well, perhaps you could recommend an inexpensive hotel in a safe area?"

"There are none." He smiled—more of a grimace, really, the grimace of the Africa veteran that said, "Pretty awful, isn't it, but that's the way things are here." It made him look mouselike. "Listen, come stay with me—I own a bakery. Here's the address." He scribbled something on a scrap of paper, introduced himself as Marcel, and was gone.

A French baker in Lagos? For six years? Why would he or anyone else stay there unless he had to? Curiosity made the stopover seem a little less menacing. I pictured the bakery as an elegant *pâtisserie* tucked away in the heart of the city (somehow Lagos had acquired cobblestones), Marcel lovingly squeezing out tubes of icing on the morning's éclairs. I seized his offer, the friendly gesture of a fellow "European" in a part of the world where whites were no longer rulers and not yet enemies. We wandered somewhere in between, privileged and uneasy, quick to smile at another white face.

"It is customary upon entering Nigeria to pay an airport fee of twenty *naira*."

The customs official at Murtala Mohammed Airport examined my passport while his hand fiddled with the rubber entry stamp. He looked up at me without interest.

"But the visa is in order. I paid for it in Lomé."

"It is customary upon entering to pay a fee of fifteen *naira*."

The custom wasn't so time-honored that it couldn't be adjusted by a few *naira*.

"I'm not going to pay fifteen *naira*. There's no problem with my passport."

"If you are traveling alone the fee can be reduced to ten." Silence. "All right, how much are you going to pay?" He was suddenly familiar and impatient; a line of arrivals, black men in expensive suits and women with fifty-kilo sacks of rice at their feet, waited behind me. I felt the pressure of the wads of *naira* I'd tucked away in my underwear and socks before leaving Lomé because of Nigeria's currency restrictions (money changed on Lomé's black market—one of the practices in Africa, like drinking bad water, I objected to but eventually found myself adopting). I fished a five-*naira* note out of the moneybag on my belt. The stamp descended on my passport.

One taximan out of several clustered just outside the automatic doors managed to steer me toward his car. I was obviously a good bet for a killer fare and he'd had to fight off the others to get me, but I'd been forewarned. Without quoting a fare he started his motor; I told him to turn it off and asked his price. I saw him smile in the rearview mirror. He said that the fare was a trivial thing between friends like us, we would work something out at the end. Then he said twenty-five *naira*. I refused to pay more than twelve. There was some good-natured arguing, he relented, and we started for the city.

From the backseat I gazed at the riot of cars on the four-lane highway into Lagos, metal glinting in the sun. Horns blared and taxis swerved across the crowded lanes, doing sixty; the rusty bodies of accidents littered the roadside. Faces of a middle-class African family beamed from a commercial billboard: "Nivaquine—Fastest Relief from Malaria!" Beyond the sea of tin roofs and the lagoon that cut Lagos into three islands, downtown rose in the haze.

Yaba Island, where the driver got lost, was a vast slum of houses pieced together from wood and corrugated iron. Garbage filled the sidewalks, battered cars lined the rutted streets, men lounged on doorsteps. A blanket of damp heat clung to Lagos; Lomé's air had been humid, but here the smell of exhaust and open sewers made it heavier, dirtier. "Which side you go for?" the driver kept asking. I had no idea which side; I had only Marcel's scrap of paper. Suddenly we were stuck in a go-slow that looked endless. Hawkers threaded through the traffic with their wares and passed my window; I rolled it up. A man, scarecrow-thin, held up baby clothes for my inspection. I started to lower the window; the taxi lurched ahead twenty feet; the scarecrow came running up alongside. "How much you pay? How much you pay?"

"Where is Adja Market?" I asked over the half-unrolled window.

"Adja Market?" The scarecrow began to laugh, and he said something long and mocking to the driver in Yoruba. The driver muttered; we tore out of our lane down a side street and left the scarecrow shouting after us, "Ten *naira*! Ten *naira*!" In the rearview mirror I saw him frantically waving a pair of pink pajamas, and saw the driver's scowl—his satisfaction at snaring a European passenger was gone.

We didn't find the bakery for an hour. The driver insisted on two *naira* extra for having gotten lost in the shamble of streets. Later I found I'd already paid double the normal fare.

The *"pâtisserie"* turned out to be an industrial bakery. Two low concrete buildings surrounded a parking lot, with an eatery on the far side of the watchman's booth at the gate, and next to it an outdoor shower and toilet stall. Across the lot, through an open door, I saw giant ovens and a crowd of African employees whose faces glistened and whose arms were powdered white. Two of them were piling hundreds of croissants and loaves of French bread onto trays in a van. Shouts of pidgin English carried all over the lot.

The watchman (younger and better dressed than the one in Lomé, and less interested in me) pointed me to the end of the lot, to a small office that had the impermanent look of a trailer. No one was there; I went in and knocked on the inner door, and a heavy French accent called, *"Entrez!"*

I stepped into Marcel's apartment—rather, Marcel and Papa's, for he had a partner twice his age, also French. It was Papa who had answered my knock. "Hello!" Papa put out a large hand from where he sat. He had his other in a bowl of raw eggs, clawing them into a mix. He added, in his own pidgin, "Long time I no see you why?"

"It's my friend from Lomé," Marcel said in French. "I hope you had no trouble getting here."

The two of them were sitting on empty two-gallon Nido powdered-milk cans at a plywood table, fixing dinner. The room was windowless, about thirty feet by twenty, and divided in half by a few colorful African cloths strung from the low ceiling. Midway across one half, a couch stood by the Nido cans and the plywood table, covered with bread crumbs and plates smeared with butter from another meal. At the far end of the room a partition separated the refrigerator and gas stove from a shower that doubled as a kitchen sink. On the other side of the cloths were two mattresses strewn with clothes, towels, and mildly pornographic French paperbacks. Someone had taped a Bob Marley poster to the wall by the front door. They had an air conditioner, but the place smelled like a bachelors' room.

The most striking thing about the apartment was the trash that overflowed from another Nido can. Instead of taking the can out back when it filled, Papa and Marcel threw garbage on top until the runoff of soiled paper towels and eggshells collected on the carpet. The Nido can was a meeting place for most of Adja Market's flies.

I'd arrived in time for dinner. I sat with Marcel—I on the couch, he on a Nido can—while Papa fried up the eggs and potatoes. Papa looked about sixty and had a long Gallic face, lined and weathered, all ears and nose. His French came out hoarse from the throat, nearly incomprehensible after years of Africa and Scotch. His hands moved like a short-order cook's between the pan, the utensils, and his glass of White Horse; he'd been in the food business in Africa for a quarter century. In the refrigerator I saw fresh butter and slabs of frozen steak, hidden luxuries. Marcel put on a tape of King Sunny Ade and the African Beats; it was a good machine and the room filled with the sound of juju music, like a fly buzzing near the ear then flitting off.

"Ade started out at a nightclub just around the corner," Marcel said. "We'll take you there after dinner."

"I'm pretty tired." And King Sunny wouldn't be there tonight— he was on his first American tour.

Employees hung around the office and the parking lot, Nigerians from the villages and illegal immigrants from Togo, Benin, and Ghana. They came in without waiting for an *"Entrez!"* and didn't use "sir" or *"monsieur"* but first names instead—a casualness, a lack of deference toward Europeans that was rare in Lomé and unthinkable in Lavié. Papa and Marcel kept the illegals from the authorities' attention. A few months before, in January 1983, the Shagari government had expelled hundreds of thousands of alien workers, claiming they took jobs that Nigerians, with the oil economy failing, needed. It was a popular move during an election year. Hundreds of those expelled had died in jammed boats and overloaded trucks, or from disease on the beach in Lomé waiting for Ghana to open its border and let them across. Busloads of Togolese had come through Lavié, mattresses and bags roped precariously on top, exhausted faces peering out the windows; a few were singing African gospels.

Papa and Marcel themselves were illegals—their work permits had expired—but for Europeans the risk was smaller. A handful of *naira* would take care of it. Somehow, as with the trash can, they didn't bother.

"They leave us alone, they don't mind us," Marcel said, pouring Scotch.

"Won't they search out your illegal workers?"

"Pssh!" Papa scoffed from the stove. "The Nigerians need them here, see. No one in Nigeria wants to do this kind of work, cooking and cleaning. People here think they are going to get rich fast—*money*," he said in English, rubbing his greasy fingers. "They think they are going to become oil executives or officials in the ministry of this or that, or best of all, smugglers. Menial labor—it's not good enough for them. You'll see. Soon enough the government will be asking the illegals back. Jobs are already easy to get." He spoke with a kind of fatherly smile, as if explaining the facts of life to his child.

"Zey are all on ze make," Marcel added in English. His was good, but Papa spoke only the version of the local pidgin he used with his Nigerian and Ghanaian workers. Marcel gave his smile-grimace, and I noticed an ugly knot of scar tissue, still red, in the crook of his jaw. It caught my eye and I found myself staring. I had probably seen it in Lomé, but it hadn't registered; it hadn't belonged to the dapper little *pâtissier* I'd imagined at the Nigerian embassy. Now, in the squalor of the room, the scar became a part of him; it made Marcel seem coarser, and a little sadder.

"Personally I am a capitalist," Papa went on. "I believe in free enterprise. You Americans have the best idea. Socialists don't understand what makes people go." He shot Marcel a challenging glance. "Nigerians do. Nigeria is the most capitalist place anywhere on earth, I promise you. You can do anything with money. And if you haven't got it, you are lost. Look at all the poor bastards out there in Adja Market. No money, nothing to do—so they break into houses on Victoria Island and steal clocks and stereos. They kill. If you're on the street and a man attacks you and a policeman walks by, he won't stop until you've reached in your wallet and pulled out twenty *naira* for him."

Marcel shook his head. "Papa exaggerates."

"Oh yes it's true!" Papa cried in English—another of his stock phrases. "The Yoruba are the worst. Lagos is a Yoruba city, you know, that's why it's so bad here. The Yoruba can go out into the bush and recite the most beautiful poetry you'll ever hear, but in Lagos—careful!" He indicated the moneybag on my belt. "You should keep that inside your pants."

We sat around the plywood and ate, broke fresh bakery bread and added to the morning's crumbs. Though the general filth and the thought of Papa's hand in the eggs made me flinch, his cooking was good and I took the food down hungrily. I began to feel more at ease in their room, sheltered from the huge city.

"The police can be very unpleasant," Marcel said, his mouth full of egg. "Just going into town and back can cost me twenty *naira*. I keep money in the glove compartment for that."

Twenty *naira* seemed to be the official rate for bribery.

"They do it in Togo too," I said, "if the driver's card is expired."

Marcel laughed ironically. "Togo is a small country. Here they do it no matter what state your card's in. Every now and then the government decides to crack down. Once I was coming back here at night from my girl friend's on Lagos Island and I was stopped by cops. I complained, but what can you do? I paid up. Another kilometer and I'm stopped again. This was too much. Before they asked for money I said, 'But I just paid your friends up the road.' 'What?!' These cops were shocked. They said they'd only wanted to see my papers. They had me get in their car and take them back to the first point. *Fwwwt'*—he whistled and slashed the air—"in prison, all of them. Of course, I never got my money back. But these periods don't last long, the government doesn't really give a damn. Every election they talk about cleaning up corruption, but that's the only time we hear of it. The police—they are small compared to the politicians." He whistled again.

We were silent and I looked at the two of them—Marcel with his moustache working up and down, Papa gulping the last of his Scotch. They lived as expatriates, disheveled, careless, and unnoticed. In a smaller African city like Lomé they would have been known, even famous; children would have trailed them down the street chanting *"Yovo!"* and cripples would have held open their bakery door and smiled for twenty-five francs. But Lomé seemed half a world away. In the chaos of Lagos, Papa and Marcel disappeared; they adapted to its rules and got by. Once or twice a week, when the city's overcharged current went black, they brought out kerosene lamps, and when the Nido can filled they threw more trash on top. This was what every African state, at least in its rhetoric, aspired to: a point where whites no longer mattered, where a hotel menu didn't have to include beefsteak and red wine to attract Europeans. But in Lagos the menus hadn't changed—the beefsteaks were now eaten by rich Nigerians who flashed business cards bearing the title "chief."

The tape had stopped. Flies were buzzing over the trash can.

"Why do you stay?"

Papa set his glass down and gave me a lank paternal look. "See"— he pointed with a crust of bread—"we're free here. No one cares about us, no one interferes. Everything is okay in Nigeria. The *francophone* countries are very repressive, no one there can speak his mind. But Nigeria has newspapers, free elections—they're preparing for one next month. Things happen here."

I had seen tabloids on the street blasting headlines about the election, and party billboards on the highway into the city: "Vote

UPN for Nigeria!" Several candidates were challenging President Shagari, and the loyalists of the three major parties held strident rallies that had led to arson and deaths in Oyo and Ondo, the states around Lagos. Violence is the surest sign of an open election in the Third World. I almost welcomed it, after a year of Togo's state-sponsored demonstrations and official slogans from the mouths of schoolchildren. Downtown the next day, I heard two Nigerians arguing over Shagari, and a year of political silence was broken for me.

"Papa has been in Lagos too long now," Marcel said. "He couldn't go back to the other countries."

Papa added, "In Togo, Benin, Ivory Coast, I was afraid to get drunk in bars. I never knew what things I might start saying that would put me in jail. Here, I drink anywhere!" And we all laughed.

One bottle of White Horse had been emptied and Marcel retrieved another from a crate behind the refrigerator. The bakers became more garrulous; tired, I struggled to follow. The air conditioner whirred futilely, and the smell of cooking grease was recycled on the humid air.

Papa was talking about his early years in Africa. "I came to the Sahara with the Legion. I was in Upper Volta—this was in the fifties. Oh, you should have seen them then! They knew nothing—*rien*. One time I was in my truck and I couldn't get the damn thing started." Marcel grunted with displeasure; it was an old story. But Papa was beaming and engrossed. "I tell the Voltaic with me to get out and push while I try to start up. He gets out and I sit at the wheel and wait. *Rien*—the thing doesn't move. *'Mais qu'est-ce qui se passe?'* I turn around—the Voltaic is *in the bed of the truck pushing against the cab*! Oh, my God!" He made a pushing motion and lost himself in laughter, rocking with hoarse gasps. Marcel frowned and crossed his arms, and the scar emerged. Papa resumed, "See, without us they would still be nothing, primitive."

Marcel said, "Yes, by the time you got the Voltaic in your truck we'd had a hundred years to teach them. And taught nothing."

Papa ignored him. "And then when we got out, look what happened. I had a *boulangerie* in Benin, up in Parakou. I had it for years,

I made lots of friends there. Just a small town—a good place to be. Then in 'seventy-one the revolution comes. No revolution, just another coup, but this time it's Marxists so it's a revolution. All of us Europeans—we're the enemy now. They take my *boulangerie*, they confiscate it." His voice moistened. "Now the people who were my friends won't even talk to me—they ignore me and act like they never knew me. I left to come here. I'm sure the *boulangerie* is a dingy little place now with flies all over the bread and the ovens at half capacity. You see what is happening in Africa. . . ." In his excitement his fingers were working the greasy bread crumbs on the plywood. "Ah, but they'll never let us go completely. They need us, see—like the illegals here. They can't do it by themselves."

Marcel became contentious. "You are an old imperialist, Papa. You talk as if we should own the place. What were we here for except to exploit them? And you want us to go on exploiting them. Your problem is they've made it difficult for us. Look at Nigeria, look at how sick the place has become. It wants to be a Western country because we've told them that's the way to be, that's development. See how developed they've become. All these people in Lagos—criminals, illegals, unemployed—while a few big ones get richer. They learned this from us."

"It's better here than other countries," Papa countered. "There are jobs—Ghanaians come here and find work. Better dog-eat-dog than dog-eat-nothing."

"And then they're kicked out and they drown or crash, all because the price of oil has dropped." Marcel turned to me. "You should go back to your Togo. The people are simple, they won't cut your throat in the night for a few *naira*."

"What do you know." Papa scowled. "How long have you been in Africa?"

"Shut up, Papa. You've been here too long, you don't know anything anymore."

They sat without speaking—Papa drinking from his glass, Marcel staring at the table. Outside Lagos was still wide awake. Tires screeched, men shouted in the street. At that moment the city felt vibrant, a place where lives could be made or lost; the room seemed passed by, and the two men small and misplaced.

There was a knock at the door. It opened, and a tall, very black young man appeared. His thin frame was lost in the flowing robes and floppy turban of a Hausa *alhaji*, a Moslem who has made the pilgrimage to Mecca and become a man of honor. His eyes, Oriental above high cheekbones, had a look I rarely saw in Togo but that was common in Lagos—knowing, wry, alert.

"Max!" Papa broke the silence. "Long time I no see you why?"

"You have the receipts, Max?" Marcel rose and went over to discuss business while Papa kept me entertained. Max's arrival seemed to cheer him. "Max is our front man, see. He drives the van and knows the city better than anyone. Today Max has become an *alhaji*." He admired Max's costume. "Max, did you fly to Mecca over the weekend?"

Max smiled as he flipped through a sheaf of papers. "Pay me better and I won't have to be a fake *alhaji* anymore, Papa."

Max spoke French; and in fact he wasn't a Hausa, or even a Nigerian, but a Togolese who'd been in Lagos a few years. So the oversized costume was a sort of ironic joke, on himself and on the rich Hausa businessmen who strode in robes through downtown Lagos—like a New York delivery boy showing up for work one day in a three-piece suit.

Papa winked. "Max is a good man. Sometimes he keeps a bit of the money he collects, but we don't mind that."

Max joined us at the table, elaborately lifting the folds of his robe to sit on the third Nido can. "You are visiting from Togo? And the people of Lomé, they're well?"

"They're well." It was an odd question from him, a trace of the village boy.

"Are you Peace Corps? I had a Peace Corps once for English. Miss Nancy—oh, she taught us too well, too well! In Ketao—you know the town?"

"Their cloth is famous in the north."

He smiled at my recognition; from Togo's smallness there was a bond between us.

"We've been talking about Lagos," Papa said. "Is it hell or not?"

"Lagos? It's not so bad."

"You must like it," I said, "since you stay."

Max rubbed his chin. "*Oui*—I like it, I stay. In Lagos I am one man—I work, I make money, I take out girls. Some people in Ketao might say I am a bad man. . . ."

"Are we bad men too?" Papa asked provokingly.

Max looked from Papa to Marcel with his Oriental eyes, smiling. "You and Marcel are all right, we like you. The rest of the Europeans in Africa can clear out. We'll do better without them. Except Peace Corps," he added, tapping my knee, as if he might have offended me.

"No more pilots," Papa taunted, "no more doctors, no more record producers?"

Max leaned toward me, elbows on the folds of his robe over his knees. "What Papa says is true. We've gone too far. We're like the drug addicts, we can't live without these foreign things anymore."

"Do you prefer Ketao?" I asked. Already it had become hard to remember Lavié, the feel of the sluggish afternoons when only roosters and goats were awake, the sound of babies crying. Lagos had crashed in, with its clipped words and horns of backed-up cars and wads of money changing hands. No one ever had coins, nothing less than a one-*naira* bill; the driver had laughed at my handful of *kobo*. But before he came here, Max must have been a schoolboy under a thatch roof by a river, reciting French verbs. After two or three years in Lagos, would one of my own students be as fluid, as sophisticated as Max, parodying himself in a religious costume?

"In Lagos I am one man," Max answered, losing his smile. "But when I go home with the money to my village, I am another man. No French, no English, no Bob Marley. I carry water like the others. I am happy there and happy here. How can I go making differences, that this one is better than that one? I have too many other things to go worrying about things like that."

Papa poked him. "And their names are Lilian and Mansa."

"Max is right, though." Marcel had been quiet since the quarrel. "Europeans analyze and worry over everything, but Africans know how to enjoy life now. That's why Papa won't go back to France. Oh, he goes at Christmas every year, but he couldn't live there. His wife understands. He gets nervous when he returns."

"The dentist bill, the *métro*, the taxes." Papa waved vaguely. "No one stops and talks with anyone else, everyone is always rushing. It's cold there, see? Lagos may be like that, too, but we have friends here. Max."

It was midnight. The ovens ran all night, in two shifts, and Papa and Marcel slept only five hours. But we talked on. Marcel's secret ambition was to leave baking and start a shortwave radio station in Equatorial Guinea; it would broadcast to all Africa a better, less Western-oriented news than Africa Number One in Gabon. "The radio is the greatest weapon in Africa," he said. But when his catering business here had foundered, Papa had come along, and they'd worked and lived together amid a circle of Africans for three years. As he described his plan for the radio station, Marcel's eyes winked with an excitement I hadn't seen; for him the *boulangerie* was not a way of life, but a resting point that had begun to stagnate. He had progressive ideas about Africa and liked local music and tribal cloth, but I imagined that one day he would go back to Brittany. Papa was a Gaullist, with a family in France, who couldn't bear to live outside West Africa and would always be a fugitive *boulanger*.

Before Lagos my picture of Africa had been of a bush taxi trundling down a dusty road; the sound of Emma sweeping the yard at daybreak; the smell of cooking palm oil. Now it was billboards with black faces, ovens disgorging piles of bread, loud quarrels, my own alertness—a filthy rushing river that swept in all the debris on its banks: Papa, Marcel, and Max; Lagos's chiefs, *alhajis*, and its jobless; the busloads of refugees leaving and the illegals who stayed; migrants from all over Nigeria and West Africa. No one had any idea where it was going. It was moving, that was enough.

Thirty years ago Lagos had been another colonial town asleep among the mangrove swamps on an infested lagoon. Independence, Biafra, oil, recession, and now it sprawled out of control like some wild tropical mutant of American capitalism. At the end of the sixties oil suddenly flooded the country with billions of dollars a year, and people fled the farms for Nigeria's cities; Lagos swelled from 300,000 to three million in a decade; by the beginning of the eighties a billion dollars of food was being imported every year and Lagos was being called the world's most expensive city. Then came the bust. The country could no longer feed itself; great numbers of unemployed in the city had to resort to buying and selling on the black market, to smuggling, or to robbery. The river did not seem to be slowing down. Soon enough it would spread elsewhere—to Togo too? Or would Lomé be saved from "development" by its insignificance? Unpaved streets with scrawny bleating goats, or rutted streets with angry choking taxis: this seemed the choice in West Africa.

Few people I knew in Togo would have hesitated to choose the latter. Nigerians may have been "wicked men," but they could speak freely and had money too. Reeking, crowded, black-eat-black, Lagos was the hope of Africa.

Papa and Marcel floated like little white flecks on the surface of the river, washed this way and that. Most of their countrymen had left at independence with cars and cocoa futures, and only came back when it was clear that a few pieces of pie were still to be had, this time at no cost. After twenty-five years Papa's slice was small and stale; if profit was the goal, he and Marcel were doing badly. But they seemed indifferent to the squalor of their life. They got by, they threw more on top.

Something had softened between them since Max came into the room. He was a reason for staying, for living with the shabbiness. Even Lagos had a whiff of the old African air of knowing people and being responsible for them: for Max, for me. In a house out on Victoria Island among the diplomats and businessmen, there would have been a cook, glass-louvered windows, and a trace of colonialism; and their tension would have snapped.

Marcel handed me a key to the outhouse and a roll of toilet paper. "You take my mattress on that side." He pointed behind the hanging cloth. "I'll be staying with my girl tonight."

"I ahm a blahck wo-mahn," Papa mocked the girl friend's low, accented English. "I ahm your guhl friend, not your play-theng."

Marcel smiled, and said to me, "As for your Cameroon visa, tomorrow we'll drive downtown and see if we can find a friend of mine from Douala who can help you. The embassy is very strict."

He picked up the dirty plates and bent to scrape them over the Nido can. Bits of egg tumbled on the carpet. "And if you go overland, careful! It's safer in a large bus, and don't travel at night. There are highway bandits to the east, in Iboland. All of Nigeria is becoming Lagos."

That was in July 1983. In August, Shehu Shagari won reelection to a second term on a promise to wipe out corruption; but he'd already lost his chance. On New Year's Eve, the day I arrived back in New York, a Hausa general named Buhari staged a coup d'état that ousted the Shagari regime, and with it the last democratic government on the continent. Buhari sealed the borders and put ministers on trial, vowing an end to corruption. Within twenty months he, too, would be gone; but not before ordering another expulsion of illegal West African workers. Seven hundred thousand of them were given three weeks to leave. Thousands of refugees massed at the Benin border, where the Marxist government refused to let them back across. They were stranded for days in the no-man's-land between the two closed borders, amid piles of pots and mattresses, waiting in the rain for an order to move.

Shortly after the second expulsion I got a letter from a student of mine. He'd quit school in Togo and gone to Lagos to look for a job, any job. He was working twelve hours a day in a chemical factory outside the city and saving money to build a house back in the village. "I know you will have concerns for me," he wrote. "But don't. I tell you this recent expulsion has been a very harsh exercise for the immigrants. As for me, I came on my own and I will leave on my own. I am a person of boldness and *savoir-faire*."

On Safari

After Lagos, after two sodden weeks of overland travel through Nigeria and Cameroon in a ceaseless rain, I flew across the desert to meet my mother and sister in Cairo. Later they said that arriving in Egypt seemed like leaving the West for the first time; as my

Egypt Air jet circled over the sprawling gray city in the sands, with its network of highways and its lights yellow at dusk, I thought I was reentering it. Ten days of climbing among ruins and tombs in the blazing sun; ten nights in lavish air-conditioned hotels; then on to Kenya, with its safaris.

This morning we were sitting out on the terrace of the Norfolk Hotel. It was the oldest in Nairobi, built just after the turn of the century, when the city was a dusty stop on the rail line that coolie labor imported from India was laying between the coast and Uganda. Lions, we'd been told, prowled a mile or two away, while hunters back from a shoot took their afternoon tea on the terrace, where this morning we were eating the "Big-Game Buffet" breakfast. What had once been a dirt road was now Kenyatta Avenue, noisy with traffic; across it, the University of Nairobi stood behind a freshly mowed lawn and beds of frangipani and hyacinth. Black businessmen in pinstripes and laborers in overalls hurried past on the sidewalk. The thousands of unemployed migrants we'd heard about were massed somewhere in shanties, out of sight. Here on the terrace of the Norfolk it was still possible to think of the country as the preserve of *wamzungu*, white men.

The place mats on our breakfast table showed a little scene of three white hunters crossing a river, rifles over their shoulders, trailed by a caravan of black carriers loaded down with luggage and game. At the other tables on the terrace real whites, dressed to goggle if not to kill, in tailored khaki safari suits and topis or sweatpants and velour leopardskin pullovers, chatted excitedly in English, German, Swedish. Others lounged in their chairs, irritated by a delay or simply bored. Kenyans—waiters, not carriers—moved among the tables, efficient, reserved, almost invisible except when the headwaiter barked orders in Swahili.

Inside the lobby, upstaging the portrait of His Excellency President Daniel arap Moi, gazelle heads and leopard pelts hung on the walls, trophies from the age when you could actually shoot bullets instead of just pictures. A signboard over the reception desk kept track of daily sightings at the four or five major parks: "Mara—6 rhinos, 25 baboons, 17 warthogs, 63 water buffalo, 378

wildebeest . . ." The signboard was like the posting of snow conditions on the various slopes at a ski lodge. That was the atmosphere
of the Norfolk—the mixture of feverish anticipation and utter boredom of a ski resort, where people dressed, ate, and talked skiing,
where everyone had come for one reason. We had all come here to
look at animals.

"Don't you want another omelette?" my mother asked. I'd been
eating everything within reach since Cairo; the unlimited Kenyan
buffets were nearly fatal.

"No, I'm fine."

"Are you sure? George has lost weight, hasn't he?"

"Your hair's thinner too," my sister added, adjusting her
sunglasses.

"It's the malaria pills," I said, like a stoical old Africa hand.
"Apparently they make you lose your hair."

"Permanently?" my sister asked. "The ones for East Africa too?"

"You never know. Maybe."

She frowned. "I don't believe it. The doctor didn't say anything
about it. God, maybe I won't take them."

"We'll all take them," my mother said. "We'll go bald together."

"I am *not* going to go bald."

My mother looked at her watch. "Didn't the woman from Flamingo Tours say nine o'clock for the van? I suppose things will be
even less reliable in Togo."

"Kenya is like clockwork compared to Togo," I said. "You just
have to expect things not to work out, and you won't get frustrated."

My mother leaned toward me. "When you're paying as much as
we are, you shouldn't have to expect things not to work out. It's
fine for you in Togo, but the Norfolk ain't cheap."

This morning Charles N' Somebody of Flamingo Tours was to
drive us north through the highlands to Treetops, a lodge built on
stilts over a man-made salt lick where animals came at night to
tongue the rocks in the glare of spotlights, while guests watched
from the balcony. It had the added attraction of being the place
where Princess Elizabeth learned that her father had died and she
would be crowned queen.

Suddenly:

"If it isn't Nancy Packer!"

Over the flowery hedge three Americans were squinting up from the sidewalk. I didn't recognize the middle-aged parents, but their daughter had been a few years ahead of me in high school in California. They were all outfitted in khaki, carried nylon traveling bags, and had binoculars slung around their necks.

The Nordstroms joined us. Mr. and Mrs. Nordstrom seemed straight off a Palo Alto tennis court—tanned, silver-haired, handsome. Susan, in her late twenties, was blond and paler and had the uneasy manner of an adult traveling with parents.

"We just got into Nairobi last night," Mr. Nordstrom said in his flat West Coast accent. "What a holdup at the airport! They didn't want to let us in."

"You see," his wife explained, "we've just flown up from Johannesburg. We didn't know it, but African countries won't let you in if you've got 'South Africa' stamped on your passport. So the officials kept us waiting for two or three hours at the airport and we were about ready to get on the plane back to London."

"Then the customs guy said something funny," Mr. Nordstrom continued. "He said, 'I will give you the opportunity to make it easier.' Of course Marge and I had no idea what he was getting at, and *he* couldn't say it right out, but clever Susan figured out he was asking for a bribe. Can you imagine?"

Susan smiled tightly.

"So we paid," said her mother.

"It would've been worth the trade-off, though," said her father, opening a menu. "South Africa for Kenya. Cape Town is the most beautiful city I've ever seen. Clean streets, flowers, the ocean. Everything was well run."

His daughter spoke to us by way of a caustic answer. "He doesn't know what we didn't see. The tour didn't take us through the black neighborhoods. They wanted us to think exactly what he's saying."

"Well, of course there is apartheid," Mr. Nordstrom allowed, "and it's terrible. But there's not much we can do about it. I enjoyed the place. I'd go back."

Susan looked away, over the hedge. A waiter came by to take their order. But the Nordstroms wouldn't have anything to eat— just iced tea.

"Nairobi reminds me of England," Mrs. Nordstrom said. "Such beautiful flowers. The people are awfully polite too. They even drive on the left here!"

"Wait till you see the game parks," my mother said.

"Beautiful?"

"Astonishing."

Using the Norfolk as a base, we'd done two safaris already. The parks to the south along the Tanzanian border, Amboseli and Masai Mara, were flat plains that shimmered in the sun like the mirage of a shallow yellow lake. Here and there in the grass was an acacia tree with its horizontal layers of branches, a thorn tree drooping with the nests of weaverbirds, a spring bordered by green grass that gave a flash of color to the tracts of dry savanna. At the southern edge of Amboseli, Mount Kilimanjaro burst out of the flatness and rose as far as the clouds; once, parting, they revealed its snow-covered peak.

The game lodge, surrounded by bungalows, stood fortresslike at the heart of the reserve. From here the tourists set out in safari vans every morning after a heavy breakfast buffet; and although the reserve spread out over a vast area, the vans seemed to keep meeting up with each other. Our driver would slow as he passed another driver on the dirt track, exchange a few shouts in Swahili, and then we were hightailing it across the plain, leaving dust clouds in our wake like an airplane's trail of smoke, to a grove of acacias where a pride of lions had been reported. And here they were: two males and four females, their magnificent slack bodies stretched out in the grass, their tails flicking at flies, a few cubs pouncing and pawing at their mothers' bellies; and six vans parked in a semicircle, safariers leaning out windows and sun roofs, snapping pictures and murmuring delight in the afternoon buzz.

But it was approaching four o'clock. The hippos and crocodiles were about to surface in the river for feeding. So we were in gear again, sped away from the lion pride; made a series of incomprehensible turns onto tracks that were barely more than paths; passed a van and then another; and suddenly here was the river. And here were the hippos—snouts and eyes and ears floating on the muddy surface. And crocodiles, too, stretched out on the banks, sun-warmed, smiling, a lower front tooth protruding dangerously over the lip.

The way back to the lodge from the river took us past thousands of wildebeest—smaller, bearded bison—spread out over the plain, all heading in the same direction in their annual migration northward from the Serengeti. They strolled past the white bones of their own kind, the ones killed and eaten by lions, then licked clean by hyenas and vultures. In one patch of grass a lion lay with its face buried in the flank of a freshly killed wildebeest; hearing our engine idling, he looked up from his meal and passed a tongue over his blood-smeared mouth. Our cameras clicked.

In the evening, at the lodge, there were steaks and fruit salads and wine for the safariers, pleasant fatigue, much talk of the day's sightings. After dinner a nature film was shown: many months in the life of one water hole. A crocodile thrashed an impala into the water with its tail; a long-necked bird sky-dove down for a water snake; one hippo struggled and splashed to mount another. Killing, eating, reproducing, more killing: the magnificent sights we'd all come to see on the plain boiled down to this. Projected onto a screen, what we'd been marveling at all day took on a new look, as if someone had adjusted the focus of our cameras to show things clear.

"Pure survival," my mother said when the film was over. "I'd rather not know. It's the feeling I have when I read about the size of the universe. It makes all our human pretense seem absurd."

Other absurdities intruded. Along the road from Nairobi to the Masai Mara reserve was a string of gift shops where tourists could buy sculptures, cowskin shields, and jewelry of the Masai tribe. The Masai themselves, who used to inhabit and graze their flocks in the game park that the state had expropriated and that we were now heading toward, loitered outside these shops. Tall and thin, dressed in red cloth, they stood about, some storklike on one leg; their looped earlobes, weighted with numerous earring hoops, dangled close to the shoulders. When a new van of whites arrived and emp-

tied, they hustled over, clutching spears, and assumed warlike pos-
tures; their smiles flashed; the tourists snapped away and then
distributed the set fee of a few shillings. In one place, as we were
waiting in our van for the driver, several Masai women came to the
windows. They were old, toothless creatures, with mutilated earlobes and lips. They didn't beg; we didn't know what they wanted.
With their hands on the windows they chatted at us and laughed.
On their grayish faces flies crawled. The women didn't brush them
away; they didn't seem to notice or care.

My sister shuddered. "What do they want?"

"They hardly seem human, do they?" my mother said when the
women, shooed away by our driver, had moved on to another van.
"I feel no connection at all."

But for the most part things worked as planned in Kenya. Neat
British-style road signs pointed the way to Nairobi along the airport
motorway; reservations from months in advance hadn't been thrown
out; giraffes and elephants made appropriate appearances out on the
reserve; hotel and tour people spoke impeccable English. Even the
teeming poor were kept more or less out of view. The tourist came
to look at animals, not people, and the government delivered the
goods.

Kenya left me at a loss. It was yet another Africa. Not the village
one I'd spent my first year in; not the new one of squalid survival—
André's, the bakers', Max's—that had exploded the first. This
seemed a fantasy Africa that Kenya and its white tourists concocted
for their mutual benefit. It brought the feeling of nostalgic adventure
to the whites and confirmed their sense of themselves at the center
of things; it brought foreign currency to the country. There were
"Isak Dinesen Tours," hot-air balloon rides over Amboseli, char-
broiled lunches at the Carnivore Restaurant outside Nairobi, glasses
of Kenya Coffee Liqueur at the Mount Kenya Safari Club, where
antlered trophies graced the walls and the voices of old British
settler-hunters still lingered in the lounge.

And the underlying sense that this safari cult was a little absurd—
after all, it was hard to concentrate on the lion cubs with half a
dozen other vans around, and the only trophies you brought home

were ebony figurines from the hotel lobby and a few hundred color snapshots—went unspoken, was taboo.

The Kenyans one met were there to facilitate the fantasy. Encountering them on "human" terms was out of the question. *"Jambo!"* I would greet the desk clerk in tourist Swahili. *"Jambo!"* he would pipe back. And I would walk away ashamed at the falseness, the condescension; ashamed to realize he was condescending to me, too, and that he wasn't offended because nothing more than this was expected. Here there were no anecdotes, and no defeats. The old strain of struggling and failing to live with Africans on something like their terms was lifted; whites were in the saddle again.

In South Africa Mr. Nordstrom had been impressed by what the white government wanted to impress him with; in Kenya a less sinister deception was at work. But unofficial Africa had a way of staring in at the windows. Only the willfully blind could ignore it completely. And when it did show its face, the Africa of Africans came as a shock. From the vantage point of a safari van or hotel terrace, the poor Africans who got through seemed more horrifying than they really were. The tourist had nothing to suggest to him that these, too, were ordinary lives.

It was easy to belittle whites for indulging a vain and silly colonial daydream. But at least there was an element of honesty in it. I knew well enough the illusions of the other daydream—going native. Traveling overland as I did through West Africa, eating in markets and riding in painful positions with local people on muddy back roads, provided no direct line to the "real Africa." Instead the days were spent in hassles over bush taxi fares and hotels, sickness and money shortages, angering yourself and the leather dealer who wouldn't come down in price. You never got out of your white skin; you only experienced Africa as a white on a tight budget. By the end, the exhaustion that came of the hassles had taken over to the point where, in your native shirt and sandals, you hated Africans for their inefficiency and bad smells.

And perhaps they didn't care for you either. The scruffy Europeans in drawstring pants and tank tops who backpacked through Africa looking for spiritual fulfillment, and spending a pittance, were called "*ameyibo-yovo*" by the Togolese, "black whites"—not in homage to the success of their effort to cross the line but in derision at its futility. These tourists were still not seeing Africans.

Travelers came to Africa in search of landscape, animals, a political utopia, a primitive release. Who could help being disappointed and a little disgusted when he encountered Africans?

We spent ten days in Kenya's exotic playground. I wolfed down quantities of beef and pie, and began to gain a little weight. I gaped at elephants eating acacia trees and vultures waiting for hyenas waiting for lions to finish off wildebeest. I swam languid laps in a sparkling pool in Mombasa, on the Indian Ocean. And through the whole of our stay, thinking of Lavié, Ouagadougou, and Lagos, and feeling the long way I'd come during the year alone in Africa, with one part of myself I stood aside from the spectacle, from my family, too, not quite willing to believe.

Out on the terrace of the Norfolk the breakfasters were beginning to thin out for the long drive from Nairobi to the parks.

"I hear you're in Peace Corps," Mr. Nordstrom said to me. "That must take some, you know, intestinal fortitude." I didn't know whether he was admiring my courage or commenting on the risks of amoebic dysentery. He laughed—perhaps it had been a pun, intending both—and patted the binoculars dangling from his neck. "I guess I'm happy to be a good old American tourist."

A van with zebra stripes pulled up at the curb. "Flamingo Tours" was written on the sliding door beside a pink flamingo perched on one leg. An anxious, round-bellied Kenyan in a khaki vest hurried toward the terrace. My mother waved, and he came over in a profusion of apologies.

"The incompetent mechanic was to have the van ready yesterday evening," he explained in the clipped accent of Kenyans, biting off each word. He seemed genuinely angry. "We'll deduct it from your fee, of course."

"That's quite reasonable," my mother said. The guide helped my sister and mother with their bags.

"Well, happy safari!" Mrs. Nordstrom cried. "See you in California."

Mr. Nordstrom sighed. "A long way from here."

We roared off toward Mount Kenya and the highlands, the white settlers' plantations, the coffee bushes extending for miles in orderly rows, the black women in sweaters and men in fedoras who stooped among them; and beyond, Treetops, where buffalo and gazelle awaited us, licking imperviously at the spotlit rock.

The end of traveling found me back in Togo, where my mother spent the last days of August. She thrilled the Agbeli kids with the toy trucks and Winnie-the-Pooh Viewfinders she'd brought in her luggage, and I was proud to see her eat Ama's corn mush and chicken sauce with her fingers on the first night in the village. But Togo was not Kenya—not the Kenya we'd been shown; and the poverty, which had become almost normal to me, disturbed and depressed her. Children with herniated navels and swollen bellies, smiling from the roadside; Christine like Mother Hubbard with her brood; the darkness that engulfed my house at night. She came up with ideas to improve the quality of life here: more lamps, candles to give the place light; projects to fill the monotonous days; money-making ventures for Christine. She was a wind of energy and will out of the West, but she saw her incongruity here.

"Americans always want to get things done," she said on her last night in the village. "For every problem a solution. I don't have that feeling here. Don't the Togolese want to make their lives better? And yet, there doesn't seem to be any way to. The people are so kind and hospitable. I've never seen children like the Agbelis. Atsu is just the nicest boy. Did you see how he divided up the peanuts I gave him with the others? But what's to become of them?"

"Sometimes I think they'd be better off without us," I said. "All of our solutions—at least Africans aren't neurotic."

"Then is it better for them to stay underdeveloped? Child mortality, those swollen bellies? Is that what you're saying?"

I didn't know what I was saying. The conversation, like most of ours in the past few days, came to an inconclusive end. I was making a point that I'd heard many times and disliked. The point was not important; it was part of the mood that was coming over me. And the mood itself—an exasperation and gloom because of my mother's presence here, the feeling of resistance and futility that had begun in Kenya—came of the fact that there was so much I couldn't share with her. She had come to Lavié—past to present, home to Africa—and they had nothing to do with each other. Or so it seemed to me. I couldn't bridge them, and in the presence of both I couldn't reconcile myself to either. Africa, with all its good and bad revelations, had set me apart. For a year I'd concealed much of myself from the village; now I was concealing myself from my mother as well.

At the end of so much traveling, which had saturated me with new impressions, stirred up an obsession with the continent and its politics, and brought me close to exhaustion, I felt her presence in my postage stamp of it as a tearing or rending. An intimation of this feeling had come just before the summer travels began when, down with a bout of malaria during a week of heavy rain, I took the strong remedial dose of chloroquine. The pills were said to give bad dreams, and that night I had the worst nightmare of my whole time in Africa.

I was standing on a clay path, carrying a pack, against a tropical background of low green mountains. It wasn't Togo, though; it was the landscape of North Vietnam, where I was a soldier, though I wore shorts and a T-shirt. What struck me most about that view of myself was my own face. It looked nothing like me: a tangled red beard, a sweaty mop of long hair, an oldness and fatigue. And then the view turned out to be a photograph, which I had brought home to California to show my family and friends. I had to convince everyone that there was a terrible change in the face in the photo, so unlike me; but the people there, including my mother, didn't grasp it, became irritated and turned away.

I went down with my mother to Lomé, and we said good-bye in the back of a taxicab. She was going to spend a couple of days at the four-star Hôtel de la Paix on the beach—her R&R before the flight to New York. I got on a bus for Kpalimé, for the start of my second year. Up ahead, the sun was going down over Ghana, the air was thin and mild after a rain shower. I enjoyed two hours' calm on the bus. But within an hour of getting back to Lavié, I was convinced I was about to have a stroke.

CHAPTER 9

Hypochondria

I HAD ALL THE SYMPTOMS. THEY WERE SITTING IN MY lap, ticked off in the three-hundred-and-fifty-page nightmare Peace Corps had given us for our medical well-being, *Where There Is No Doctor*. Headache. Dizziness. A little lump on the back of my neck, on the right side just below the skull. Wasn't that where the carotid artery ran on its way to the brain? And what about these waves of blood rushing through my face?

I grabbed my lamp and went outside.

"Christine?"

"Fo Georgie?"

"When Benjamin gets back I need to see him. I'm sick, he has to drive me to Agou."

"What is it?"

What was it? "I'm going to . . ." I gave up and left her standing there bewildered. Back inside, I sat with the book open on my knees. "Stroke," it announced, next to a drawing of a Central American peasant lying on the ground. I couldn't dislodge the word from my head. The word was a little time bomb that was going to go off, in an hour, in ten minutes, in five seconds, with an explosion of blood. My head would blow up. *Stroke.* I took another roll call of the symptoms: all present.

"Put the person in bed with his head a little higher than his feet. If he is unconscious, roll his head back and to one side so his saliva (or vomit) runs out of his mouth rather than into his lungs. If possible, seek medical help." Where there is no doctor, *find one*. Pray. But I couldn't pray. I was from the West, where God was dead and the ancestors were rotting underground. My immediate ancestor—my father—had had a stroke that paralyzed his right side and ended up killing him. That was when he was—yes, just about twice my age. Did this mean something?

The American military hospital where they flew critically ill volunteers was three hours away by car and then another five by plane, in Frankfurt. But my time bomb was not set for eight hours. There was the Lavié dispensary—two bare rooms and a half-trained nurse: closed, and useless. The Kpalimé public hospital was open, but worse than useless. If its needles missed the sciatic nerve, they would give you hepatitis anyway. The Presbyterian hospital at the base of Mount Agou, on the road from Kpalimé to Lomé, had one of the better reputations in Togo. So it was Agou.

I'd had other close calls here. There was the week when my right pinkie wouldn't stop twitching and threatened to degenerate into muscular dystrophy. The lump on my right testicle that could easily have developed into cancer if a British doctor in Nairobi hadn't assured me it was a seminal tubule. I'd had less drastic diseases than muscular dystrophy and cancer: three days of fever and blinding headache with malaria, a week when amoebic dysentery turned my bowels to blood, food poisoning, continual fits of diarrhea. Nothing was lonelier than being sick in the village, waking up in the middle of the night to run and squat over a foul toilet hole with the black smoke from the kerosene lamp at my feet drifting into my nostrils. Yet I wasn't afraid of any of these. It was the incurable Western afflictions I kept almost coming down with, the ones that Togolese hospitals had nothing for.

There was a pattern here: right pinkie, right testicle—the right side. The lump was on the right side of my neck. A wave of blood washed up through my face.

"Christine?"

"Fo Georgie?"

"Ben is going to be out all night. Let's go find a driver. We have to go to Agou right away."

Christine ran inside for a shawl while shouting things to the children. They stared at me, baffled.

The Moslem driver who garaged his orange van in Ama's yard was eating. He told me he would leave as soon as he'd finished his supper. *"Now!"* I insisted. *"Kaba kaba!"* He grumbled, wiped his mouth on his sleeve, and led us to the van.

We rushed along the road to Kpalimé. It was pitch-dark; trees flew past us, a blur of green in the long glare of headlights; other headlights appeared, blinded us, flew by, a horn sounded, and then everything ahead went black again. The driver was scowling, but he had the pedal to the floor and kept checking his watch.

Sitting in front between him and Christine I readied myself for the moment when the clot would burst the vessel and snuff out my light like the bush going black as we raced past. I quietly admitted that this whole African venture had been a mistake. A feeling of fatalism was sinking in, bound up with the rush of trees, the driver with his hands still greasy from his supper, the miserable tropical hospital that would try and fail to save me, the phrase Christine kept repeating: *"Ça va passer."* In America none of this would have happened. There wouldn't have been months of loneliness and strain bringing me to the brink of a stroke. There wouldn't be the bush, the driver. I would be in grad school, in my own carrel in the library, reading Donne's lesser poems.

Could you bring it on just by thinking about it? I closed my eyes to empty my brain of all thoughts and give the blood some room. Christine held my hand the whole way.

The driver turned off the Lomé road at a cluster of huts where a "Guinness Is Good for You" sign marked a bistro. The hospital had no sign. A hundred yards down a rough paved road, a three-story concrete building appeared dimly on the right. Christine shouted. The driver slammed on his brakes, pulled up by the gate, turned off the ignition, and looked at his watch. He turned to us; he was beaming.

"Seventeen minutes."

The Hôpital Bethesda-Presbytérien was as dark as the bush. Inside the gate a flight of steps wound from the courtyard up to the second-floor balcony. A figure was lying asleep in the courtyard on a bench. We approached, Christine and the driver supporting me on each arm.

"*Ago!*"

The old man grunted, stirred, and sat up. He had a patchy gray beard and wore a knitted ski cap. Christine spoke to him in Ewé. He was the night watchman, he knew nothing of receiving hours, we would have to wait. He wandered off. Christine and the driver exchanged a few fast words that were lost on me; the driver shook his head. I stood up. What were they saying? Christine smiled. "*Ça va passer.*" She motioned for me to sit, and like a child I sat down again.

The old man came back and told us to go upstairs. With Christine on my arm I began the ascent along the railing. At the first landing we met a woman on her way down.

"No, no, you'll have to go back down. The nurse on duty hasn't given permission yet."

I was about to tell her that my time bomb was ticking very loud; instead I gave in to the flow of events and let Christine guide me back down. After five minutes—two eternities—a young woman appeared in a white smock that might have been dead *yovo* medical wear. I could go upstairs now. And then I lost track of Christine and the driver. I didn't see Christine until the next morning, and the driver for several days, at which point he calculated my bill as the equivalent of twelve round trips to Agou.

On the way up the nurse prodded me with questions. What was wrong with *monsieur?*

"Do you know," I asked, "what *l'hémorragie cérébrale* is?"

She screwed up her face. "Eh?"

I hadn't thought to look up the right translation. I pointed to my head. "*L'hémorragie cérébrale.*"

"*Oh, oui, oui,*" she said, smiling. "*L'hémorragie cérébrale. Oui, oui, oui.*" And we continued up the stairs.

A familiar feeling. She was one of the boys hanging out at the station who fed you a line that a nonexistent taxi would leave any minute now. She didn't understand, no one seemed to understand; my *baché* was bound for an undiscovered country. But a thought flashed across the swamp of my brain: I am walking without support. Shouldn't I be prostrate and barely conscious? Is it because of this that she's smiling?

We went along the balcony into a room bright enough to make me squint. The nurse led me to a counter where a man, also in white, was sitting among a jungle of rubber tubes that carried liquids from suspended sacks into test tubes and containers. This was the receptionist—a familiar sight! I approached him with relief.

"Please, I'd like to see a doctor. Right away if possible."

He looked up with all the concern of a customs agent. "I'm here to receive registered patients," he said. "I have no time to be bothered if you haven't registered yet."

For the first time I had an urge to laugh. So African bureaucracy was going to follow me into the grave. How many forms, I wondered, did a man in the throes of cardiac arrest have to fill out before he could see a doctor? The nurse had seemed one type; the receptionist was another—an Aboï, Eyadema, *patron*, the driver of the vehicle. He wasn't about to let me get past without a whiff of his power.

A shriveled old man appeared at my side, a chew stick mashed in his mouth. He led me into the first room off the corridor. He had me lie on a table, which was damp under my shirt, and stood over me asking the same questions as the nurse. He kept repeating, *"Palu"* ("Malaria"). He spoke some French, but *l'hémorragie cérébrale* flew over his head, and he missed my *sang* on the first two tries. He took my blood pressure: 130 over 90. I breathed a little easier. Did *monsieur* have *frissons*, chills? No, I said. In his booklet he jotted down *frissons* anyway. How could *monsieur* fail to have *frissons*—everyone with malaria had *frissons*. He told me to wait while he got the doctor, and went out. The masticated chew stick had disintegrated over his teeth and lips.

I lay still. The *tick-tick* had temporarily stopped; instead, I was hearing the groans of a woman lying on the table against the opposite wall. I hadn't noticed her before. Her age was impossible to tell, but it wasn't hard to see that she was dying. Her *pagne* had slipped off, exposing the upper part of her body. The breasts and belly were shrunken, and the contour of her skull was visible beneath a thin layer of skin the color of bad coffee. Intermittently a hoarse moan came out of her mouth, followed by a trail of drool. She was unaware of me, unaware of anything, it seemed. Was she dying of starvation, or of some wasting disease? Had they left her in this room to die? Where were the doctors?

The door flew open and a white man wearing a doctor's coat and stethoscope breezed in. About forty, he was tall and had a light brown beard and cold blue eyes. All at once the racism that whites in Africa feel deep down without even knowing it came welling up in a flood of relief. That the face peering down without much interest into mine was white meant everything. It meant I wasn't going to die.

"Vat seems to be de problem?"

He spoke English!

"I think I'm going to have a stroke, doctor."

He put his fingers on my pulse. An ironic smile pursed his lips. "Come, aren't you a beet young for a stroke?"

I described the dizziness, the headache, the lump, the waves of blood—which already seemed to be subsiding.

"But dese are wery subjectif reactions, you know."

My reply was a sheepish whisper. "I know."

Dr. Jakobi, the German director of the hospital, informed me I would spend the night here and be given a series of tests in the morning. He breezed out again, and in a few minutes the old man came back to show me to my room. As we went out, a moan escaped from the woman dying on the other table.

The way upstairs took us past an open door through which I heard a low murmur of voices. Two rows of cots, a dozen in each row, were squeezed together like passengers in the back of a *baché*, so that one had to turn sideways to move between them. All the cots were filled, and at the foot of each one four or five family members were camped out on the floor, adults and little children lying on mats amid bowls of corn mush, jugs of palm wine, and scattered pieces of clothing. Some of them were talking in tense, hushed tones; a baby was crying; mothers fed their children. I remembered how people in Lavié disappeared for days at a time when a relative went to the hospital. But nothing suggested that medical treatment was going on here: no intravenous feeding tubes, no bottles of pills, not even institutional bed sheets. The sick lay under the brilliantly colored *pagnes* their families had brought. It was like a holding room: either they would get well here in the presence of their relatives or they would die. It smelled of sweat and pepper sauce.

My room was upstairs. It looked like a cheap motel room without a TV set. But it was obviously the VIP room, since a made-up bed, a night table, and privacy were great luxuries. Apparently a "European" was automatically assigned here. For a peasant, its thirty-dollar rate would exhaust a month's income in a single night.

I undressed, crawled under the stiff white sheet and bedspread, dozed, and woke up to the sight of the young woman who'd brought me up from the courtyard. She was brandishing a hypodermic needle. She flung the bedspread aside and told me to turn over.

"What's that?"

"Valium and chloroquine."

"I don't have malaria. I'll take the Valium but I don't need chloroquine."

"Oui, oui, oui."

I felt the prick of the needle in my buttock.

"The doctor has prescribed Valium and chloroquine," she said tonelessly. You were malarial until proven otherwise. I muttered something about my rights as a patient, but it didn't make much impression on the nurse. She left as the fluid spread out coolly through my buttock, and in two minutes I was unconscious. A last thought occurred before I sank into the profoundest sleep of my life: *I hope she missed the sciatic nerve.*

I woke up, not only alive but also unparalyzed, to a blur of faces—some of them vaguely familiar, as in a condensed dream of the whole night; others strange. Men and women, black and white, all in medical coats, all standing over my bed staring down at me. I had no idea how long I'd slept; I was conscious of a vague sense of well-being.

"You see?" came a guttural German voice. "Wery subjectif reactions."

"His eyes are extremely red," said a Frenchwoman.

"But of course," a Togolese man answered. "He's just woken up."

Hands were placed on my forehead, my chest, as if I were a specimen; more scientific observations were made; and they paraded out.

Before releasing me the hospital put me through a battery of pointless tests. I managed to fight off another injection of chloroquine, but preserving my urine sample in a test tube without a stopper and squeezing my stool sample into a vial the size of my little finger proved more difficult. The hypodermic nurse served me a hospital breakfast of Nescafé, toast, and an egg, and then I waited four hours for the test results. Christine and Benjamin had come in his taxi first thing in the morning, with a potful of chicken and sauce, three grapefruits, and the concern of the villagers. Embarrassment was beginning to catch up with me. Christine and I sat together in my VIP room. I nibbled at the chicken, she looked uneasily at the opulence around her. We hardly spoke, but at one point she said something that struck me and stayed with me like a proverb or a confession.

"If you are never sick and you always keep yourself from sickness," she said, "when it comes it will beat you, it will knock you down and you can't get up. You have to let the sickness come—then it will pass. The people who are always well—they die easily!"

Christine and Ben left around eleven. At one the test results came in. The Frenchwoman showed them to me and drew my attention to the protein count.

"Seventeen!" she exclaimed cheerfully. "The Africans, they dream of that!"

"What is their count?"

"For the children, eight or perhaps nine. They dream of seventeen!"

Before leaving I went for a walk. It had rained during the night, and the air outside was fresh and cool. In daylight the hospital looked like a welcoming place; beds of orchids around the grounds were brilliant in the sunshine. For the first time I saw that we were at the foot of Mount Agou, the lower slopes covered with lush woodland, the upper slopes and the peak fogged over. I felt as if I'd woken up from a feverish, delirious dream. My senses had been thrown open and were almost overwhelmed by the flowers, the mountain, the smell of rain.

On the way back I ran into Dr. Jakobi. He handed me my discharge booklet. On the front he'd written: "Beg. nervous breakdown."

"Many German wolunteers come in here vit de same ting," he assured me in his slightly supercilious manner. "You are wery alone in Togo and dese tings build up. Haf you no one to talk vit?" I mentioned the Agbelis. "Ach, you cannot discuss your intimate problems vit an African family. You should treat yourself vell, go down to Lomé and haf a trink in a nice hotel sometimes."

"I suppose not too many Africans come in with this problem."

He raised his eyebrows. "On de contrary. All de time. Teachers, students who haf failed deir exams, dey come in vit dese ailments vich dey do not understand but dey are de symptoms of breakdown."

"Only educated Togolese?"

"Of course. Never de peasants. Deir lifes haf not yet been torn in two."

I went home by public taxi. Less than twenty-four hours ago I was hurtling along this road at a hundred kilometers an hour, my hand in Christine's, the fear of death at my throat. Now it was the road to Lavié again, the same potholes at the bottom of each hill, the same pack of passengers babbling in Ewé, and, except for a slight sense of unreality and a soreness in one buttock, the same *yovo* who'd taken this road fifty times.

The children greeted me as if I were a wounded soldier home from the front. Christine told me they hadn't slept well and had been badgering her with questions. Mawuli had even cried and kept asking, *"Fo Georgie e la ku a?"* Other than me, he was the only one childish enough to think I might actually die.

One of the first things I had noticed in Lomé, after the smell of cooking oil and the hordes of children chanting *"Yovo,"* was cripples.

Young men with withered legs crawled through the streets near the movie theaters, rubber pads under their palms and nothing under their knees, which looked like uncured leather from scraping across dirt and pavement. Old lepers sat outside the Christian bookstores and held up their fingerless hands to shoppers. A handsome, smiling young man sat in a tangle of poliomyelitic legs and held open the same *boulangerie* door for two years; I am sure he's there today. Women with goiters in the throat the size of grapefruit, old blind men led by boys rattling a cup, children whose navels were swollen up with air, lunatics, and everywhere the cripples—the sheer numbers on the streets were staggering. Some begged, but many found little useful jobs to keep themselves alive: newspaper boys were usually crippled; every modern glass office building had its unofficial mutilated doorman; the boy at L'Amitié had taught himself to play songs on his nose; others hung around hotels and kept watch over the cars of tourists and businessmen. They had to be equally inventive in their means of locomotion: a leg curled round a stick, go-carts with steering columns, one-pedal bicycles.

Initially the sight of so many diseases and deformities in public was horrifying, and a little fascinating. After a while you got used to it; eventually you stopped noticing. The ill, the insane, and the dying were out on the streets because they were too common a part of everyday life to be worth hiding. But when I got out of the hospital, health began to preoccupy me. Not so much my own—the "Beg. nervous breakdown," my imagined illnesses, embarrassed me and I didn't want to hear of them again. Suddenly, though, I had a series of encounters with sickness and death that kept bringing to mind Christine's observation that those who are never sick die easily, and Dr. Jakobi's, that the Togolese who came in complaining of mysterious pains had had "deir lifes torn in two."

Medicine was a complicated business in Lavié. For their endless headaches and stomachaches, diarrhea, and fatigue, villagers were willing to spend a thousand francs (three dollars, or two days' wages) on the products of Togopharma. For any complaint short of a bullet wound, the nearby dispensaries and hospitals had the answer in a needle filled with chloroquine. A friend of mine was unfortunate enough to check into Agou with an actual case of malaria; after days of injections he had absorbed almost enough quinine to kill him, and didn't completely recover for five months. A hypodermic needle and the typed label on a bottle of pills inspired a faith that wasn't so easily distinguished from the faith in herbal medicines and fetish powders. But Western medicine, unlike fetish healing, wasn't understood so much as simply believed in. And the same faith villagers attached to the prescriptions written out by the old village pharmacist drove them to my door with their medical problems: a woman with a son going blind, an old man with chest pains, Christine with her many children's many ills. My Peace Corps medical kit quickly emptied out. Yet these "consultations" always ended abruptly, with my implied admission, in spite of skin color, of helplessness: *"Je ne suis pas docteur."*

Every Friday afternoon the two-room clinic under the iroko tree between the primary school and the market stayed open for market day. Women who'd spent the morning buying and selling waited in line on the bench outside, babies on their backs or at their breasts. The women never looked panicky or irritated. Something in their wordless patience, the babies' big-eyed stares, the sun overhead, and the complete inadequacy of the clinic for anything but weighing and taking a temperature, made it a picture of despair week after week.

When the pills, injections, pharmacies, and clinics did no good, and hopelessness was closing in around the family, they fell back on tradition. The fetish priest was called in at the point where Catholics call in their priest—not to administer last rites, but as a last-ditch effort to heal. In a village not far from Lavié I once had the chance to see traditional medicine at its most public and dramatic.

The earth, soaked by a recent rain, was veined with rivulets, and the two dancing girls scuffed it with their bare feet and kicked sand against the villagers, who had formed a semicircle around them. The fetish priest stood aside, robed in white, smoking a cigarette. Three men at the front of the group beat out the rhythm on leather drums, punctuated by a cowbell, a whistle, and a rattle, and the crowd lifted its voice on the swell of the beat. The music started fast and somehow got faster and fiercer, the crowd chanted louder, and the girls responded as if the drums and voices controlled them, with wild spins and turns, gyrating, rolling their eyes, flailing their arms, colliding and caroming off each other. They were no more than ten or eleven years old, rail-thin, one in a green flowered frock, the other in an ankle-length nylon dress, blue with dyed white streaks that spiraled and blurred as she spun.

The girls had been ill for days. The clinic in a nearby town had prescribed medication, but there was no improvement. This dance came at the end of a week of consultation, not with a doctor or nurse, but with the fetish priest. Dancing now, they were helpless, sick with their own motions. One of them reeled, fell, lay breathing like an animal that's been shot, then staggered to her feet. The drummers, as if they smelled the moment to strike, brought the music to a climax; the voices crested; and all at once everything broke off. The drums stopped with a terrific final slap of fingers, the cowbell clanged, the crowd raised a shout. Both girls had collapsed on the ground. They lay at an oblique angle to each other with their faces pushed against the dirt, arms twisted behind the back, mouths open, the whites of their eyes showing. Only the frantic rise and fall of their chests suggested that the dance hadn't killed them.

A man dragged the girls outside the semicircle and seated them on a hyena pelt, their backs propped against a hut. The drumming started and the villagers resumed their dance, calmer and milder now. The girls sat dazed, legs spread flat on the dirt; they emitted little groans, and their heads rolled and lolled as if there weren't a muscle left in their necks.

The fetish priest set his sandaled heel to the cigarette butt. He had been watching with the detached assurance of a big money changer or a maître d'. His cult, the village cult, was of a river god: When a villager went fishing in the Akebu region and didn't return for three years, the village assumed that a wild animal had eaten him and performed funeral rites. All the while the river god was holding him; and when he finally came back he came with a sword, sickle, and spear, emblems of the cult he now served. A shrine was built, a hollow mud block with molded stars and crescents studded on the surface with cowrie shells and a strip of corrugated iron over the opening. Inside, a jar held water from the Akebu River. After the dance the priest would give some of it to the girls to drink; their families would pay him fifty francs and a bottle of gin; and the girls, having regained the consciousness they set out to lose, would be cured of sickness and spared future sickness, in body and mind.

Possession, which seemed brutal, frenzied, and irrational, a surrender and destruction of personality, was considered a good thing, a sign that the possessed was welcomed by the god. It happened under the eyes of the entire village; it exposed the sick to greater sickness, but also to the healing power of the fetish priest. Christine had said to me, "You have to let the sickness come—then it will pass," and she had been talking about something like this: the inevitability of sickness, the healing that goes on in the mind, implicit in the dance, implicit in everything I knew about traditional medicine.

But there was another name for a fetish priest in Togo: *charlatan*. And, Western and skeptical, I wasn't always sure that these healers were the real thing. If you looked at health in the Western way, statistically, Togo's life-expectancy of 49 and its infant mortality rate of 110 per 1,000 births were no plug for the fetish profession. One weekend a trip up on the Danyi plateau brought me face-to-face with a local *charlatan*.

A line of people waited under the thatch shelter in his courtyard, but not expressionlessly like the women outside the Lavié clinic; these fidgeted and looked tense. And instead of babies they carried bottles of gin and schnapps or chickens bound at the feet, payment on the spot for services rendered. The priest himself sat in a dark room on a plain wooden chair, looking quite unremarkable. I'd expected an old man in robes and a white beard, but this one was young, dressed in jeans and an Adidas sweat jacket. On his lap he held a round dime-store mirror with a picture of the young Liz Taylor on the back. Through this medium he communicated with the ancestors, and other tools of his trade were scattered around the floor: a bow and a quiver full of arrows, chains of cowrie shells, horsehair fly whisks, leather drums. I had wanted to pay for a session, a divination; but he took me for just another tourist with a camera and said he would allow me one photograph, with his priestesses. Of course, the picture wouldn't come out without the consent of the ancestors—a French television crew that had tried to film him found their work ruined when they replayed it—and the ancestors wouldn't consent without some tribute. Two thousand francs was the going rate.

I paid it, got an uninteresting pose with the *charlatan* looking grim and his priestesses in white skirts looking bored, and left with the impression that this was an enterprising young fake. The people waiting under the thatch obviously didn't see him that way. As I went out, I passed a man on his way in with a bottle of gin in one hand and stony earnestness on his face.

In the center of the *charlatan*'s village a taxi was filling up to make the trip down to Adeta and Kpalimé. I was given the front seat; behind me a well-dressed young couple sat on either side of their son. In the back two more seats remained to be filled. From a glance the boy seemed to be about six, and he didn't look well. His head lolled on his neck, his eyes drooped shut. The parents did not seem concerned; they were looking out the window.

His tongue came out, and he drooled. Now his parents were looking at him, and his mother was smiling, trying to wake him up.

I asked, "Does the driver know that he's sick?"

They shook their heads. A man in the back said something to me; and in one of the lunatic misunderstandings that happened to me whenever anything important was going on in Africa, I misheard him to say: *"L'enfant n'est pas gravement malade."*

"Look at him!" I said. "He's very ill."

"That's what I said," the man replied, exasperated. *"L'enfant est très gravement malade."*

I jumped out and told the driver that we had to go straight to Kpalimé. When I returned the parents had grown anxious. The father kept shaking the boy's head and saying his name—no response. The mother was suddenly panic-stricken. Already it seemed useless to go all the way to the Kpalimé hospital; that would take at least an hour. The driver hopped in, turned around, and roared out of the village center in the opposite direction of Adeta.

On the way out of town, on the right, at the back of a dirt lot, there was a clinic—an old, peeling, cream-colored colonial building with a veranda and balustrade. We pulled up in a cloud of dust. The father gathered the boy and carried him up the steps of the veranda; his wife scrambled behind. He tried the front door: locked. The driver went around to the side of the building calling, *"Docteur! Docteur!"* No answer. It was two-thirty in the afternoon and the village had shut down. If there was a doctor he was home asleep. The *charlatan* was busy communicating with the ancestors. The hot silence of siesta lay on the place.

Now the wife was pacing frantically on the veranda. Her husband sat numbly in a wicker chair with the boy in his lap. From time to time she rushed over to get the child's attention, smile, play with him—then turned away, her face a mute scream. The driver came from around the building, followed by two men who didn't look anything like doctors. They strode up to the veranda. The father's hand was on the boy's chest; the boy's eyes opened wide once or twice, and then closed. One of the men went up the steps and looked at the boy. He turned away and said to no one in particular: *"Eku."*

The mother stamped her feet and broke into sobs. With her hands on the balustrade rail she wailed and wailed. Her husband, who hadn't moved, said something sharply. She didn't stop; the wails rose to the pitch of the bereaved. The driver came down off the porch, saying—offhandedly, it seemed—*"Eku. Oui, l'enfant est decédé."* I looked at the body lying in the father's lap. Its limpness, its stillness were unmistakable. The mouth was partly open and the face had already turned waxen.

The driver instructed me to get back in the car. Mechanically I complied. We left them behind—the two unknown men talking on the steps, the father sitting perfectly still in the wicker chair, the mother at the rail hurling her cries like curses into the sun-drenched afternoon.

"Jaundice," the driver said when I asked what the boy had had.

"The child falls ill on Wednesday, and his parents wait until Saturday to take him to the hospital? Ah, no, it's not serious." He clucked in disapproval.

We made our way down the plateau.

The death had hardly rippled the surface of the day. A boy had slipped away noiselessly, a taxi had been interrupted on its way from Danyi to Adeta. The driver's postmortem: jaundice, and delay. His *"eku"* had sounded casual and even callous, but I didn't think that the driver was indifferent to what we'd seen. He was only recognizing what was learned young in Africa: that death comes suddenly, with few reasons and few preventions, that it is, after all, ordinary. And when this recognition sometimes seemed like heartlessness, I remembered the mother at the veranda rail.

Toward the end of September an old woman died in Lavié. *"Une vieille là-bas,"* Christine explained, gesturing vaguely toward the middle of the village. What of? She shrugged. Of death. It was Ama and Faustus's mother, Madame Ketekou. And so, wanting to show my sympathy, and curious to know what happened to Africans after they died, I went to her burial. The body had gone to Kpalimé for cold storage, since Lavié had no electricity and no morgue. "I have an older brother in the frigo in Kpalimé," a farmer once said by way of informing me of a death in the family.

The three-room Ketekou house was packed with at least fifty mourners. Outside, on the clay shoulder of the road, where women usually squatted with trays of peanuts and soaps, a couple of Peugeots and Renaults were parked—wealthier relatives up from Lomé. The late afternoon sky was gray and streaked with woodsmoke from the first evening fires; the air was chilly and yet oppressive. From inside came the sound of voices, a commotion, and then mourners began spilling outside in a hurry, as if to beat the rain. Functionaries in suits with starched collars, city women with their hair in elaborate coils, villagers wearing the usual motley patchwork of *pagnes* and dead *yovo* clothes; and in the middle of the crowd a group of young women in plain white cloth tied above their breasts, their bodies and faces painted in lines of blue, yellow, and red. Two boys beat drums, a third banged a cowbell. The coffin appeared, borne by four men in suits. It was the gaudy, overpriced box, its polished mahogany ruined by brass ornaments glued around the sides, that most Africans seemed to favor, the sort of tacky coffin an American family without much money but "wanting to do it right" would buy. As the doorway cleared I glanced inside and saw a sea of bouquets.

We moved down the road, the drums beat, and the painted women in white began to dance and sing—not radio gospel, but something older: the funeral chants I'd heard the night of my arrival. A student near me explained that these were official mourners, paid to go from funeral to funeral. The rest of the crowd took up the chant and all the women moved in stutter steps and swayed their hips, even the ones from Lomé in chiffon dresses and high heels. We passed my house; and as we did I remembered the burial of the CEG girl I'd seen on the rainy day of my arrival, watching from the roadside surrounded by my boxes and mobylette. That was almost exactly a year ago; now I was in the file of mourners, moving past my own house, seeing myself double: here and still on the roadside, marcher and spectator, today and not today. Only now there was nothing remarkable in my presence. As we went along I savored this recognition, even now a private one.

Four hundred yards out of the village, we turned right off the road down a path about six feet wide. We were among great trees, kapoks with round leaves the size of platters, iroko, baobab, a tree whose name I didn't know that had roots rising twenty feet aboveground like flying buttresses supporting the trunk, the upper branches wreathed and choked with creepers. The sky was darkening fast. Amid the chants there were scattered conversations, even a few bursts of laughter. Behind me two men were arguing about some money owed. A couple of old women sobbed. As we came into a clearing of the kapoks, a hush fell.

I had never seen the Lavié cemetery before today. A few dozen old graves, barely mounds of dirt, were marked with crude wood crosses; elsewhere a cement slab, a slate headstone, and one or two of the statuettes you saw in all Togolese burial grounds, painted red and blue and looking like tourist-trap renditions of gothic sculpture.

The graves weren't in rows; the cemetery was laid out as if a battle had taken place and the corpses had had to be buried in a rush.

We assembled around a hole, into which the coffin was lowered. A pastor in black and white robes read from the Ewé Bible. There were prayers, songs—gospel now, the painted dancers silent, as if the older chants would be inappropriate at the verge of the grave. Aboï had once told me that jeers and reminders of debts or misdeeds might follow a coffin into the grave; but Madame Ketekou received a respectful silence. I spotted Ama, in her best *pagne*, looking somber; Faustus was beside her, red-eyed—whether from weeping or drink, I didn't know. The pastor finished his sermon to *amens* and the first shovelfuls of dirt were tossed on the coffin. The crowd began to break up and start back for the village. On his way by, the chief stopped to greet me.

"Monsieur Georges! You are here? *Ah, c'est bien, c'est bien.*"

I asked if the woman had been very old.

"Oh, yes yes. At least, let us say, seventy years old. I'll join her before long," he added with a grim twinkle in his eye.

"But you're only fifty-five."

"I will die by seventy, that's sure. It doesn't matter, by then my youngest son will be grown and I'll be tired."

I ventured, "And—after death?"

"It is Paradise. For both you and me—we'll be together up there."

"I'm afraid I'm not a believer."

"That doesn't matter, just so long as you are a good man."

"Well, I'm a little afraid of dying," I admitted. "Rotting in the earth, and never seeing or feeling anything again. . . ."

The chief frowned and nodded, as if I'd reminded him of something. "*Oui*—there is that. There is always that. Sometimes I fear too. But, Monsieur Georges, we'll both be caught in the rain—come on back to the village."

But I stayed awhile by the grave, and watched the gravediggers fill it up with the mound of red earth alongside. Three of them took turns standing on the coffin in the pit and using a short-handled shovel and a hoe to pull the dirt down around their legs as rapidly as a dog covers its excrement. A couple of others hung around and egged them on. After the solemnity of prayer and song, the scene degenerated in a hurry: raucous laughter, insults, tobacco snorting. A lunatic I knew, about five feet tall with an incomprehensible stammer, flitted back and forth between me and the others, giggling and trying to get me to take some snuff. One man, a member of the deceased's family, was shouting at the gravediggers to get it done right. "I'm here to make sure you do your work!" he bellowed. "You'll close up the hole properly before you get your palm wine."

The gravediggers laughed, and one of them alluded to the morning crew who'd dug the grave but couldn't make it for the afternoon shift because they'd already incapacitated themselves on their payment. At last the pit was closed up; bare feet stamped on the mound. We left just as the first drops were splattering on the graves and the kapok leaves.

I began my second year of teaching with a keen sense of irrelevance. Sickness and death seemed all around, and I was going back to the blackboard with "Showing Grandfather Round Lagos." I and my friend Mensah, who had already helped me build four latrines at school, decided to give a series of *causeries de santé* (health chats) in different quarters of the village. The point was to address the villagers directly, especially the women, about a few essentials of preventive health: nutrition, origins of common diseases, water, and the "fecal peril." We collected Peace Corps posters, drew pictures, diagrammed pathways of disease from fly to excrement to baby to mother to food to family. We told the chief to have his *gong-gongeur* assemble the Agbeli quarter for the first chat at his house. We would keep it brief and simple, and Mensah would do the talking in Ewé.

Our first mistake was to hold it on a Friday—market day. We waited in the chief's courtyard until five o'clock, but fewer than twenty people showed up: old men, a few farmers in ragged shirts, and little children. The women were still at the market, so we missed our main audience. None of the men could understand why their wives' presence was needed, but they promised to take home what they heard.

I doubt they took home much. The posters drew mainly laughter;

Mensah's talk, blank stares. He would make a point, ask if they understood, and receive an unconvincing murmur of assent. The only villagers who participated were the old chief and another octogenarian who sat next to him on a bench. Whenever one of them answered a question—which foods were good for you, which baby in the picture was sick and which was healthy—the other flatly contradicted him. Then they quarreled vehemently, and if Mensah was obliged to disagree with one of them, the other gloated and showered him with rebukes to shut up the next time, while the children exploded in giggles.

The problem with this *causerie*, I realized later, lay in the whole idea of prevention. Preventive medicine had informed the fetish dance from start to finish, synonymous with the cure. But here it was an abstraction; it warded off some hypothetical ill, but did nothing about the real ones all around us. Keep the animals penned in and your children won't get sick with diarrhea—what *yovo grigri* was this? The pills required no *causerie de santé*; their magic was there for everyone to see. An old man in my quarter had heard from his daughter that a health chat was being given and asked her to get something for his tuberculosis. She came to me; I explained that we could educate about prevention but had no medicines to give, that we had to go by the public health slogan, "Better to Prevent Than to Cure." She nodded, and relayed this message to her father, who sent her back to me with another question: Then what good was it to him?

I took a photo during the *causerie de santé*, and it sums up the failure of our health campaign in Lavié. Most eyes, as usual, are on the camera, and the two old men—the old chief in his orange cloth tied around the chest, the other with a flowery blue robe and rubber sandals—sit rigidly side by side, hands on their knees, staring at the photographer. But some of the small children are watching Mensah, who points at a poster he is holding under his chin. It is the "sick baby" poster. One little girl stares at it in what seems to be a shock of recognition: for like the child in the picture she has on nothing but a pair of yellow shorts, and her arms and legs are matchsticks, her belly a swollen balloon, her navel hanging out like an enormous valve.

. . .

The hospital in Agou took its cues from Western medicine—badly, but it would be sentimental and wrong to say the villagers were better off without it. They didn't think so. They paid enormous sums for pills and injections. The parents on the plateau had counted on the clinic, not the *charlatan*, in the dwindling minutes of their son's life. But in my last months in Africa, in encounters that began to repeat themselves insistently, as if all along I'd had my ears plugged with wax, I discovered that the pills bought by prescription and the injections delivered on a hospital cot left out what to the fetish priest were the twin centers of healing—the village and the mind.

Kuma Kumahia's village was far away, and now his mind was playing tricks on him. A teacher of agriculture, he'd been assigned by the inspection in Atakpamé to a remote spot among the Akposso people an hour's hike up the plateau from the Kpalimé-Atakpamé road. No road went up here; access was impossible except on foot. Apparently he had fallen out of favor with one of the *patrons* at the inspection; this posting was his internal exile.

I made the hike to visit Kumahia one Saturday morning at the end of September, my back pocket stuffed with a wad of bills. My volunteer friend Isaiah, who'd returned to the States, had entrusted me with a hundred bucks to help Kumahia start a school garden and a cooperative among the farmers who were his new neighbors. I sweated and panted up the rocky switchbacks, passed no dwellings and no people, and didn't reach his village until midmorning. It wasn't really a village at all, but a few farmhouses scattered across the hillside near a cacao grove, two open-air thatch huts in a dirt clearing, and a courtyard bordered on two sides by iron-roofed houses. These had to be the functionaries' dwellings. I hadn't been able to send word in advance that I was coming, but Kumahia was at home and came running out of one of the houses like a colonial officer in a remote river outpost who's just spotted the monthly mail boat.

"Oh, George!" he kept repeating in delight. "No no no no no." Thin as a prisoner, a rough beard graying on his chin, he was as alone up here as any African I'd met. No wife, not even the usual cousins and nephews teachers brought along to do chores for them. He shared the compound with the family of the primary school principal, who was the only other teacher. Together they had been charged with starting a school. The cacao farmers on their own initiative had organized a crude cooperative and taken up a collection to build the two thatch huts I'd seen coming in. These were the school. Fifty children, from farms miles away, crammed each hut. There were no desks, no books, no pens, and most of the farm kids didn't even have the khaki uniforms that were normally essential to the impression that education was going on. Kumahia and the other man were starting from scratch.

"The farmers here have a good spirit," he told me as we sat on a bench outside his concrete wall. He'd gone into his house for a calculator—the Texas Instruments gadget, up here on the empty hillside, seemed as absurd as a miracle—to figure out what exchange I'd gotten on the black market in Lomé for Isaiah's dollars. "They want the children to be educated and they have raised the money themselves. What Isaiah has sent me will help us, but we have so far to go, so far. You see how we are underdeveloped here. What do you think Peace Corps can do for us?"

As long as the village was only accessible on foot, it was unlikely Peace Corps or anyone else would commit funds to the place. One of development's numerous ironies: it limited itself to the more convenient locations—those already more "developed."

Kumahia looked haggard. The domed, balding forehead and the intelligent eyes were deeply lined as if from too much squinting. He reminded me a little of the stock absentminded professor, gentle and prematurely senile. "Yes, that's it. Always the problem of access. Last year there was an effort to build a track up here to the farmhouses so the cacao could be transported more effectively. But a certain someone, who has a government relation, insisted that if the track didn't detour by his house off in the woods down there, he would prevent it from being made. And so it never was."

He didn't mention his own situation, but a tight smile conveyed the idea that "government relation" meant everything, that it was responsible for his being here.

"Oh! When Isaiah and I were together in Amlamé, we were well, we were well. He helped me with many things. My parents are both dead, and I was thinking too much." He tapped the creases by his eye. "Isaiah talked to me and helped me to understand why I was unhappy. Now . . ." And with a weary gesture he spread his arms wide and indicated the circumstances I'd found him in—the single compound in the middle of a fallow field, the huts dotting the hillside, the grassy slopes leading up to the shade of cacao trees, the buzzing of insects, the inhuman silence of the place. "I had headaches then, but with Isaiah they went away. Now he's gone, and who is there for me here? The pains in my head return, and I haven't eaten well."

Food reminded Kumahia of his host's duty. He apologized profusely, went inside, and came out with a loaf of bread, a tin of Cook's margarine, two glasses, and a bottle of the cheap Spanish wine sold in bistros. He must have bought it in Amlamé, one last indulgence before setting out for his post. The bottle was still nearly full.

"Now that you know the way up here," he said, raising his glass to me, "you will visit me often and things will be more cheerful."

Kuma Kumahia kept himself amazingly free of bitterness. There was nothing he could do about his situation, and though it might have seemed to someone else a dead end, a place with no exit, he was already going about the task of starting a village school where there had been no school—no village, really. He didn't try to palliate his lot with rationalizations an American would have used about "career challenges"; he hadn't given in to self-pity either. Up here that might be fatal. And yet, as I sat with him in the courtyard, it seemed plain that things had gone terribly wrong. He had no family, and wherever his village might have been, this wasn't it. The local Akposso gave him problems; in a sense he was as much a stranger here as I. Education and a profession had led him a long way from his own home, to a city, to Peace Corps training and friendships with Americans; now, by some twist, he'd ended up in a village again, only farther removed than ever. His mysterious headaches had come with him. If he'd never left his own village, I thought, he would be taking the cure of a fetish priest. In America he'd be on a shrink's couch. But there seemed nothing for him here: he was alone. Like the man who'd gone to fish in the Akebu river, this was his three-year spiritual ordeal. What cult would receive him at the end of it?

"Dey come in vit dese ailments vich dey do not understand," Dr. Jakobi had said, "but dey are de symptoms of breakdown."

Kuma Kumahia escorted me out to the path. We stood together looking out over the hillside. "At least it's calm here," I said, and breathed the thin plateau air, faintly redolent with ripening cacao pods.

"Yes," he agreed, "it's calm." And after a moment's thought: "It's too calm."

CHAPTER 10

The Kiss Is European

WHEN SHE VISITED ME IN THE HOSPITAL AT AGOU, Christine told me the story of the family's years in the Ivory Coast. And she told it as a *"j'accuse."*

Benjamin had spent much of the seventies traveling around West Africa and trying to make a living as a driver: across the border in Benin, up in the hot desolate sands of Niger, and finally in "the Paris of Africa"—slick, glamorous, sprawling Abidjan, with its skyscrapers, its indoor skating rink, and its forty thousand Frenchmen. It had become a swamp of French-speaking migrant labor, just as Lagos had of English-speaking.

In Abidjan Benjamin achieved a measure of success. For the first time he owned his own vehicle, and lived in a small house in one of the immigrant slums that had electricity and even a refrigerator. When Christine and the children joined him for the last three of the seven years he spent there, she found the city to her liking. She learned market French from the local trader women, and prepared new dishes like potatoes and garden vegetables. They were living a little better than in Lavié, and the huge city must have been an exciting place; the children's eyes always lit up when Abidjan was mentioned. But what Christine emphasized in my hospital room was the years before she joined him, when she was fending for herself and the kids in the village, with only in-laws for family.

"I had Dové in me," she said, "and there wasn't any money. A long, long time Ben wasn't sending money. The chief, the family, no one gave any. I took care of the children alone. I sold the clothes I was making on the machine. To have Dové I needed the operation." She meant the Caesarean section scar she'd already shown me. "I wrote Benjamin for money. Nothing."

"He sent no money?"

"Fo Georgie!" Her voice rose and her eyes filmed over. "I sold my sewing machine to have the operation and make Dové. After that I had nothing to make the clothes, after that I was poor." She stared at me. "That's why. That's why I'm angry with him. I can't forget."

Something about the Abidjan period was missing. If the Ivory Coast had brought relative success, why did the Agbelis come back at all? At different times Benjamin gave different reasons—that he wanted to build a house (our house) in the village, that the chief needed him, that it wasn't good to live abroad too long. All of these sounded plausible to me; but a phrase he used in unguarded moments hinted that there had been problems even in the steel-and-glass paradise of Abidjan. It was a joke among his drinking friends, a sort of refrain that made light of and at the same time confessed the hardships of migrant-labor life. *"Pays là,"* Benjamin would say with a dismissive wave, a smile dimpling his flabby cheeks, *"c'est pas la peine"*—"That country, it ain't worth the trouble."

I could only guess what the trouble had been. But there was the evidence of my own senses to go on: the migrants I'd seen all over West Africa—Lomé, Ouagadougou, Lagos, Onitsha, Douala. If I had to find an image to convey contemporary Africa to Americans as I grasped it, it wouldn't be a refugee camp full of half-starved ghosts, or natives in loincloths outside their grass huts, or a guerrilla army training in the bush, or black youths throwing stones at a smoking bus: nothing so picturesque. I would show an African man I saw once in a busy street near the Grand Marché in Lomé. A trader in the bolts of navy blue, gray, and beige cloth that trousers were cut from, he stood, bolts draped over each shoulder, behind his table outside a shoe store, counting out a wad of money. He counted with a fair amount of show, and at first glance he looked well off and at ease; but certain details began to contradict that impression. His stance behind the table, his mouth and jaw—the eyes hidden by sunglasses—were taut. And his clothes didn't match the wad in his hand: dead *yovo* corduroys too tight around the thighs and too long, a cream shirt missing buttons. He was taller and blacker than most Togolese. The first impression gave way to another: he was neither wealthy nor *chez lui*. He sold the bolts for someone else; and he was a migrant in Togo.

Lomé was full of Ghanaians driving taxis, Senegalese selling coffee, Nigerians changing money or peddling pirated tapes, men from Niger selling embroidered shirts, Malian Tuaregs in robes and turbans hawking leather sheaths and boxes "from Timbuktu." Lagos had its Togolese, Ghanaians, and Cameroonians, Cameroon its Nigerians and Chadians. A Mauritanian merchant traveled over thousands of kilometers of desert to sell cloth in Lomé; a Togolese made the trip in reverse to drive a taxi in Nouakchott. Every time I went down to Lomé I seemed to hear less French and more English— the result of an influx of Ghanaians expelled from Lagos and Nigerians fleeing the oil bust. The idea that drove these millions, mostly villagers, back and forth across the West African diaspora was a simple one: it must be better somewhere else.

The stories began to accumulate with a numbing sameness— details of harassment by the police, of large sums gained from a shipment of clothes at the port and then lost to a Nigerian con man; nostalgia for families and villages left behind; affairs with indifferent bargirls; the insider's lowdown on how to pay off border guards, hide currency; the strutting and joking that masked a deeper anxiety. Above all, the rootlessness. *"Pays là, c'est pas la peine."* It might have stood for a thousand small defeats.

Back in Lavié, I was always reminded of the other side of migrant labor: the female side. The tall woman who lived across the hedge from us had a husband working in the oil economy of Gabon, in Central Africa. Plucky and good-humored, Irène took care of the four children, tended the cornfield between the house and the woods, sold flour, and waited for the installments of money to arrive from Libreville. But in the brief moments free of work, her handsome face—flecked, like her neck and shoulders, with light patches of skin from a peeling fungal infection—looked pursed, lugubrious. Over a period of fourteen months her husband came home once. Well spoken and well dressed, he made a point of introducing himself to me and mentioned with satisfaction that he'd heard I had "shown an interest" in his wife. He said Gabon had treated him quite well. Within a week he was gone, and had taken the oldest daughter so she could attend school in Libreville. Irène went back to waiting.

She and Christine were contemporaries, both outsiders to Lavié, and great friends: their bond was their common experience. In Irène's solitary days, burdened with responsibilities and chores, I had a view of the years when Christine had been alone in Lavié. She was virtually alone even now. As far as I could tell, her sex life had ended. "After the first months without," she said once, "women can go for a long time and it doesn't matter. They aren't like men." At night I would hear the two women talking outside Christine's kitchen, always with a peculiar intensity, voices rising and falling on the swells of emotion and the musical inflections of Ewé, blending and separating like a duet of sopranos.

Some months the installments didn't arrive from Libreville, and Irène had to make do. I began seeing her in the mornings sitting on her steps across the yard, head resting on her open hand; instead of her usual call across the yard, *"Fo Georgie, efoa?"* she stared mournfully. She had an ache in her teeth and gums, and no money to buy something for it. I made her a "loan" of nine hundred francs, and she came back from the pharmacy with a liquid anesthetic in a bottle whose English label dated back to those quaint family-medicine ads from the forties. The stuff worked so well that she insisted I rub some over my own gums. It had a foul taste of eucalyptus menthol and quickly rendered my whole mouth numb.

Within half a week I found myself embroiled in two family quarrels. In a sense they were the same story.

A couple of nights after my loan to Irène, I heard loud voices from her house across the yard: long accusatory male shouting, Irène's brief angry answers. The next morning, looking as if her teeth were aching again, she recounted the showdown to me. Her brother-in-law, the primary school teacher who lived behind the bistro, which he owned and his brother Kodjo ineptly ran, had told her never to ask money of me. She was her in-laws' responsibility as long as her husband was in Gabon, and they were quite capable of taking care of her. I decided to have a word with the teacher.

That evening I took a path to the house behind the bistro and found him in his courtyard eating supper. Thin and angular, his face a shrewd and sharpened version of his brother Kodjo's dullness, he greeted me with a curt nod and invited me to sit. He came right to the point, making his case as a fellow teacher, in cross-cultural terms. They appreciated my concern for Irène, he said, but it wasn't necessary. Irène was in good hands in the village while her husband was away. Perhaps in America women living alone had to fend for themselves, but in Africa the ties of family were supreme and no one was ever left to go hungry. Besides, he added—and now we were talking man to man—this woman was a wasteful woman. If she had no money for medicine, it was because she'd spent the money her husband sent home on who knows what. By giving her money whenever she asked for it, I was only encouraging her to be careless. I had to be wary, as with a child. I knew how women could be.

"She didn't ask for it," I said coolly. "It was a gift."

He shrugged and turned back to his supper.

When I reported the conversation to her, Irène said, "He doesn't love me, Fo Georgie." She wasn't making a defense but stating a fact. "This family doesn't love me at all."

I steered her around to the subject of the money from Gabon, trying and failing to avoid phrasing it as a question about the truth of her brother-in-law's assessment.

"Fo Georgie," she said, slapping the back of one hand into the palm of the other. The gesture seemed to ask what proof I might require that would be more convincing than the sun-bleached, torn blue *pagne* that she wore today, and every day. I required none. "No money."

"That woman wastes everything. She is lazy, careless."

Now it was the chief speaking; now the woman under consideration was Christine. He had stopped by to say good-evening, and I'd used the occasion, impulsively and with misgiving, to get at his version of the sewing-machine affair. Had there been no money? Had Christine sold her prized possession in order to give birth to a child of the Agbelis?

The chief heard me out, and then shook his head in disgust. "The woman has lied—that's all. She was provided for when Benjamin was away—there were four of us supporting her then, my brothers and I. She told you she had to sell it? It's a lie. She gets money from the Agbelis and then she spends it all. We don't know where! You mustn't believe her, Monsieur Georges. Who do you think Lucien learned his ways from?"

It was bad strategy for the chief to bring up Lucien. But he'd succeeded in fluttering up a slight doubt in the pit of my belly. For the second time in a week I was asked to choose between a woman's word and the word of the family that was ostensibly bound to support her. And for the second time it came down to whether I could believe the evidence of my own eyes. What did she waste these generous amounts of child support on? Jewelry she kept locked in a box, clothes she never wore, forays to Kpalimé between midnight and three in the morning? Except for a *pagne* I brought her from Upper Volta, I hadn't noticed a single addition to her wardrobe in a year: four or five faded *pagnes*, two sleeveless blouses with flower patterns, the lace camisole she wore as a shirt. The longest trip she'd taken this whole time was the fifteen miles to Adeta when the Lavié market ran out of yams. The children's clothes were in rags. Atsu was wearing outgrown khakis to school, and Christine had to sew—on a machine she rented from another woman—their book bags out of scraps of cloth. Shirts and trousers went through four or five owners: Markie's clothes last year were Dové's this and would be Mawuli's next. And now Christine had begun selling *egble*, balls of cold sour corn mush wrapped in leaves, every day in front of the bistro. Emma, who watched the tray when Christine was at the market or cooking supper, came home one evening twenty-five francs short. She'd lost the coin, she cried; her ears were boxed anyway.

On the whole, not a picture of conspicuous consumption.

In fact, there had been a deterioration in Christine's circumstances since I'd gone off on my summer trips and spent more money than she could conceive of. There was an air of urgency about the *egble*; money was scarcer than ever, her temper was shorter. One morning, after I described a dream I'd had, she said she'd dreamed the night before as well: she'd been in a crowded market, selling pretty cloth out of her own stall.

"*Nana Benz!*" I joked, grouping her with the powerful Marché Mamans in Lomé who pulled up outside the Grand Marché in Mercedes sedans. Christine laughed with pleasure at the thought. Suddenly she said:

"He doesn't give me any money now."

"Who?"

"Ben. Benjamin. He gives nothing."

She'd appealed to the chief—not exactly her natural ally, but the only court there was—and he was going to make a *jugement*. She asked me to intercede on her behalf; and, like an inept shuttle diplomat, I only got to the heart of the matter after several trips back and forth.

Benjamin was withholding money, the chief said, because Christine had stopped cooking for him—the second-to-worst wifely rebellion. Why had she stopped? Because, Christine told me, she found out while I was traveling that Benjamin had taken a woman up in Kpelé-Elé; he visited her during the Kpalimé-Atakpamé runs he now made. Yes, the chief said, it was true about the woman in Kpelé-Elé, but irrelevant; as soon as Christine started cooking for him again, his brother would give her what he owed her.

This was the *jugement*.

By now I was hard-pressed to say exactly what an African husband owed his wife. Obviously not fidelity. That was the last thing—"irrelevant." Adultery, it seemed, was as natural to village men as drinking *sodabi* and sleeping at noon. It wasn't kept secret either; in fact, it carried a certain amount of prestige. Of course, faithlessness only went in one direction. For a village woman it was unthinkable. Adultery was the "development" version of polygamy, a necessary substitute for a practice that had become less common among the younger husbands because of Western, Christian strictures and, even more, the financial straits most of them were in. A mistress wasn't free, but the woman in Kpelé-Elé probably didn't ask of Benjamin what Christine asked.

While the women were confiding their problems to me, village men were trying to procure me a "wife," meaning someone to do the cooking and share my bed. "Marriage" proposals suddenly started coming in. Some men offered their own daughters, others made more general suggestions. One old man in farmer's garb—torn shirt, grimy corduroys, tire-rubber sandals—nudged me as I was eating my morning bowl of rice and beans outside the bistro. When I looked, he was thrusting a finger through a circle formed by the thumb and forefinger of his other hand. "Fo Georgie." He smiled, raised his eyebrows, and asked why I didn't take one of the village girls to do this with me. The life I was leading was not decent!

I'd had my chances. A female student appeared at my door one night, with two male classmates making oblique offers as pimps; but this was taboo, and one of the teachers later told me the intention had been blackmail. There was Ama, eighteen years old, daughter of a Protestant minister in Atakpamé, who met me one harmattan day at John's in Hiheatro, informed me she would come to visit sometime, and appeared in Lavié the next Friday with four changes of clothing. It was clear pretty quickly that we had nothing to say to each other—the subject that interested her most was her pimples—but it seemed she was going to stay the night anyway. Conversation had not been the idea. I made up a mattress for her in the living room while she went into my bedroom to change. When she didn't emerge for fifteen minutes I went in after her and found her curled up under my blanket.

"Ama, you can't sleep in here."

"Why not?"

"I made a bed for you in the living room."

"Oh, no, it's too cold there."

"Then I'll sleep in the living room."

"You won't sleep in your own bed? Why not?"

I went back into the living room, and spent the harmattan night shivering under a sheet.

My friends among the teachers heard this story with something between disbelief and outrage. The poor girl had come all this way— there she was, in my bed—at least I could have directed her to one of their houses. Sex was not a choice you made but an irresistible force in whose presence you found yourself. Whatever you thought of each other, once you ended up alone in the same room there wasn't much question what had to happen.

Perhaps that was the thinking of Yawa, a twenty-year-old who sold eggs in the market. Yawa was lithe, full-lipped, and (the rarity of this combination helped account for my celibacy) neither a student nor married. She was enjoying a sort of free ride for a couple of years until a young man with the right number of goats came along with a marriage offer. Every Friday for weeks we carried on a flirtation in the market, so that the market women started referring to her as my "wife" even though she hadn't performed either of the two wifely functions. I liked her, and my chance of sampling the first came one Friday when, after I'd bought enough of her eggs to make omelettes for half the village, she invited me over to her house for *fufu* the next afternoon. We were to meet at my house at one o'clock.

I sat in my living room as the hot hours crawled by: one, two, three o'clock, and still no Yawa. In the end she never came. Eventually I deduced what had happened. *Fufu* could not mean just *fufu*. The two of us alone in her house inevitably had to lead to the second function. And she'd decided that she didn't want me or didn't want the gossip (for nothing stayed secret in Lavié) that would hound her for weeks.

The other teachers and I had long, spirited exchanges about the fine points of marriage and sex. I took the side of women, which struck the men as a baffling betrayal. Their arguments drifted between biology and sociology, the physical needs of the male of every species and the cultural imperatives of African life. They reasoned that polygamy and adultery were in the interests of women, lightening their load of chores in both kitchen and bedroom. The cannier among them took the offensive and pointed out that their way was better than ours, with our skyrocketing divorce rates and broken families. At times the arguments began to make sense to me, until I remembered they were rationalizing a system that left them and only them free to screw around.

The farmers were more blunt.

"I can give you two reasons why a man needs two wives."

The old man—the one with the expressive fingers—had me cornered over my bowl of rice again. I had just told him that in my country we threw polygamists in prison. His indignation had subsided enough for him to show me why we were fools.

"One." A knobby finger stuck up in front of his eyes. "Who will cook for you if your first wife is sick? What can you do?"

To provoke him I said, "You can cook for yourself."

The women selling rice and beans guffawed, as if to say, "That I'd pay to see!"

"Two." A second finger in the air, my answer not worth consideration. "What do you do if your first wife has given birth? For a year she is unclean and you cannot touch her. Who will please you? Or," he went on with disgust, "in your country do you touch your wife when she's unclean?" Now he moved in for the kill. "And what if she is pregnant? How will you do then?" He leaned back, folded his arms across his bony chest, and rested his case.

"Lie on your back," I suggested, "and she can get on top. Try it, I promise it will work fine."

He slapped my knee and wheezed with laughter. But as I stood to go, he remarked rather grimly that he was quite happy not to live in the village where Fo Georgie came from.

All of these were the arguments of men. No woman ever offered me any rationale for the men's infidelities. Even Ama—as "traditional" a woman as I knew in Africa—once said that the two worst things about men were taking more than one wife and eating snake. As for Christine, I didn't need to solicit her opinion about men and their behavior. But when, in the thick of their family crises, I asked her and Irène why they, too, didn't take lovers, they shook their heads vehemently. Christine's answer was feminist and antifeminist in the same breath, a reminder of the limits of her ability to think outside a system she plainly knew oppressed them.

"No, that isn't done," she said with finality. "What they do is bad. But God didn't make woman like that—only man."

CEG Lavié had a new principal. The authorities in their wisdom had finally sent away Aboï, and in his place we received a man who'd been principal here five or six years ago. Dossavi, a Mina from Anécho on the coast (and thus far more acceptable here than Aboï the Kabyé), was a good-looking man of about thirty with very dark skin and a mild scowl on his face. At six feet he was unusually tall for a southerner and one of the few in the village taller than I. He wore a light gray cardigan, flared double-knit pants, and gray shoes with tassels—in America what an orthodontist wears on his golf days, but here the attire of a sophisticate. And, in my experience of Africa, Dossavi was a new kind of man. His French flowed out easily, in an accent that sounded closer to Paris than to Anécho, sprinkled with slang like *pute* and *mec*. Most functionaries walked on the crushed heels of their dress shoes like slippers; Dossavi wore his Western-style, heel up. Son of a minor functionary and a market woman, he'd never been farther than Nigeria, yet he managed to convey great worldliness.

At the first *conseil de prof.* he was businesslike to the point of arrogance. He had heard that Lavié was a problem school, he was the *chef* now, and he wanted things to change quickly. After school he liked to play sports and drink beer, he announced, but here at school, it was work, work, work. I'd never heard anyone make the distinction before. And he was as good as his word: the *conseil* was mercifully short, and instead of spending the usual two weeks watching students cut the grass that had overgrown the grounds during vacation, we began classes the next day. "He's a little brusque, isn't he," Agbefianou said to me after the first *conseil*. But no "*J-J-Je refuse!*" followed. We were all relieved at the new principal's self-assurance; no one had forgotten last year's chaos, Aboï's neurotic tyrannies.

Dossavi was the first Togolese who didn't seem in the least impressed by my skin color. At noon on the first day of classes I approached him outside his office to get the letters for me he had on his desk. He was starting up his Vespa to go home for lunch, a briefcase clenched under one arm. Frowning, he got off. "All right, but you're costing me five minutes of my time."

"Is time as valuable as that?" I was incredulous. No one in Lavié fussed over an hour lost, let alone five minutes.

"It's because we don't care about time," he said, his back to me as he unlocked the office door, "that we Africans are still under-developed."

Dossavi breathed *le développement.* That evening after sunset I heard the motor of the Vespa puttering into my yard. A gruff voice called out, "Monsieur Packer, you're home?"

He hadn't clapped, hadn't greeted the family in the yard first. It was the way an American would come for a visit. He had changed into a new pair of trousers but was still wearing the cardigan.

"Can I use your *monsieur?*"

I stared. "I'm sorry?"

"Your *monsieur.* You see, I haven't got one at my house."

It took me another moment to realize he was talking about my toilet.

"I'm not yet used to the village life," he said as he came into the house. "Where I'm staying there's just a simple latrine, a hole with a seat made of clay. You have to squat all the way down. The lodgings aren't at all satisfactory. Do you mind?"

I showed him through the kitchen to the WC, warning him that it didn't flush.

"That doesn't matter, the children will fetch a bucket of water." And as if he'd been giving them orders for years, he yelled through the back door for one of the Agbeli boys to go to the river with a bucket. Christine appeared, shouting at Claudie, and then turned to us with a modest smile and a slight curtsy for the new principal. *"Bonsoir, madame,"* he said. They exchanged a few words in Ewé. Already Dossavi, the southerner, had gotten further with the village than Aboï had managed in three years—even if things here were a bit primitive for him.

"You know this was my house when I was here before?"

"No, I didn't. Then I've stolen it from you."

"But the family wasn't here then. I had plenty of space, five rooms for just me and my wife. We slept in that same bed you're using. Now I'm stuck over in the Amedanu quarter in three rooms with my brother and niece. I need to find a new place."

He disappeared into the WC, threw his trousers up over the half-shut door, and spent a quarter hour inside—muttering, exhorting himself, rambling on, about what I didn't listen to find out.

On his way out he invited me for a *déjeuner* of *fufu* tomorrow at his unsatisfactory lodgings in the Amedanu quarter.

Even Dossavi's niece was cosmopolitan. In his living room she served us bowls of *fufu*, her hair done in elaborate beaded corn rows, her shoulders bared by a sheer blue blouse with thin straps, her fingers thick with rings. When I asked how she liked Lavié, she shrugged and curled her lip like a Manhattan girl contemplating a year of school in West Virginia.

"She's spoiled," Dossavi said, reaching to pinch the glob of yam that floated in a greasy red sea of palm oil. We had started with green oranges, which he peeled entirely and ate in sections, *yovo*-style; Africans skinned the rind in strips, sliced off the top, and sucked the juice dry, then tore the fruit open and devoured the pulp. The *fufu* was served with a bottle of Chianti. "Nineteen eighty was a good year for this wine," he said.

I asked whether his wife lived with him here.

"She's in Kpalimé with my son. She works in a bank there."

"Do you see her often?"

"Oh, from time to time. I visit her to see the boy. He's almost three now. Soon enough he'll come live with me." He leaned forward and looked at me frankly. "You see—can't we use *tu* with each other, Georges?—I don't get along with my wife. We quarrel when we're together. It isn't the way it was before, when we were living in your house. We were happy then. We slept together every night in that bed, with the straw mattress. She's become a disappointment to me. I can't tell her things, she isn't involved in my work. She is a woman who frowns a great deal. She's—like a stone."

He told me that before his wife there had been another woman,

Christine, the one he'd really wanted to marry when he was a university student—beautiful, understanding, "smarter than any other woman. And she knew how to make love exceptionally well." But her family had been opposed, and when a blood test showed that they both had sickle-cell anemia and would produce unhealthy children, they agreed to stop seeing each other. It was a tragic event in his life. Now she was married to someone else in Lomé. She was still the one he went to with his problems.

"Does your wife know that?"

He waved away his wife. "She doesn't care, she knows I don't love her anymore."

"Do you think that African men and women have the same feelings for each other as Westerners?"

I was asking a question that had been forming in my mind for weeks. I'd never seen teen-agers get misty-eyed listening to Bob Marley together; never once seen a kiss, a touch, a sentimental look; never heard a soft word between students or married couples, in the capital or the village. Love here seemed to have nothing to do with pleasure, freedom, and fulfillment. The strongest ties were the necessary ones, between parents and children, siblings, cousins; the hives that broke out on Christine's neck the week that Aku had measles were the clearest token of love I could find. Romantic love was another luxury import out of the West, like tape decks and tinned strawberries. I'd never heard a Ewé word for "love," though I knew the word for "kiss" was *kissi*—borrowed from English to refer to something that might have been as exotic as bottled whiskey when the *yovos* arrived.

"For example," I went on, "I never see people kissing here—"

"The kiss is European," he said at once, defining in four words what I'd stumbled onto after fifteen months. "Africans do not kiss—at least they didn't before you people came. Even now it is uncouth to kiss your wife or child in public. Villagers will tell you that another man could see they're dear to you and try to harm you through them. And as for kissing your wife before you go to work in the morning . . ." He made a kissing noise, thick with disgust. "No, never. It's weak."

"But in private—"

"You must understand. For Africans, there isn't the same affection as for whites. A man can never love his wife as much as his own brothers and cousins. We marry for children—that's all. Or, if one is a peasant, for help in the field too."

"An African never tells his wife he loves her?"

"He tells her by allowing her to prepare his food. That's his affection. It is difficult for Europeans to understand this. You have a very idealized view of marriage, don't you?"

Dossavi and I became fast friends. He was informed, blunt, ambitious, and had been thwarted more than once in his life by the education bureaucracy. This man who couldn't get used to the privations of village life, who marveled at my "ease" in Lavié and complained of his own "ennui" after the stimulations of Lomé, became my link to a modern Africa from which I'd been surprisingly cut off. After school, over beers in the bistro, we talked about education and women and world politics. Two or three weekends we went down to Lomé, where we frequented nightclubs with names like Tabu, Jungle Bar, Café des Arts.

One Saturday night, a humid Lomé night at the end of the October rains, we had gone to drink at Tabu, on a sandy side road near the ocean. At the bottom of a narrow flight of stairs, sitting by the doorway, an old man collected the three-hundred-franc entry fee—high enough to keep out most of the students, immigrant laborers, and assorted *voyous* who made up a nocturnal subculture here and in the provincial towns. The men and women upstairs were in their late twenties and thirties, elegantly dressed and coiffed, and doused with choking quantities of perfume or cologne. The air was close, damp, and briny; the reggae blaring out of oversized speakers was too loud for talk. From our corner table by the bar we had a view of the whole floor.

It took me a few minutes to see that, at the far end, where people were dancing, what I'd taken for a ceiling was actually the open air. Along the glossy bamboo walls African kitsch was on display: plastic potted palms, pictures of village life—huts on a lagoon where swans floated, elephants and water-fetching women sharing a riverbank— landscapes that existed nowhere in Togo, painted in lush, nostalgic reds and blues. Even their kitschiness belonged to the elegance of the nightclub. They were reminders that this place wasn't the village, that the village had to be recalled in these distortions.

The dancers two-stepped slowly in the heat, the men with a hand resting lightly on the small of the women's backs, the other hands joined at the shoulder. They didn't talk as they danced, or even look at each other. They gazed past, as if their thoughts were far away from their bodies, which never lost the rhythm and seemed to move automatically. Some younger men danced alone or with each other. They danced with their whole bodies, smiling, eyes closed, their open shirts revealing glistening chests; they alone seemed to have come here for the release of music and dance.

At the tables groups of men and women sat amid bottles of Bière du Benin, and watched the dancers; the men spoke very little, the women not at all. In the flash of red and green strobe lights the faces of the women, silent, drinking beer, heavily made up with lipstick and mascara and—on some—skin lightener, looked glamorous and bored. It was an expression I'd begun to recognize as specifically female: on secretaries and bargirls and functionaries' wives, on women being escorted into the passenger seats of Mercedes, women behind the reception desks at hotels, women sitting alone in bars. It was a modern face, a city face—well tended, unhappy, compliant, the face of a woman whose own life held no interest for her.

"What do you think of her, on the right? Do you like her?"

Dossavi was pointing two tables away, where three women were drinking unaccompanied. The woman in question was small, very black, no more than twenty-five, hair tressed in corn rows. When she opened her cherry-red mouth to drink, she revealed a broken front tooth.

I shrugged. "She's fine."

"*Bon.*" Dossavi stood up and went over to the table. Ignoring her friends, he spoke to the woman directly. I couldn't hear what he said, but he was using French. She looked startled, nervous, then a little amused. As he spoke she glanced over at me; our eyes met and hers darted away. Dossavi went on, still in French. He seemed to be persuading her of something. There was no giggling or teasing from her friends; they sipped beers and watched the dancers. Finally she smiled, gathered her purse, and followed Dossavi back to our table. She was wearing jeans, a rarity among African women, rolled up to the knees, and a white silk shirt untucked and belted around the waist—not a costume I was used to. I saw, too, that she was pretty despite the broken tooth, and that she had the barely formed body of a twelve-year-old.

"Georges, may I present Yvette. Georges teaches in my school in Lavié."

Yvette shrugged. We shook hands; hers was thin and cool.

"*Bonsoir, m'sieur.*"

"*Bonsoir. Comment ça va?*"

"*Ça va très bien.*"

The pleasantries teachers and students exchanged in the village. Dossavi looked at me. "Do you like her?"

I didn't know what to say. This hadn't been planned with me. I said I liked her.

Dossavi said, "Yvette, are you interested in the cinema?"

Yvette nodded. She was looking at me more boldly, a long, silent look that ended with the slightest parting of her lips and the sight of the black gap where the tooth was broken.

"Then let's all go see a film. There's an excellent one at the 24 Janvier."

We paid our bill, left, walked to the ocean road, and hailed a taxi for the center of town. Dossavi sat in front with the driver, Yvette and I in back, hands on our knees, knees in danger of touching. Her shins shone smooth. No one said a word.

As a rule the cinemas in Lomé played the worst American or French films, but I wondered how Dossavi's choice even found its way here—a soft-core American porn flick, dubbed in French and titled *L'Eté du Bac* (the English title must have been something like *Graduation Summer*). The father of a rich boy in LA wants his son to go to his own Ivy League alma mater; the boy would rather go to aerobics classes and ogle the women. An F in German at the end of his senior year imperils his college chances, and the father hires a live-in Swiss tutor for the summer—a gorgeous blond older woman, of course, and of course the lessons turn to sex. We were sitting in velvet seats in an air-conditioned theater with a balcony and a vast screen. The allusions were all remote from Lomé, but the audience of city bourgeoisie (tickets at this luxury cinema cost a thousand francs) found it unfailingly interesting and funny. The "romantic" moments got the biggest laughs.

Yvette, too, liked it. Sitting beside me, she would check her grasp of the latest plot twist with me, ply me with cultural questions. How did the machine wash the clothes? What was "Harvard"? When the boy took out a box of Camel filters, she turned and sang a jingle in my ear: "Camel! *Le goût de l'action.*" Perhaps an ad she'd seen at another film; perhaps she came to films all the time. Nothing surprised her and everything absorbed her. After her boredom at Tabu, the movie that did not seem strange to her and the glamor of the plush theater brought out a playful excitement in Yvette. By the end her hand was in mine.

Outside the cinema Dossavi left us. He said he would see me tomorrow, told me to "take care," and went off in search of a taxi back to his brother's. Yvette and I did not look at each other. The mood of the movie—trashy and intoxicating—was already wearing off. We were not in LA but in Lomé again, on a paved street with one electric light, coconut husks strewn in the road, Renault taxis rattling past, the salt breeze sultrier than ever after the chill of the air conditioning.

A woman in a white *pagne*, a night *commerçante*, passed us balancing a basin of coconuts on her head. I stopped her and paid for two; the *commerçante* expertly hacked the tops off with her cutlass.

Yvette said, "We have so many in my hometown."

"Where is your hometown?"

"In Ivory Coast."

"You're from Abidjan?"

"Not Abidjan. From Bouaflé."

It explained a lot. Why she and Dossavi spoke only French; why the name Lavié meant nothing to her; perhaps why she'd been without a man at Tabu. So she was a stranger, another migrant—a migrant, and a woman. The night had brought us around to this point. I hadn't anticipated or arranged it, but I understood the thing expected of me, and I felt it as something that had been missing from my time here, something welcome now. Drinking from the coconuts, we began walking in the direction of the Boulevard Circulaire, toward the Hôtel Ahodikpé, a cheap place, a favorite haunt among volunteers.

Yvette made it clear that she didn't care for the hotel. The desk clerk was brusque with us and Yvette curled a lip at her. On our way upstairs she told me that we wouldn't be treated this way at a better hotel. I said I was a volunteer, not a salaried worker, that my money was tight.

"But you are white, no?" Yvette asked ironically.

In the room—a bed with a sheet, a small table, one overhead light bulb, a bathroom with only cold water and a dank smell—I spoke about my work and about the country I came from. Yvette listened a few moments, yawned, took off the jeans and blouse, and told me to turn on the air conditioner (she'd insisted on a *chambre climatisée* because of the Lomé mosquitoes).

She obviously had no interest in what I was telling her. The movie had spoken to her of glamor, but the country itself and the words of someone who'd lived there were nothing but abstractions, unconnected to the feeling of the movie or to her.

She went into the bathroom and shut the door. She spent a long time with the water running. When she came out, her twelve-year-old's body was naked. Unselfconsciously she walked across to the bed and lay belly-down on top of the sheet. She had brought out a chew stick from the bathroom and began cleaning her teeth over the pillow. She smelled strongly of soap. I sat on the side of the bed, my shirt off. I asked her:

"Why did you come to Lomé?"

She hunched her shoulders in a shrug. "It is a small city."

"And Abidjan?"

"Abidjan was too big, too many people, not enough money. The people there are wicked, they take your money, they break you."

"And Bouaflé?"

"My hometown?" She gave a derisive laugh. "There was nothing for me in Bouaflé. Nobody can stay there."

"Lomé is better?"

She cleaned her teeth. Another shrug. "I have to stay someplace. Lomé is good. I stay with my sister in Tokoin."

I knew that "sister" did not mean flesh and blood, only friend; she had no relatives in Togo, she said. I asked her how she could live so far from her family.

"I was always thinking of them at first. Now, I forget. It happens like that." She turned to look at me, smiling acidly, showing the broken tooth. "You talk so much!"

From the moment when she'd said she wasn't from here, was a foreigner, I felt drawn to Yvette. Why she came, how she survived, did she survive. I wanted to know. In the way she described Abidjan, there was something of Benjamin's *"Pays là, c'est pas la peine"*; there was something of Christine and Irène, too, for Yvette was not just out of her milieu in Lomé but alone. The migrant's vulnerability, the vulnerability of a woman. She compensated for these, I thought, disguised them, with the curt indifference that had been lifted only inside the cinema.

I pried out of her that in Abidjan she'd gone with a man who'd had some money and had been abusive to her, who had finally cut her off. After she arrived in Lomé—she'd come with another woman from Bouaflé who'd since gone back—there were some months of hardship when she lived along the waste canal off the Route de Kpalimé and tried a series of ventures in the Grand Marché: selling *kolikoes* (fried yams), unloading produce trucks, cleaning up the meat and tobacco markets in the evenings. For one reason or another none of it worked. All this she described in a neutral monotone. She became a prostitute through the good graces of another Ivoirienne, slowly, telling herself at each step that it was temporary until she found better work. But nothing had come along.

Here our conversation ended. With a gesture of impatience—a flick of the fingers across the pillow—she rolled over on her side and huddled in her own arms and stared at me, as if to say that with talking so much we were going to miss what we'd come for. But I'd been lonely and was grateful, and we didn't miss it.

In the morning, shivering from the air conditioner that had run all night, she looked tired. She had a stomachache, she said, and turned irritably away from a kiss as if it were a crude thing by daylight. We dressed and I arranged the bed. On the way through the door she stopped; her back was to me.

"When I go home I might find there is nothing to eat."

"I can give you money for it."

"How much?"

I took out my wallet. "Here's fifteen hundred francs."

She turned in the doorway and looked at the bills without taking them. "Fifteen hundred francs? That is nothing."

For food it was plenty. But I understood. Somehow I'd managed to imagine, despite her occupation, that Yvette and I had met at a nightclub, had seen a movie, had been lonely, gone to a hotel together, confided in each other, enjoyed each other, spent the night together—that that was all. That the food was food and not a way of sparing me or both of us the embarrassment of having to spell out what should have been as clear as the nose on my face. Now it was clear. I took out another thousand. She folded the bills away in her belt. She was smiling now, and smiling when I hailed her a taxi on the Boulevard Circulaire. We were both smiling when she gave me her address in Tokoin and I said I would look for her there or at Tabu. But I didn't see Yvette again.

CHAPTER 11

Wait a Little More

NEAR THE END OF OCTOBER, WITH HEAVY RAINS FALL-
ing every afternoon, the old chief finally came to tell
me the history of the village.

Summer travels had sparked my interest in African
newness, in its cities and politics, the lives of migrants and of
women, the wave of change that seemed to be washing up human
debris everywhere I looked. It all fascinated and depressed me. The
happy, pastoral village of my first impression had been an anxious
newcomer's fantasy. Now nothing was as it seemed; everything was
ambiguous and contaminated, passed through and fragmented in
the lens I thought of simply as Lagos. I suppose what I was craving—
though I could hardly have articulated it at the time—was something
old, fixed, and absolute, through which I could see things clearly
again; something, in fact, like the authenticity that the regime had
corrupted into slogans and leader worship. It seemed that the thing
to do was go into the past.

But the past was gone, and hadn't left a trace. Once you started
looking, it was astonishing how completely precolonial history had
been erased in Africa, especially tropical Africa. The oldest buildings
I saw in Togo were the stone ruins of a group of German military
garrisons outside Atakpamé. Nothing made of mud and thatch lasted

more than a generation in the wet and rot of the bush, and so when you talked about African historical architecture you were almost always talking not about anything indigenous and truly old, but the whitewashed villas and offices, with their balustraded verandas and shuttered windows, that the early Europeans built when they were establishing the colony, less than a hundred years ago.

And these, too, had a way of fading, even when they remained physically. The town of Anécho, situated on a lagoon forty kilometers up the coast toward Benin from Lomé, had been the capital of the German colony: a center of power and wealth, hometown of the Afro-Brazilian families—Olympios, DeSouzas, Lawsons—who had been the Togolese elite for several centuries since they arrived as traders from the New World and intermarried with the Ewé on the coast. The French moved the capital to Lomé, and Anécho began to languish. The languishing turned into decay after independence, when Eyadema took power and, perceiving in the Anécho families the biggest threat to his rule, cut the city off from state projects and began pumping money into the north. By the time I visited Anécho in 1982 it was a ghost town floating on the lagoon, stagnant and faintly sinister, with its abandoned colonial buildings, its voodoo market, and its smell of drying fish. A tropical orange sunlight dissolved on the water and blurred into indistinction the outlines of the peeling structures along the lagoon.

Or there was Hiheatro, the Atakpamé suburb where my friend John and dozens of other whites lived. Between 1963 and 1966, during the chaotic regime of Nicholas Grunitzky—the ineffectual half-Pole from Atakpamé—grandiose designs were drawn to set up the capital of the local prefecture, Amou, in Hiheatro. After Grunitzky's fall and Eyadema's second coming, the prefecture was moved to Amlamé. Hiheatro continued to draw whites and wealthy blacks, but the half-finished buildings of the sixties went to seed. The only remnants of Grunitzky's vision were unused concrete market stalls and broad unpaved avenues, their island dividers choked with weeds, leading to an empty plaza with a concrete-ringed mound that was to have been a stage for festivities. All of this had the mystery of an archeological find, for it was overgrown with elephant grass, and you could easily walk across the village without knowing that the idea of a major political center was underfoot.

The neglected past was reclaimed by the bush. I never saw a single physical object in Togo that I could say for certain had been there a hundred years earlier. "Ancient Africa" was brand-new and constantly being made over again, by whites, by other whites, then by successive ruling blacks. There were no books, no archives, to verify anything; its history was tenuous and manipulable. If the past existed anywhere, I decided, it existed in the minds of the handful of Togolese old enough to remember.

So I made a point of getting to know the old chief of Lavié. I already knew about several of his personas. There was the legendary figure, at least as old as the century, who ruled with an autocrat's grip during a period that spanned five American presidencies, from the Jazz age to the Space Age; patriarch of the Agbeli clan, vengeful grandfather at the trial of Lucien. Then there was the magician Christine described with awe one night. Years before, the people of Akata, the next village down the road toward Adeta, had marched on Lavié with *coup-coups* and sticks. The old chief came out alone—everyone else had taken cover indoors—and met them on the road just outside our house. He carried a fistful of black powder, a supremely potent *grigri* that he'd concocted himself; when he hurled it in their faces, the people of Akata threw up their weapons in terror and ran back down the road. His knowledge of the fetish secrets saved the village.

And there was the mysterious figure at the center of a scandal that, rumor had it, ended his reign as chief. At the end of the fifties—so went this story, as I pieced it together out of oblique and reluctant snippets from various people in Lavié—a villager had been accused of killing someone through black magic. As usual in such cases, punishment consisted of forcing him out of Lavié to the next village, where he would be escorted by those villagers on to the next, and so on till he was too far from Lavié to come back. But on the way out of Lavié, a group of villagers beat him up so badly that he died of his wounds. Unfortunately for the old chief, the dead man had a relative in the French colonial administration. The relative brought charges, and the old chief, who was responsible for the sorcerer's safe conduct, was convicted of negligence and sentenced to twenty years in jail. If the story was true, he hadn't been out more than a few years.

All of these old chiefs I tried to square with the one I knew, the withered octogenarian who slept long hours with other old men under the mango tree outside the bistro. He almost always wore an orange shirt with half the buttons missing, green pants, rubber sandals, and a Buster Keaton hat, flat and floppy. The clothes looked comical, but the face, with its fiery eyes, grizzled beard, and toothless cheeks, commanded respect; the body was tough, with an old farmer's loose muscle hanging on the bony arms and chest. Whenever I walked or motored by and called out, in respect, *"Wofo!"* he would lift his head and shoulders off the rock, raise a stick-thin arm, and shout hoarsely, *"Georgie! Egbe fedo!"*

One evening I was in the bistro drinking beer with Erasmus, the current chief's secretary. The old chief was inside with us, taking shots of *sodabi*, having left his spot on the rock like an old walrus slipping into the sea at the end of the day.

"I wish I spoke Ewé better," I said to Erasmus, whose French was pretty good. "I'd like to hear the old man talk. I'm sure he has a lot to tell."

"A lot! You only need to ask him. I can translate easily."

"You don't think he'd be offended?"

The old chief had finished his *sodabi* and gone outside. It was past six o'clock, nearly dark, and lamps were appearing on the road. The bistro radio was playing African gospel. I followed him out and spoke to him in Ewé.

"Wofo! Fié lo! Will you come to my house on Sunday to speak to me of the village?"

The old chief turned. His face, quite black except for the knots of white beard, was withered like a prune; layers of wrinkles ringed the eyes. But the eyes themselves, hard and alive, fixed me with a long stare, as if to weigh my sincerity. He knew exactly what I'd meant about speaking of the village. It seemed he'd been waiting for this request.

"Georgie, moi—je suis vieux—tu connais?" he said, not rumbling or slurring like most people who've lost their teeth, but in a voice that was almost choked with passion as he just about depleted his French. *Vieux* as he pronounced it suggested the potency of his years.

From behind me Erasmus interpreted. "He says he has many experiences that only he can tell you about."

"I was born long ago and I saw the white man's war. I won't hide anything from you, teacher; you can ask me what you want. I am old and know many things. If you want knowledge about Lavié, no one can answer but me."

We were sitting in my living room on a hot Sunday afternoon, all three cradling cups of beer. The tape recorder I'd been given permission to use was whirring on the table. The old chief had dressed for the occasion; his faded orange *pagne* was wrapped above the nipples, and he wore dyed leather sandals. Erasmus had to translate much of what I heard, and I suspected I was losing a fair portion of the original: abstractions replaced metaphors; a proverb was dropped here and there, a telling detail omitted as irrelevant. But what got through held me rapt.

It was the old chief's manner, as much as his story, that made the afternoon fly by. What he had to tell me wasn't ancient history, but a living matter to him. He acted out every scene, took on at different points the roles of rifle, gatling gun, French soldier, schoolboy, big game, young chief, village elder. He gestured sharply, inflected the telling with a range of emotions from fury to sorrow to exultation, shouted, whispered, created special effects. His story transported him, so that he seemed to live more intensely in his memory than he lived in the present, in the village, on the bistro rock. To him the past was full of drama, abundance, order, meaning. He reminded me of old Nestor in the *Iliad*—"A stone that takes ten men to lift today was lifted in those days by only one." It hardly mattered whether his narrative was accurate, though I had no reason to doubt him and later was able to corroborate certain details. What mattered was that he saw the past in this way, gave it this greatness.

"My father and mother were farmers of the land. They had so

many fields and we always ate well—the meat of deer, *agouti*, wild boar. My father had a gun from the Germans: gun, powder, bullets, everything. We hunted zebra and buffalo, but no lions or elephants—these weren't here. *Prang!* I was a good shot, from boyhood on. My father took me hunting. Back then it rained as it should and we had enough of everything—corn, yams, all. It's only today that the world is no longer full of rain. I have never seen anything like this. I planted corn and yam this year—nothing, all ruined. My age, I still go to the fields—*moi, cultivateur!* That's all I can do, since I couldn't go to school after the war came in 1914. I was at the school in Lavié, the German mission. It was only one hut of thatch. I began school in 1910, four years before the war. I knew the alphabet fine: a, f, t . . ."

"Did you fight along with the Germans in the war?"

He had been too young. But other Togolese fought for the Germans, as Dahomeyans fought for the French and the people of the Gold Coast for the English.

"Now I want to speak of the war. But you know, Georgie"—he leaned forward—"because you are hearing my voice it is good that you give me some *cadeau*. You keep making me remember so many things; you want me to earn this *cadeau!* What will you give me, teacher? If you give me a gift worthy of my name I will tell you many other things. You know, I like all strong drinks."

I told him I'd bought a bottle of the whites' whiskey.

"Fine. I'm ready to talk about the war. I was there when the German troops came through Lavié. *Moi, la guerre!* The Germans were strong, but the war surprised them. That's why they lost. They knew nothing of what was going to happen—the war came suddenly, *bwam!*"

He re-created the great battle outside Atakpamé, where a colonel from each of the European powers was killed and the Germans had to surrender.

"Did Togolese die too?"

"They died too! And ones from Gold Coast died, and from Dahomey died." He opened his black-gummed mouth and made a long hoarse roar like the sound of a machine gun. "Many black men died."

The Germans had conscripted their African soldiers, and no one resisted. But the Germans never killed civilians. He said he liked the Germans. They built schools and churches, and under them the Africans lived well. I asked if the French had done things for themselves and not the Togolese.

He corrected me. "No, that's not what I said. I didn't say the French weren't good. I don't want to judge the Germans or the French. You said that. Perhaps you'll tell somebody what I say. . . ." He folded his arms and sat back as if he weren't going to say another word.

I reminded him of his promise to tell me everything. He eyed me suspiciously. "Georgie, you are a teacher, a *yovo*; I am *ameyibo*, a farmer. And one day it could happen that you bring me before some tribunal and they would ask me, 'Did you say this? Your voice is with us here in this machine.' "

"No, *wofo*." I clasped my hands. "Why? I live here in Lavié, I invite me over, we share beer, I'm a friend to the Agbelis. Why would I try to harm you?"

"If you did, God would ask you why."

"Exactly."

He was placated. "Very well. Then yes, I agree. With the Germans we were well—but the French turned the good of Togo for themselves. With the Germans Togo was big, so big! After the war bad things came to us. The Ewé are not together today because the French and English tore Togo in two pieces, and they gave half to Gold Coast. Was that good?

"Now I'm convinced you didn't invite me here to report me, because you are a good man, teacher."

"You're the teacher today; I'm your pupil."

"Do you say so? Ha ha! Fine, fine. Now I am going to tell you the whole truth of how we came to Lavié."

The origin of the Ewé people was in Notsé, halfway between Lomé and Atakpamé. At some time—and he gave no hint whether it was a hundred years ago or three hundred—they fell under the rule of a certain King Agokoli. He repeated the name slowly, with awe.

"This Agokoli was an evil man. He did evil things to his people, demanded human blood and human heads to make himself glorious. Every year, so many heads! He did to his people things no one should do. So the people fled this evil king—they left Notsé. *'Midjo!'* they said to each other. 'Let's go! Let's leave this king!' And they divided up: some to Agou, some to Danyi, some to Gold Coast. The people of Lavié went toward Gold Coast.

"They settled first on a mountain called Lakletodji, 'The Mountain of the Wild Animals.' For there were fierce beasts on this mountain. These were courageous men. *Tsohh!*" he shouted. "There were hyena. The hyena is a wicked beast. From Lakletodji they went to Assadzatodji, 'The Mountain of the Big Ants.' Two peoples were on this mountain, the people of Lavié and another. The chief, Agbedo, decided to go on to Gold Coast. The Tsamenyi followed him, but the people of Lavié stayed on the Mountain of the Big Ants."

"Tsamenyi?"

"Tsamenyi—they took that name before they left Notsé. *Nyi* is a poisonous bee and *tsa* is a tree with bitter bark. The *nyi* live in the *tsa* tree. And so they called themselves Tsamenyi, for they wanted others to know that if anyone tried to harm them they would sting like this bee. Careful! The people were venomous. So Agbedo led the Tsamenyi to Gold Coast. But our people didn't go. Each year Agbedo sent his royal scepter back and told the people to come join him in Gold Coast. But each year they sent him a messenger who said, '*Lalaviadé*. Wait a little more.' They said they would come soon, but the harvest of the first year was good on the Mountain of the Big Ants, and so they delayed. '*Lalaviadé*,' they said that year, and the next year, and every year after that, for the harvests were always good. '*Lalaviadé*. Wait a little more.' And in the end they never went to Gold Coast. And so when they finally came to this place where we are sitting, they gave it this same name, Lalaviadé, or as we say, Lavié. This is the only true meaning of the name."

A troubling thought came. His eyes filled with indignation. "It does not mean 'little beast' or 'little meat'—no, never!"

I mentioned a man from Kpalimé who'd told me, with a laugh, that Lavié meant just that, giving the word an inflection that signified this debased meaning instead of the old chief's etymology.

The old man's arms shook, his voice trembled like Lear's in the storm, and he raged, "No, that's not true at all! *Aghhh, ohhh!* It's a lie, a lie! They in Kpalimé are jealous of the courageous people of Lavié and so they say it in such a way to mean—oh, they know the true meaning but they want to insult us! Those people—you know the war between the Ewé and the Ashanti. The Ashanti were fierce people, but the people of Lavié fought them bravely, right here in the village; we drove them out and left many houses in Gold Coast without a man at the head! But because Kpalimé is a city, they say they were the ones who fought. They fought nobody! Kpalimé isn't even a single people, it's just a sauce with people thrown in from everywhere, Hausa and Kotokoli and Kabyé . . . The name means only this: 'Wait a little more.' Where was I now? Ah, the line of chiefs."

He settled back and let the insult pass. "After Agbedo left for Gold Coast, the people on the Mountain of the Big Ants came down and settled in Didofedomé, 'The Place of Two Baobabs.' But at Didofedomé they were too many. And so the chief and others left and came here to Lavié. I am the only one in the village who can tell you the truth of this—the others will tell you almost all lies. Now I want to go out and urinate, and then I will tell you of the leaders of the people who settled in Lavié, ever since the time they left King Agokoli."

When he came back, I had a lamp lit on the table. Gloom was gathering around the house and woodsmoke drifted through the windows. The day's heat had eased, and in the dusk the old chief recited the royal genealogy—a list of chiefs' names, from Notsé to the present, that sounded biblical to me. In the lineage he came sixth.

"I am Gbaga VI—Yawo Nafo Gbaga VI."

"What does *Gbaga* mean?"

"Gba-*ga*," he corrected me. "It is the name of a river. We took the royal name because of the strength of the river. But today this river is almost dry."

"Could you tell me how you elect a chief?"

He clapped me on the knee. "Ah, Georgie, you ask the best questions, you are making me work for my white man's drink! If you are chief, and you grow old or else you die, all the elders of the village are called together to meet." He put his hands to his mouth and made the long hollow sound of a summons. "And they sit down and decide who in the family is going to mount the throne. It does not have to be the eldest son. The chief today is not my son, he is my nephew. The man they choose mustn't know, for if he does, of course he will try to run away."

"Doesn't he want to be chief?"

He stared in astonishment. "Do you think it's an easy thing to be chief? He truly doesn't want it. So they collect a gourd of palm wine and twelve bottles of *sodabi*."

"And how did they tell you the day you were chosen?"

He fell silent and put his hands to his eyes. The sun had fled over Ghana, and his face and arms were lit from below by the yellow glow of the lamp. "It is nighttime. The children and the chickens are asleep at my house. Ah—I know nothing, I have no idea. I am just a young man. A friend comes to my house. He sees my wife is with me and he tells her to go away, he has something important to tell me. We sit and drink, and while we do the dead chief's assistant and the other elders come into my house, all quiet, because it's night and through the village you can hear nothing. They had red and white chalk with them. I hear something; I call out. *'Ago!'* But there is no *'Amé!'* And now they're in the room, they are seizing me and I shout, *'Nuka edzo?'* 'What's happening?' "

He had himself by the throat, his legs flailed, his face was contorted in agony.

"We struggle and I try to get away but they hold me and throw the chalk all over me. Now I can't escape into the night—I'll be seen! I hit and kick but can do nothing. Oh! They take me away. I hear the tam-tam, and I'm still struggling, but it's no good. *Moi!*" he cried in horror. *"Chef de canton!"*

He stared at me, thumped his chest, and sat back panting. Erasmus gave me a look that said, "There, you can't say you haven't got your money's worth!"

The old chief wasn't finished. "All the villagers come from every house to play the tam-tam and rejoice. I sit for nine days in a room where they keep me. On the second day they take me down to the river to wash. I eat chicken, rice, corn. I drink palm wine. Old men come to calm me, but I can't leave."

"And what were you thinking in the room?"

"When I was locked in the room I was thinking, 'Ahh. If I knew, if I knew, I would have escaped, gone to Gold Coast like the Tsamenyi. But now here I am, an important man—it's not good.' After the ninth day they washed me again, then they led me back to my house and my wives and children. The French official called together the chiefs of Agou, Kpelé, all the villages to see me crowned. I had the throne, the crown, the sandals of gold. Even the Frenchman couldn't refuse me as chief! And so I began to work."

He spoke of the duties of the chief, the taxes to collect, the disputes to judge. At the end of it I asked him why he stopped.

A long sigh. "I alone can tell you the truth of this. *Metsi, metsi.* I was old, I was tired."

"Not because of politics?"

"What do you mean, Georgie?"

I repeated an explanation the chief had given me: that at the time of independence there were two factions, the Unités and the Progrès. The Unités wanted immediate independence, the Progrès gradual decolonization from France. The old chief had been a Progrès, and when the Unités won a popular vote, they replaced him with the present chief.

He slowly shook his head. "That wasn't the reason. I could go on being chief after that if I wanted."

So, finally, I asked him about the rumor: the murder, the trial, the imprisonment. He listened with his eyes averted, his sunken jaw working. Even when he spoke, he didn't look at me.

"It is true, there was a man killed. He was an evil man. We have two kinds of magic. There is the kind I do—I heal the sick, settle quarrels, drive away evil spirits. But there is also black magic, which men use to kill people and sow strife. He was a sorcerer, a jealous man. I have never done black magic. If you want, you can come to my house next Sunday and I will perform a ceremony with a cock."

I said I'd like to very much; and then I pressed him once more about the rumor. He didn't answer, but instead stood up, and said that as it was very late, and he was very old and had spoken at length, he would leave me now. I took the lamp and led him to the door. Passing my bedroom he paused, looked inside, and wagged a finger at me.

"Georgie, you must find a girl in the village. There are many— only, you are too cheap. It's not good for a man to sleep alone."

A week later, at eight in the morning, I was standing inside his house, watching him handle a rooster over a basket of leaves. He lived behind the chief's compound, in unassuming quarters, with a concrete stoop and a corrugated roof—reddened with rust—and a skim coat of concrete chipping off the mud-brick walls. These rough-casts always gave a village house a decaying, defiled look, but they carried prestige.

The night before, the old chief had collected three basketfuls of leaves of the *ama* vine, wood from the vine's roots, and dried stems of the *notsigbe* plant. This I knew from Erasmus, who stood behind us, sleepy-eyed, grinning foolishly, my ubiquitous interpreter. The old chief had already laid an armful of fetish objects on the leaves: three small bottles twined with bark strippings, tarred together and smeared with chicken feathers, and tarred to them the wood figure of a man eight inches high, his wild eyes painted white, his lips thrust out; two brown gourds; and a horsehair fly whisk. The old chief looked solemn; his eyes were hard and clear.

With his free hand he took a flask of *sodabi* from Erasmus and poured a few drops on the floor, splashed more over the leaves and fetish objects, and then started speaking in a rapid monotone. It sounded like a chant.

"He says he's going to kill the cock for the ceremony," Erasmus said near my ear. I could smell that he'd already gotten a start on drinking. "He says they must answer."

"Who?"

"The ancestors!"

Sodabi was passed around in a shot glass and I steeled myself for a dose on an empty stomach. The old chief spat his on the leaves.

"Now he's asking the leaves to be efficacious."

With a flourish he dangled the cock, bound at the claws and squawking, over the basket, and held out a hand for a kitchen knife from Erasmus, first assistant surgeon. The old chief plucked feathers from the throat, placed the knife against the pimpled skin, and sawed back and forth as blood spurted over the blade. The bird screeched and flapped its wings, but the knife sank deeper until blood was flowing freely and the head hung from just a few sinews. The body twitched several times, then went limp. The old man dripped the blood over the leaves like a chef pouring salad dressing, ripped a handful of feathers from the breast, and scattered them on the pile. They stuck to the bright red trail.

A little boy with a shaved head who'd been lurking in the corner took the cock away for preparation. The old man put a handful of seeds and bark in his mouth, chewed, and spat into the basket.

"The seeds of the *tenyui* plant," Erasmus muttered. "They give the leaves force."

The old man grabbed his own crotch through the *pagne* and flexed a loose bicep. *"La force! Tu connais?"*

The big basketful of leaves, *sodabi*, blood, and spittle was reduced by scorching, pounding, and grinding into a bowlful of black powder fine as soot. The old man said nothing was stronger than this medicine, *zoglozo*. It cured all kinds of ailments—malaria, snakebite, impotence, jaundice. Stirred into liquor—*sodabi* or white man's whiskey, but useless with the weaker drinks such as palm wine, millet beer, or even white man's beer—it was poured into incisions made on the ailing part of the body, where it entered the bloodstream and began to heal. Drunk, it entered the spirit and protected you against the evil eye of sorcerers like the one who'd been dragged out of the village and beaten to death. A miracle juice, medicine for soul and body, it sold for an astronomical sum—six thousand francs for one cup. But the old chief had to avoid the reputation of a quack and couldn't sell it to get rich, only for healing purposes. I offered to buy a thimble's worth, but he gave me gratis three generous spoonfuls in a miniature bottle of Long John Scotch. Then he took out his razor blade and moved toward me.

The sight of it broke a spell. I'd been light-headed, captivated almost as much as during the oral history. I felt the privilege of an initiate; the old man's trust moved me. Perhaps if I'd found a bottle of rubbing alcohol to clean the blade, I would have gone along with his treatment. But a dirty razor blade brought me to myself, and I passed in favor of a glass of powder mixed with *sodabi*. I knocked it back. Dregs clung to the roof of my mouth and stained my tongue black.

We were standing out in front of his house, the smell of roasting fowl heavy in the air. The old man put a bony hand on my shoulder.

"Georgie," he said, and fixed me with a long steady look, as he'd done in the bistro. But this time he wasn't sizing up my intentions. *"Wonye amé enyo."*

Erasmus had disappeared but I didn't need his help to understand that the old chief was telling me I was a good man.

"Wonye Laviéto." I was one of them; I should stay here with them. I only needed to have my body covered with charcoal, he told me, and I would be his true son. The hand lay on my shoulder like a blessing. He asked when I was leaving.

"At Christmas I'm going to Europe."

"You will come back?"

"I will come back. I'll be here until June."

He smiled. Suddenly he looked quite frail and old. His eyes were moist. Perhaps we each had the same thought in our heads: that after June we wouldn't see each other again.

It didn't rain that afternoon. The next day was windy and bone-dry. And it didn't rain again for months. The final harvest had been even more meager than the summer's; the late heavy rains had rotted much of the corn crop. The village was already hunkering down for the long parching, the wait for March. The next evening, thinking of the sadness in the old chief's eye, I remembered T. S. Eliot's "Gerontion":

> Here I am, an old man in a dry month,
> Being read to by a boy, waiting for rain.

In his essay "The Crocodiles of Yamoussoukro," V. S. Naipaul makes a distinction between two African worlds. "There was the world of the day; that was the white world. There was the world of the night; that was the African world, of spirits and magic and the true gods. And in that world ragged men, humiliated by day, were transformed—in their own eyes, and the eyes of their fellows—into kings, sorcerers, herbalists, men in touch with the true forces of the earth and possessed of complete power. . . . To the African—however much, in daylight, he himself appeared to mock it—it was the true world: it turned white men to phantoms."

Naipaul is writing about black slaves on Caribbean plantations in the nineteenth century, but his words also describe the spiritual divide he found in the Ivory Coast, in Abidjan. "The new world existed in the minds of others. . . . The skills could be learned, but faith in the new world was fragile. When the President went, and the foreigners went away (as some people wanted them to), would the faith survive? Or would Africans be claimed by another idea of reality?"

It seems a simple idea—simple enough to border on the facile. But in its simplicity lies a deep insight. The worlds of memory and magic into which the old chief decided to initiate me—worlds that most younger Africans either were ignorant of, despised, or kept behind doors—made up this separate realm of the "night world." The secrets of the past and fetishism lived in his imagination, presided over his better half, realer than anything Lavié had become. They peopled the world of the night self, born in the deep past before the white man's war, attuned to the hidden power of nature and words, at one with the village, the woods, and the dead.

But the old man had to live in the day world too. And that self (just out of jail? who knew?) was tired and useless, the walrus sleeping on the rock every day, ignored or secretly ridiculed by the schoolchildren who, I heard, used to stand at rigid attention when he walked by. Now he was an uneasy ghost in the day world; I imagined him waiting for death to release him from it.

Naipaul's paradigm makes sense of a good deal of the mess of contemporary Africa, until you come across a man like Erasmus.

I ran into the chief's secretary inside the bistro a few nights after the ceremony with the cock. A big, stooped man with a grizzled beard, he usually expressed a sort of hangdog lugubriousness, his lips spreading into the beginnings of a besotted grin. Tonight the expression was exaggerated with his third or fourth *sodabi*. To me Erasmus had always been a comic figure. As the chief's all-purpose assistant who never had anything to do, a paper pusher in a village of farmers and artisans, he seemed as absurd as his name. Never roaring drunk, he was always buzzed. More than once I heard the old chief make fun of him; in the old chief's shadow, translating the sacred rituals into sixth-grade French for the benefit of a *yovo* visitor, Erasmus got the worse of any comparison.

Tonight, standing at the counter in the harsh light of an Aladdin's gas lamp hanging overhead, he reminded me of his labors as interpreter. I'd given the old chief a bottle of Scotch for his tales, a bottle of schnapps for his magic. Wasn't there anything for Erasmus? Why hadn't I come by to greet him since the ceremony?

I quickly stood him another *sodabi*. Kodjo, the half-idiot *boutiquier*, poured out two shots from a green glass jug. Erasmus tipped a dribble onto the floor—the ancestors' portion—then the rest went down the hatch.

"You also owe me four cigarettes," he said.

After another round of *sodabi*, on me, I discovered that the Aladdin's lamp was moving across the ceiling. I leaned with Erasmus on the bar while he smoked a foul filterless Gauloise.

"You know," I sniped, "smoking is bad for you."

"Eh, yes, I know. But I only smoke one a day, and at night, when it's not so dangerous." He paused while this theory sank in, then added: "I smoke and drink *sodabi* to forget my cares."

We went outside and sat on a stone bench against the bistro wall, looking out at the road. The old men were gone from under the mango tree, home for supper. Lamps came swaying up and down the hill like swollen fireflies. Across the road women crouched with paraffin wicks flaming out of tin cans; old men and children wandered over to buy matches, soap, peanuts; they kept their voices low out of respect for the night. A breeze blew and the moonlight was watery and already beginning to disappear behind dust clouds. Harmattan was coming. Erasmus's words hung in the air with his cigarette smoke.

"What cares?" I asked.

There was his father, who'd died when he was still a boy and left him with no one to give advice in times of trouble. There was his first-born son, deaf at birth, deaf to this day at age twenty-three. There were his other children, struggling to finish primary school when their peers had already gone off to CEG. There was his own position as the chief's secretary.

"I'm not considered in the village, Georgie," he said plaintively. "I work as secretary, I'm head of the RPT in Lavié, I'm on the water committee, the building committee—I do all these things which are important for the village. Still, I'm not considered."

He threw away the butt, and the red ash fell apart in the dirt.

"I don't know what role I play anymore, here in the village. If I knew that my children considered me and did well for me, then inside myself I would be at peace. But no, they don't listen to me. I've become nothing here. *Nul.*"

He poked his thick belly; and his eyes, bloodshot with drink, watered pathetically.

To which world did Erasmus belong, the day or the night? One might answer, "He's a man of two worlds," but on this night it occurred to me that he was really a man of none. The old ways weren't alive for him as for the old chief; he had pinned his hopes on new ways, but now he found he was without a firm identity in the village, ridiculous, "not considered." Erasmus wasn't attractive to me, as the old chief was, and in fact his confessions embarrassed me; but he was a half-drunk reminder that something had changed since the old chief's days and that the change could claim victims.

What disturbed me was not the notion that the night world was the "true world," but just the opposite. The night world was true for the old chief and a few others, lingering in fragments of memory and ritual. In a year or two, when they died, it would go, too, leaving the residue of Authenticity. The faith in the new world would survive. It already snaked through on the paved road, the *yovomo*; it coated the mud walls with a concrete roughcast; it showed up in Emma's sky-blue dead *yovo* dress and the sewing machine Christine had sold for her Caesarean and the dreams of selling cloth that still broke her sleep. It hardened every time a village boy left for Lomé, or Abidjan, or Lagos. It throbbed in the head of Kumahia, the agriculture teacher stranded on the plateau, and in Dossavi's village "ennui," and in Yvette's fantasy of movies and cigarette ads. The Africans weren't in danger of contamination from the ideas of foreigners like me. Their faith in the new world was stronger than mine.

What disturbed me was this: that, having lost or been robbed of or abandoned the old chief's world, they would find that the new world didn't come, and they would go on planting and teaching in the margins of the new state, under the new chief, waiting a little more for the chance of a better life that always eluded them.

CHAPTER 12

The New Chief

NE HUNDRED DEGREES, AND THE MIDMORNING SUN burns through early harmattan dust clouds onto the schoolgrounds, where students, teachers, and village VIPs await the arrival of the distinguished visitor. The students stand in rows, shifting their weight, shielding their eyes from the sun. Teachers, Dossavi, the chief, the elders, the parents' committee, sit facing them on benches under a flimsy shelter of palm branches laid across split-bamboo slats that are supported on a frame of bamboo trunks. The students hurriedly put up this *apatome* the day before yesterday, when word reached the village that the provincial governor of the prefecture of Kloto—the *préfet*—was coming to deliver an important speech at CEG Lavié. The shelter won't last out the day; its only use is for this occasion of state. In the meantime, classes have been suspended and the sound of drums and chanting has carried on for two days, punctuated by the barks of Agbefianou, the teacher in charge of *animation* rehearsals: "Not like that! Together!"—the goatskin stirring.

We have waited in the sun for ninety minutes. It is eleven o'clock; the *préfet* is an hour late, and the students are finally permitted to sit on the grass. The elders who aren't dozing have started to cluck. Dossavi turns to no one in particular and says wryly:

"The chief is not *late*. The chief has been *delayed*."

A *3ème* boy posted as a sentry on the far side of the primary school by the paved road sprints onto the grass.

"He's coming! He's coming!"

Students scramble to their feet, dusting off their bottoms, and try to form orderly rows. Drums behind them strike up, and the dancing begins out of sync. Faces under the *apatome* that a moment ago were yawning or quarreling or laughing drop into the neutral, closed-mouth expression fit for a public occasion. Voices are extinguished. There is the sound of an engine on the dirt trail winding down past the primary school between the first-grade room and the latrine. It is unlikely that a four-wheel vehicle has ever come this way. A green Peugeot 504, emissary from the world of the state, history, and progress, bounces through the dust, scaring up two chickens.

A week before the *préfet*'s visit I was taking my morning bucket shower, with the shortwave radio outside the stall tuned to BBC. Suddenly I realized that the news reader was talking about Togo.

". . . the government of General Gnassingbé Eyadema has announced the discovery and suppression of a coup plot believed to have the support of Libyans . . . unidentified Togolese involved . . . local press has been denouncing unpatriotic elements . . ."

No one in the village had uttered a word about a coup; perhaps no one knew. Lomé might as well have been a thousand miles away. Aside from the constant public celebrations, which had nothing to do with the actual business of running a country, politics was the unspoken secret here. It was the affair of *les grands* in the capital; it vaguely concerned the village; but nothing the village could do would change anything. To the peasants the Eyadema regime was always there, an accepted fate like malaria or drought. Every now and then it intruded on their lives, in the form of a drop in the price paid for farmers' cacao or a speech by a functionary. But the villagers wanted to be left in peace, and so they accepted the price cut, they listened to the speech, they didn't ask questions. *"Pas d'histoires,"* one taxi driver had painted on the side of his van: "No stories—no trouble." Better to mind the family and the fields, and leave politics to the crazy men who want to touch it and get burned.

Functionaries preached the state gospel more willingly than farmers, partly because they knew it better but mainly because anyone with a job had something to protect and owed a kind of debt to the state and its ruler, paid in loyalty and fear. When news came of political turmoil in Upper Volta, Aboï had told me, "That's why all of Togo prays for General Eyadema. As long as he lives we have peace." Those with something were too afraid of losing it in the maelstrom of African life to oppose the government; and those with nothing were too busy toiling their supper out of the soil to think of the government at all.

Aboï had believed what he said. Among others who doled out the state pieties, I was never certain that I was not hearing a tape recording played back for reasons of self-protection, self-promotion, or sheer indifference. Sometimes mildly critical remarks were lobbed in the general direction of the government, but never on the really crucial points. I once heard a farmer muttering about the year's bad rainfall; somehow the government was responsible. Teachers objected to taxes on their low salaries and to rules against taking their students to bed. These complaints were fairly safe because they steered wide of the points—corruption, artificially low prices for crops, political imprisonment, the complete suppression of free speech, the sham democracy—that could hurt, that brought up the basic question of Eyadema's legitimacy. And when conversations drifted dangerously onto that course, Togolese detoured them with innuendo, ironic euphemism, subtle analogy, or silence.

"When we touch on African regimes in my political science course," a student at the Université du Benin told me, "we never mention this one. We speak of Senegal, Guinea, Ghana. Those we are free to criticize. Everyone knows that a comparison is being made with Togo; it is like a joke that we are all in on but no one can laugh at. So the comparison comes out indirectly. A really brave professor might say, 'Any students who want to discuss this further can come to see me later, but I don't want to pursue this in class.'"

I was aware mostly of the silence. Even Eyadema's name went unspoken in private conversations, especially at night, as if the sound would attract undesirable spirits like the other dreaded name, Sakpaté. People went to elaborate lengths—"the big man," "the one in Lomé," even "that guy there"—to avoid it. Silence meant fear, apathy, ignorance. And so by well into my second year in the village the regime seemed to exist only in *animation* songs and gaps of speech.

Then, in November, came the voice over the BBC, and the *préfet*'s visit a week later. Things began to change.

The chief of Lavié has finished his introductory remarks. They are addressed to the students in a highly inflected, formal Ewé, and the tone is cautionary. The chief's domed forehead shines in the sun and is creased with his usual public expression, worried dignity. Sweeping his *kente* aside he retreats back under the *apatome* to take his seat among the VIPs.

Drumbeats pop in the heat. The boys and girls—a moment ago rigid—are swaying in another round of *animation*, singing out a welcome to the president: *"Woezo, woezo, Gnassingbé!"* But Gnassingbé himself is not here, and the village has to settle for his local incarnations, the *préfet* and the head of the RPT in Kpalimé, seated side by side in the low armchairs provided, under the spidery shade of the *apatome*. The RPT man stands up to speak.

He is nearly obese, squeezed into the functionary's uniform of trousers and a matching leisure jacket; his fleshy face has a naturally jolly, benign look, and the solemn frown he has turned on the students squinting out on the grass seems to require a constant effort, like a man sucking in his paunch. Applause rises among the kids and the VIPs behind him, then dies. The sun on the white blouses of the girls is dazzling.

"There has been a *laisser-aller* in this school, a lack of discipline and conscience here. You avoid responsibility. You should devote yourselves to study, but instead you go into Kpalimé to enjoy yourselves with city types of ill-repute."

Using French, he has skipped the usual formalities and gone straight to the point. A low murmur spreads among the students— neither protest nor assent, but a mixture of surprise, amusement, and the simple acknowledgment that he is speaking about them. A few of the elders grunt in agreement.

"Your teachers must set you an example, for they are your parents at school, your moral guides. Instead, they neglect their work and expect the state to pay them at the end of each month. And your parents, too, instead of forcing you to do homework, have no interest and distract you with too many chores at home."

The grunting of the elders has stopped. The VIPs sit stock-still, their faces unreadable. From the students come scattered "uh-*huhs*" at the mention of chores.

"It cannot go on. It must stop. The future of the country is in your hands. The eyes of Togo and of its leader, General Gnassingbé Eyadema—"

Here the RPT man stops, a mechanical stop, and at once the assembly bursts into the applause required after public mention of the name.

"—are upon CEG Lavié. Discipline, work, patriotism, duty. The country has set the task for you. School doesn't end at twelve or five o'clock. It should continue when you leave the schoolgrounds and go home. Togo wants—Togo demands—independent initiative on your part, individual research and study. The *crise économique* must be broken, and you can all do great things for your country. But if things go on as they have started here, in this climate of *laisser-aller* and laziness, then shame and ostracism will fall on you. The Rassemblement du Peuple Togolais, avant-garde of the people, and our president, founder of the RPT, His Excellency General Gnassingbé Eyadema"—pause; applause—"are counting on you."

In spite of its harsh content, the speech doesn't sound like a diatribe. The RPT man has purged his voice of any trace of ire, harangue, or mockery; he uses a monotone. And the response is equally neutral. Three or four times, when he reverts to Ewé— talking about the goings-on in Kpalimé, he uses the Ewé word for prostitute, *ashawo*—a titter or guffaw escapes from the audience, and he and they are bound by a sudden intimacy. These asides are the only sign that he is speaking to them and they are listening; as soon as he returns to the official French, detachment sets in again. At the end, as the RPT man sinks back into the armchair next to the *préfet*'s, the faces of the assembly, students and VIPs alike, betray nothing of what they've heard. Dossavi, for whom the speech has been an indirect humiliation, is sitting with one arm draped over the back of his chair, his lips slightly pursed—the smallest hints of displeasure. The others have fixed the RPT man with expressionless black eyes.

Vendors crowded the unpaved streets of Lomé, selling Seiko watches and unpackaged socks. One of them, a small, barefoot boy, hawked a comic book called *Il y avait une fois . . . Eyadema* (*Once Upon a Time . . . Eyadema*). On the book's glossy color cover, against a background of village scenes, battles, and parades, the face of its hero stands out under a military cap: the coal-black, unsmiling face, eyes slightly dull and ill at ease, of the early photographs of President Eyadema.

If you showed the slightest interest, the eager salesboy would trot alongside, open the comic book, and flip through its pages. A series of cartoons told of the president's simple life as a village boy; how the scowling, square-jawed French killed his father doing forced labor on the *route nationale*; how on January 13, 1963, as a sergeant, he bravely shot the evil Olympio, who was trying to climb a wall into the American embassy; how on the same day four years later, as a lieutenant colonel, he toppled the corrupt new government and took power; how today, as general, he continued to rule in peace and justice. Climactic moments punctuated the tale—Eyadema pardons a would-be assassin, Eyadema emerges from the flaming wreck of his plane as an onlooker exclaims, "*Zut!* He's alive!" The boy would close the book and try to bargain the price with you.

The comic book was a token of Togo's political life. Eyadema displayed himself in a collage of heroic images; its short history was a fairy tale told with poetic license. Though Togo had only one major road, electricity in just a handful of towns, and a population that was overwhelmingly illiterate, for over twenty years he had kept himself constantly in the public eye and ear. He blended a mythic aura, ideas stolen from here and there, and force.

I saw Eyadema once, in my first few weeks at the Peace Corps training center in Atakpamé. He had appeared at a military base nearby in Temedja, and afterward his motorcade cruised into town and wound its way through the hills above. We heard a siren and rushed to the gate to look down at the road. A few police cars flashed by, seconds later two Mercedes, and then a black convertible, top down—and standing in the backseat, in a double-breasted suit with wide lapels, Eyadema. Seeing a band of cheering Americans, for a moment his stern face broke into a smile. He waved. The motorcade rushed by. On a muddy road lined with banana trees and crumbling huts, where little goats scurried out of the way, an African president appeared like John F. Kennedy, a mirage of Western power.

In the middle of Lomé another mirage appeared. Near the commercial center, the Hôtel 2 Février rose thirty-seven stories into the humid air. Nothing nearby—nothing anywhere else in Togo—was more than a few stories high. Alone in a huge empty parking lot, the luxury hotel imposed a skyscraper's steel and glass on a shantytown where chickens shared the road with taxis. Uniformed doormen stood idle outside. Only three or four floors were ever occupied, since tourism and business—despite Togo's best efforts at P.R.— brought in just a trickle of visitors. The tower's upper floors were as empty and silent as the asphalt desert below. Eyadema had built the 2 Février a few years before with French investment when he hoped the Organization of African Unity would take up quarters in Lomé. It didn't, and now the Togolese government and the French backers lost millions of African francs every day. But profit hadn't been the main purpose of the hotel: the 2 Février was a monument to Eyadema's glory; its name came from the date of the triumphal entry into Lomé, nine days after Sarakawa.

In the parking lot's center, atop a pedestal on a green knoll, stood a twenty-foot bronze statue of General Eyadema. Dressed in an officer's uniform and beaked cap, feet apart, face unsmiling but benign, he extended an open hand toward the lot. The image presided like a giant idol over the new complex, and the hand gestured to invisible throngs that the hotel, the ministries with their gold-tinted windows, the glittering convention hall of the RPT, which Eyadema founded—all were his. In this gaudy, deserted landscape the rain-stained bronze was Togo's Statue of Liberty, but it commemorated a man who had real power; running the country, Eyadema became the country.

Regularly, every five or six months, an event transformed the capital: President Mitterrand's visit, the All-Africa Trade Fair, the pope's visit, the summit of the Economic Community of West African States, President Mobutu's visit. Grandstands sprang up on the ocean road, posters were plastered onto downtown walls, T-shirts went on sale at the Grand Marché, banners were strung up over the main avenues. Dancing went on for days, and the event itself became the climax of a frenzy of anticipation. Then, when the moment had passed, and the grandstands (like the *apatome* at the CEG) had been removed, and the banners taken down, the city was already preparing for the next time. Like a couple keeping a marriage afloat by throwing party after party, Togo survived politically on these periodic spasms. The celebration that attended these events served the same purpose as the fear generated by the suppression of the semiannual coup "attempts." Each was another proof of Togo's unity and importance; each redounded to the glory of Eyadema. And his trips abroad provided more proof, more glory. When he visited the U.S. in 1983 begging for aid to stave off bankruptcy, his half-hour audience in the Oval Office managed to produce this triumphant aphorism in the official government daily: "It isn't only the great countries which produce the great leaders."

La Nouvelle Marche (*The New Course*) was the only daily newspaper in Togo—a dozen tabloid pages with the irregular lines and typos of a college rag. It reached Lavié two or three days late, the north after a week. A congratulatory letter from Eyadema to another head of state on that country's national holiday, affirming Togo's warm friendship, made headlines—even if the country was hostile, like Benin next door. A photograph of Eyadema receiving the ambassador of Brazil might occupy the lead space. These sorts of "news" stories relegated the real news of African wars and the dire state of the economy to distortion on the inside pages, or to oblivion.

Mention of Eyadema at the top of a story required five lines alone, for day after day he was "President of the Republic, General of the Army, Minister of Defense, President-Founder of the Rassemble-

ment du Peuple Togolais, His Excellency General Gnassingbé
Eyadema." The titles returned throughout the story, spiced with
heroic epithets like "The Man of Peace," "The Man of January
13," and "The Father of the Country" (rewriting history, for in fact
while Olympio lobbied the U.N. for independence from France in
the late fifties, Eyadema was fighting in the French foreign legion
against Algerian rebels). His American equivalent would be George
Washington, Abraham Lincoln, Ronald Reagan, and Caspar Wein-
berger—all stuffed into one large-sized pair of shoes.

His face, and only his, appeared everywhere. There were no other
public figures. Across the lot from the 2 Février, at the convention
hall of the RPT, you could buy a watch whose face showed that of
Eyadema fading in and out as the second hand swept past each
quarter minute. Policemen, functionaries, and careerists in general
sported on shirtfronts a gold badge bearing his image; market women
wore *pagnes* printed with row after row of images of his face. In
every restaurant, hotel, school, even in the Lebanese shops on the
ocean road in Lomé, from the capital to the most remote town in
the savanna, his picture was displayed—either the earlier one shown
on the comic book's cover or the newer black-and-white close-up,
smiling in a business suit, more confident and plumper. The recent
photo hung from the mezzanine balcony in the cavernous lobby of
the 2 Février, a ten-by-ten-foot blowup staring down on guests.

The name was no less ubiquitous than the face, appearing on
Eyadema schools, stadiums, avenues, T-shirts. The repetition of
name and face mesmerized like the chant of a new national myth.
And, as myth, it produced a vague suspicion in me that this was all
a grand illusion, that the real Eyadema looked nothing like this face
and had another name, that he was nothing more than the man
behind the curtain. Sometimes I wondered if he existed at all.

The *préfet* stirs and rises. He wears the standard functionary's suit,
in olive green. A gold badge gleams on his breast pocket. Like most
Ewés he is short and round-faced; his features have the dullness of
a man who listens to requests, if at all, from across an ornate desk
and with no need to justify his answers. But buried somewhere must

also be the sycophant's fear: he is a creature of the regime, and the same power that has exalted him to this level of blandness could disgrace him in a day. He lives in the official residence of the *préfet* of Kloto prefecture, an estate in the hills on the far side of Kpalimé, along the road toward the Ghana border, where, in the middle of kapoks and banana trees, streetlights magically spring up for a hundred meters, turning down an asphalt driveway that descends to a villa half hidden in the trees. The *préfet*'s green Peugeot is chauffeured by his bodyguard, a big policeman who is now leaning against the tree outside Dossavi's office, in khaki shorts, black knee socks, and a black de Gaulle cap, dusting off his uniform.

"*Eyadema—toujours—au pouvoir!*"

The *préfet*'s shout immediately echoes in the crowd: "*Eyadema—toujours—au pouvoir!*" the students cry. "*Eyadema—toujours—au pouvoir!*" the teachers, the chief, and the elders cry, as automatically as Catholics repeating the Hail Mary. It is an invocation, a piece of political cheerleading, an oath of fealty, a summons to the spirit that presides over this occasion. And an irony underlies it. The *préfet*, an Ewé, is leading an Ewé village, in the region of Togo that has always produced the country's civil servants and its cash crops, in uncoerced cheers for the Kabyé president, the *petit nordiste*, who in shooting the Ewé president took all power for himself, for life.

In the glare of the sun, now directly overhead, irony is hardly perceptible. The *préfet* is stalking back and forth just inside the shade of the *apatome*, raising the shout again, and getting the same echo:

"*Eyadema—toujours—au pouvoir!*"

In power forever? It might just happen. Some African presidents were great figures in the nationalist movements of the fifties and ruled godlike after independence: Zambia's Kaunda, the Ivory Coast's Houphouët-Boigny, Tanzania's Nyerere, and Senegal's Senghor are examples. Others—in Burkina Faso, in Nigeria—have come and gone in semiannual turnstile coups. On a continent where leaders are either fly-by-night soldiers or near-divines, Eyadema is almost unique in having been both. The only comparable ruler is Mobutu

Sese Seko of Zaire, from whom Eyadema took "Authenticity" and much of the other paraphernalia of his reign.

By the time the *préfet* came to speak to CEG Lavié, the reign, in its various borrowed forms, had become set in stone, Eyadema's will and goodness as unquestionable as a father's to young children. Rule by personality cult had an advantage over sheer dictatorial force. It appealed to affection as well as fear, and part of Eyadema's success in surviving (the first priority of any dictator) lay in not having been as ruthless as other African autocrats. There had been no massacres of the Ewé, nothing like the tribal slaughter in Burundi or Zimbabwe. The army hadn't run amok in the bush, unlike Uganda's, nor was its loyalty being bought off with the national treasury. Soldiers wore badly fitting uniforms and boots pieced together secondhand, and a few of them stopped me in Lomé to ask for spare change, making the fingers-to-mouth gesture I was more used to seeing from children.

Eyadema's corruption was in scale with the size of the country. Mobutu made himself one of the world's richest men in a dirt-poor land, but Eyadema, though hardly ascetic, had a smaller appetite. The steel skeleton of his new villa, looming on a hill over his tiny home village beside the *route nationale*, was left half built throughout my years in Togo, a road sign not just of harsh economic conditions but of Eyadema's relative restraint. When a whale was spotted, he flew out over the Gulf of Guinea in his helicopter and machine-gunned her as a hunting trophy—a petty corruption. He was an African hero-chief in a business suit, but not vicious. War and genocide were two ideas he had not borrowed.

Of course, he was not above the more common methods of dictators. No free speech was tolerated, not even the whiff of an opposition. Only in my last months did any Togolese friends speak about politics. There were the usual rigged elections and rubber-stamp national assemblies. Amnesty International reported frequent detention without trial of suspected "opponents," and state torture was less than authentically African—electric shocks. Most of this was impossible to learn inside the country—easier in Boston than Lomé—but toward the end I began to hear stories of political imprisonment and murder. One student who refused to join the RPT was held for eight years, and died shortly after his release. After the periodic coup "attempts," a few suspects were put on trial in the State Security Court, convicted on meager evidence, and left to rot in jail without light, air, or decent food; a few have been executed. A rival general named Koffi Kongo, who had favor with the French, was said to have been murdered in his bed. And in 1985, after a series of anonymous bombings in the capital that came in the wake of the pope's visit, a number of people were arrested, including several university professors, for "distributing subversive literature." One man died in prison; there were wide reports of torture and abuse; an Amnesty team was turned away at the airport. The government eventually gave itself a clean bill of health through an official commission that included a suspect Eyadema had magnanimously released.

Eyadema's Togo was a country that would have been totalitarian if it had had the means; but without electricity, access to the bush, and a large army and well-trained police, it fell short of absolute control (perhaps this qualified it, in the current jargon, as "authoritarian"—a totalitarian country with kerosene lamps). Underneath his costume—whether the business suit of the president, the uniform of the mythic hero, or the white robe of the African chief—Eyadema was, naked, a dictator: "The Father of Togo" shot his way into paternity. Yet he demanded nothing of the Togolese except attendance at the annual political fêtes and applause when his name was uttered in public. Students sang of how "happy" the country was, old men turned ancestral chants into new hymns of thanks to their "liberator." But these were easy words, symbols of obedience. Once villagers took care of the superficial signs, they were left alone. Eyadema had not published a little red or green book of sayings, "Eyademism" wasn't taught at the Université du Benin. He had no ideology to impose.

The regime's garb was patchwork. "Authenticity" came from Mobutu. But the black Mercedes and double-breasted suit that appeared on the muddy bush road were Western. Togo received transfusions of money from the U.S. and from France, which trained the army; and the foothold of these two countries on the west coast of Africa won Eyadema a reservoir of goodwill. When the American ambassador to Lomé said in an interview in our Peace Corps paper that one of the first duties of any president was to keep order and that Eyadema had done a good job of it, he was giving the American blessing for sham elections and for the arrests, torture, and indefinite detention without trial that were going on in the city where he spoke—assuring Eyadema that dollars would flow in spite of the necessary unpleasantness of internal security.

And although by the end of 1983 Togo was surrounded by three "leftist" states, *La Nouvelle Marche* made no reference to "Communist infiltrators"—in fact, Eyadema had close ties with Kim Il Sung of North Korea. More than once I saw a boy at the Kpalimé station in Lomé peddling works of Marx and Engels alongside the women with oranges and peanuts. The newspaper provided the obligatory slogan, *"La Révolution Togolaise."* Still, the wife of a French businessman shopped in the elegant SGGG foodstore in Lomé and carped at the slow cashier; her children attended the Ecole Française; her husband did a good business to the benefit of nobody but himself and his French company, and didn't even bother to close the office on Economic Liberation Day. The Europeans' and Asians' houses and businesses were never confiscated as in Uganda and Zaire, nor did the Lebanese shopkeepers have to worry that this week's radio would announce a "radical, authentic action"—meaning forced exodus. Eyadema demanded African names, but the shops stayed in Lebanese hands.

Democratic, Communist, revolutionary, authentic: the slogans, like the political costumes, meant very little. Most African leaders have adopted one foreign ideology or another, but Eyadema changed his shape as often as Proteus. National tourist posters called Togo *"L'Afrique en Miniature"* because the terrain went from tropics to savanna; politically, too, with its confusion of borrowed identities, the country was a small image of the continent, lately decolonized, now adrift. Togo was all things to all people, as mutable as the chameleons that scuttled in the bush. When Eyadema wrote to Mobutu in the paper, he used the Zairean's preferred title, *"citoyen"*;

Kim was "comrade"; on Mitterrand's parade route, signs proclaimed "RPT—Socialist Party: Same Objective, Same Ideal." Public life became an elaborate ritual of contradictions in which everyone agreed to play along.

The sergeant-president of this sliver country, with its artificial boundaries and its chimerical history, spent a lot of money and words on the endless assertion of his legitimacy. When the old chief of Lavié was seized at night in his house and colored with chalk and locked away for nine days, legitimacy did not need to be asserted. But that past was erased; and out of the void the new chief of the new state could invent himself and his myths. It hardly mattered that these had nothing to do with tradition or the village. Eyadema told the people they were happy, and they wouldn't say he was wrong. Togolese politics didn't go beyond this balance. Caught between a dying past and a dangerous future, between African soil and Western development, and between the two hungry super-powers, Eyadema's Togo reflected them all and had no real face of its own.

"Recent events in our capital have compelled me to address you on a weighty matter. A perfidious attempt against the government of Togo has been uncovered and swiftly put out. A group of students at the university and some of your older brothers up in Adeta involved themselves unwisely with certain Libyan spies in order to bring about a coup d'état. Their fate is sealed, and it is not a happy one."

The *préfet* announces this grim news like a pharmacist reading a prescription. By the time he begins it is past noon and the students, swaying in the sunlight, have been allowed to sit again. A few of the younger ones, cross-legged, lean together and whisper. No one seems to notice or care, because the *préfet*'s speech is not directed at any of them individually, or even at the abstraction of the group, but for the benefit of the absent chief, *le grand* in Lomé.

"We are in a time of great threat to the security of the country. The primitive disorder that reigned before the restoration of peace must never overtake Togo again. New ideas are always welcome within the cells of the RPT, and we encourage them. But nothing in human enterprise can be accomplished without discipline. The RPT is large enough to allow everyone to have a word—but no one who goes outside it can be tolerated. Togo has no need of some"— for the first time he pauses and gropes for a word: in the lull the mumbling of an elder is audible behind the *préfet*—"some 'natural socialism,' the democracy of foreigners. Togo has its own democracy. The people have spoken. In 1972, again in 1979, they decided, *Eyadema—toujours—au pouvoir!*"

He has been losing his audience in the meanderings of abstract nouns; now the cue line catches them off guard. The shout comes back raggedly.

"We have our democracy, we are happy with it," he continues. "Don't be seduced by the false ideas of the UB [Université du Benin] traitors. Disorder, disunity, must be uncovered and crushed." Suddenly his voice rises with what sounds like anger, as if he has finally realized what he is saying and has seen the patient black faces out on the grass for the first time. Their sun-drenched gaze stays blank. "I urge you to denounce dissent wherever you see or hear it: at school, in the village, even among your family and your friends. Togo will thank you for it. But as for the possibility of dissent among any of you—well, great pain would lie in store for you, and you could be sure never to make Lavié your happy home again. *Merci.*"

The drums strike up again. The students, unmarked by any trace of the speech, are back on their feet, doing what they know to do, their bodies moving in synchronized rhythms: "Eyadema—*eh!* Eyadema—*eh!*" The *préfet* doesn't wait to hear out the song. He climbs into the backseat of the Peugeot, and the policeman in shorts and knee socks gets into the driver's seat next to the heavy bulk of the RPT man. The engine grinds and starts; the car is quickly lost in a cloud of dust as it trundles out of the grounds, along the trail between the first-grade room and the latrine of the primary school, to the paved road that will return the *préfet* to Kpalimé and affairs of state. A farewell cheer goes up from the VIPs, but they don't wait for the end of the song either. Already they are on their feet, their thoughts going ahead home to the midday meal, now an hour late. By three o'clock the *apatome* is gone.

In the weeks after the suppression of the coup "attempt" something in the atmosphere of the country seemed to change—though not in the way a Westerner would expect. There were no public protests or even rumor mills grinding away. On the surface very little changed at all. If I'd been here four months and not a year and a half, I would have noticed nothing. The daily "Word of the President" in *La Nouvelle Marche* exhorted vigilance for a few weeks, and checkpoints on the roads into Lomé increased, but there were no mass roundups and arrests. Life was going on as before. And yet, for the first time, there was a kind of politicization of the general mood.

From the beginning politics here had struck me as being a child's game. It was a story told in a comic book that a little boy peddled. If Eyadema was the "Father" of Togo, the people were politically his children. Cheerfulness about public issues and a willingness to wear the Eyadema blazon defined the awareness of nearly everyone I knew. The spectacle of photogenic Togolese adults singing mindless slogans of praise, the cringing before any superior, the bogus elections, the badges, the lies—the mental atmosphere had filled me with loathing and despair, and above all boredom. I'd forced myself to lose any interest in it.

Now I felt a change in the air. After a long dry season, the slightest breath of moist wind carried a smell of suspicion and discontent from the coast. For the first time the dictatorship became palpable to me.

"Let's not talk about it any more now."

The teacher sitting in the bar in Atakpamé had been telling me about the Mouvement Togolais pour la Démocratie. I hadn't heard before now that a Togolese resistance existed, in exile in Paris, led by Olympio's survivors. Barely a movement, inept at penetrating and organizing inside the country, less Togolese than Ewé and less democratic than pro-Olympio, all the same the existence of the MTD startled me. So a handful of Togolese actively opposed the regime. Perhaps they'd been involved in the latest coup attempt.

The teacher, Amewolo, a small, intense man I'd become friends with through a volunteer in Atakpamé, was talking about the MTD not as an advocate but in neutral, descriptive tones. Now he said of the regime, "There are many who oppose it. I don't know anyone down here who is pro. Only, they are all afraid to speak."

"Down here" meant in the Ewé south. And to illustrate his point about fear, the pervasive sense that anyone could be an informer—to the extent that it was risky not to turn in someone who spoke *"contre"* in your presence, since he might be acting as an *agent provocateur* and turn in *you*—Amewolo told me a little story.

"The MTD publishes a newspaper—*Le Combat*. You don't see it in Togo. But I heard of a guy working in an office in Lomé who had a co-worker, and this co-worker wanted his job. And to get it, he smuggled a copy of *Le Combat* from Ghana and planted it on the guy's desk, and he attached a note: 'For your subscription.' Things worked perfectly. The guy was thrown in prison, and the co-worker got the job. That's all it takes."

But just then there was the noise of a motorcycle outside the bar, and the teacher abruptly shut up.

Another teacher came in. Lanky, with four thick horizontal scars across both cheeks that signified he was a northerner, the man was introduced by Amewolo as the physics instructor at his CEG. There was the usual round of handshaking, finger snapping, greetings. The physics instructor joined us for a beer. The conversation turned to school, to the trimestrial exams coming at the end of November. A notice had been issued from the Atakpamé Inspection that the country was going onto a trimester school year and that from now on exams would be written by the regional authorities. As we talked, night fell quickly, and the physics instructor—with another round of handshakes and pleasantries—got up and left. The sound of his motorcycle faded up the road. Amewolo turned to me.

"I know the noise of a Honda motor. I never speak to this guy about any of these political things, or even talk in his presence. He's an agent for the government—we all know that. He reports on the rest of us. If he'd heard us speaking, it could have been quite disagreeable."

It was a breakthrough to find out that people thought about politics at all, but in this atmosphere I had to work hard to find out anything of what they were thinking. A regime that threw a man in jail on an obvious plant—as if a subscription to *Le Combat* could be delivered in Lomé—didn't pay much attention to the difference between innocence and guilt, still less that between thought and action. The dictatorship didn't need to find the few real subversives if it could make enough examples of its law-abiding citizens. In a country whose political consciousness was so raw, arbitrary cruelty was a better weapon against opposition than an organized campaign of suppression.

What really worked in the state's favor was Togo's minuscule size. Everyone knew everyone else; everyone knew an informer. And so I was careful whom I spoke to, for others' sake and mine. It was a remarkable achievement for the regime that a Togolese, in his own house, in a bush village, at night, had to glance out the windows, close the door, and lower his voice to a whisper, before admitting that his government was repressive and corrupt.

But Togo's smallness worked against the dictatorship as well. Not long after the coup "attempt" I had to go to Lomé to publish the Peace Corps paper with a few other volunteers. On the way down from Kpalimé something happened that was revealing about the political climate of these weeks; in a sense it was typical of the whole time I spent in Togo. It happened at an army checkpoint.

I had seen roadblocks in several African countries, and no two countries ran them quite the same. In Ghana the police lowered a railroad-crossing barrier to make sure the driver stopped, put him through a lot of hassling questions and ironic banter, bargained a bribe, and then let him proceed. In Nigeria the submachine guns dangling off the shoulders of policemen served the purpose of the barrier; the bribes were steep, nonnegotiable, and paid off with a minimum of time wasted in arguing or wisecracking. Togolese checkpoints were signaled not by railroad barriers or Uzis but by women seated along the roadside with tables and trays of brochettes, oranges, and laundry soaps. And, since Togo was a military regime and dirt-poor, the guards' shacks were manned by ragged soldiers rather than smartly dressed police. A driver had to do more cringing here than elsewhere, but he stood to lose less money.

Our taxi had hit eight or nine checkpoints in the last ten or fifteen miles; a normal Kpalimé-Lomé run had no more than four. As we passed the outer suburbs, the *gendarmerie* camp, and the Lycée Technique Eyadema, we were stopping every five minutes. Today, four weeks after the attempted coup, the troops looked dead-serious.

"Unload all of that!" a big soldier yelled at the driver as he stepped out of his van for the fifth or sixth or seventh time.

"Mon patron," the driver reasoned, "your comrades just searched everything, back in Assahoun."

"Unload all of that, I said!"

Unless they really thought that we might have taken on a few sacks of pipe bombs in the bush outside Assahoun, they had coordinated nothing between posts. It didn't matter: they were not looking for bombs, only a way to assert authority. Two dozen bags were hauled out of the back and off the top. Three or four soldiers stood by, leaning on wood-butted rifles that looked antique, and barked orders while the passengers unzipped bags and opened baskets. The soldiers plunged their hands in and explored shirts, *pagnes*, and mounds of tomatoes. I had two bags. A young soldier with a shaven head, wearing fatigues that were much too small for him and lacked a name tag on the breast, was feeling something interesting in my backpack.

"It's your valise, *yovo*?"

I nodded.

"What's this? Show me."

Out of the backpack I fished my Sony Walkman. I held it up. *"Magnétophone."*

The market women were milling about with trays on their heads. Passengers counted change for snacks while they waited out the search.

"Magnétophone?"

He took the Walkman and studied it carefully from several angles. Then he looked at me. "You're lying."

"I'm not."

"You're lying! I don't like lying, *moi*. I serve the president of the republic. I like the truth!"

"I'm telling you the truth, *mon frère*."

"What's going on here?"

The big soldier, obviously the boss, had come over to check things out. He glanced at the tape recorder.

"It's yours?"

Wanting to laugh, and also feeling my throat parch up, I nodded.

"May I see your identification?"

I took out my Peace Corps card. It had long since smeared with sweat, the photo gumming in the fold.

"Corps de la Paix?"

That's what the card said. I said, *"Oui, patron."*

"What's your work?" This was a highway interrogation. He was challenging me, trying to make me slip on something.

"Prof. d'anglais."

"Prof. d'anglais?" I nodded. "You are where?"

"Lavié."

"Lavié? Lavié here?"

"Oui, patron."

"Mon vieux! My uncle is in Lavié! He's the pharmacist!"

I ransacked my memory. A face appeared, wizened, a wart the size of a jelly bean beside one nostril, a shelf of miscellaneous pills in the background. "The pharmacist—Eklu?"

"My uncle!"

"He's a good friend of mine!" I said, lying now.

A friend of the pharmacist's was a friend of his. He laughed over the coincidence, and I laughed, too, and at his insistence I wrote down my mailing address. The soldier without a name tag had wandered back to the guards' shack. Bags were being loaded into the van and both of mine were returned to me, *magnétophone* and all. The big soldier said he would write me—he'd always wanted a European pen pal. He said he understood how lonely it must be, away from my mother and father, since his parents lived up in Badou and he'd been stationed out of Lomé for three years. But the soldier's life was meant to be hard, he reminded me, just like the volunteer's.

As I boarded we shook hands through the window. I liked the man. It wasn't until we were approaching the next checkpoint that I realized they'd forgotten to look at my other bag. I might have had a high-powered rifle in it.

It was happening all over again. I'd seen a stampede here before, at the grass-roofed bar outside the Hôtel Concordia in Kpalimé, the Africans at tables or on the dance floor—sudden shouts, tables upset, the sound of glass breaking, people running for the gate, scaling the wall onto the street. Fifteen months before, my first thought had been, *Someone has a gun.* Instead, the thatch over the bar had started smoking and a fire-panic broke out. This time the image of fire came first; I was wrong again. Someone had a gun—soldiers, dressed for action in green fatigues and mesh helmets, clutching rifles, hustling through the open gate. A few people were being seized, but the soldiers didn't approach me and Amewolo, my friend visiting from Atakpamé. He grabbed my sleeve and pulled me to a hasty exit through the gate.

We rode my moped in silence across town to another bar. Closed, dark. The same at the next. The only place in Kpalimé still open was the bar-restaurant at the luxury Hôtel 30 Août.

"They don't harass the *grands*," he said, "only the *petits*."

Troubled, and tired of motoring through deserted streets, we started out of town. By now only market women were about, and soldiers standing in groups of three or four; their helmets gleamed in our headlight. On the hilly road back to Lavié the noise of the Motobecane filled the night and insects flew out of the cool blackness into our faces. Behind me Amewolo was thinking out loud.

"Oh, my country! It's martial law, this curfew. They just want to make their power felt, intimidate the young people. My country!"

He explained what I'd already guessed, that since the "attempt" the government wanted to let the citizens know who was in power and the danger of opposing him. Just a gesture, as superfluous as the *préfet*'s visit. People knew the power, and the danger.

The next morning, before he returned to Atakpamé, Amewolo and I had breakfast in my living room and talked over the night's events. He repeated what he'd said, that the purpose had been intimidation, that it had been shameful and unnecessary. One would have hoped that after so long in power the regime would have been secure enough to share control and allow divergent views to be aired. Instead, oppression only grew.

I asked what someone like him could do. He shrugged: nothing. Speak out, and lose part of your salary, your job, even end up rotting away in a dank tropical jail with no light, far from your family and village, without a woman, without music, without the things that made life, in spite of its hardship, worth living. I pointed out that others elsewhere had done just that: the French in the resistance, the Algerians in their war, the peasant militias in Central America; thousands had gone to jail and died for this cause—

Amewolo held up a hand to wipe away my romantic image of the African freedom fighter. "Those are different cases, they are not the same people as us. Yes, thousands have died. But we Africans are different. It isn't cowardice," he said, *"mais nous aimons trop la vie"*—"we love life too much."

CHAPTER 13

Cicada Philosophy

EGIMES, LIKE COAL MINES, PRODUCE SLAG. THOSE that elevate their own survival above everything else, and devote as much time and scarce money as Togo to smelting history out of myth and unity out of apathy, don't pause over a few wasted lives. Wastage is necessary to survival. And even pausing over such lives here is not easy to defend. On the scale of African horrors these have to rank fairly close to the bottom, well below famine and forced resettlement in Ethiopia, apartheid in South Africa, or civil war in Angola, less spectacular than the cloud of poison gas that swallowed up hill villages in Cameroon, less lurid than tales of cannibalism in the old Central African Empire. No headlines spring to mind.

The only compelling reason for me to write about three of these Africans is that I knew them well, almost from the beginning of my time in Africa, though I grew particularly close to each of them toward the end. Their stories are different in many ways; nonetheless they belong together for the intensity with which they've stayed in my memory and the pattern they've formed there. If pressed to phrase it, I might say that they all made the mistake of taking the state seriously when it talked about the idea of development. They paid in varying degrees of failure and humiliation, but the drama here was psychological, staged in schools and iron-roof compounds, not battlefields or death cells. None of them joined the resistance, since no resistance existed inside Togo; they didn't have revolutionary ideas or even political ambitions; their ambitions were pathetically conventional.

If these stories—stories so slight next to the greater nightmare of contemporary Africa—are worth telling it's because they don't often get told, yet they are probably being lived out, in different versions, across the continent: a residue of its recent history.

I met Simon Tamekloe during my first week in Africa, at the Peace Corps training center near Atakpamé, where he'd been hired as a technical instructor for the new batch of volunteers. My first impression was of a barrel-chested, bass-voiced man standing at the blackboard in front of a class of thirty or forty twelve-year-olds, staring them down.

"What's this? It's a pen!" he would boom, brandishing a Bic and moving up and down the rows, pointing rapid-fire at the children— "You? You? You? You?"—until, within thirty seconds, the entire class (breathless, on the edge of their seats) had repeated the catechism, "It's a pen!" When a boy wandered in late, Simon Tamekloe swept his arm toward the door and cried, "Next time you come late I will not let you in, I will drive you away!" And when another boy's brother missed several classes, he called the boy to the front and demanded: "Akpo, where is your brother?" Taking notes on his technique in the back of the room, I silently filled in the answer: "I know not. Am I my brother's keeper?"

He was a god in any classroom he entered—the God of the Old Testament, terrible and just. He never carried a whip, and he didn't need one. He mastered his pupils with a judicious mixture of glares and praise, and no one felt safe from the staccato bass voice. "You? You?" Every class was a piece of theater. The round face, with its prominent ears, broad nose, and wiry strands of beard, took on and then threw aside a series of masks: the impish grin with tongue between teeth when he was pleased or amused, the fierce stare with the mouth contracting to a frown when he wanted to intimidate.

Self-caricature played a part in Simon Tamekloe's teaching, and even more in his expansive, literate, ribald wit. He savored the English language like slices of expensive foreign cheese; his sentences flowed out in elegant shapes colored by elaborate metaphors that always seemed a little archaic—"She would howl like a fox on a cold windy morning!" "Power is sweet like honey to taste but it will stick to your fingers and you can never let go of it"—the usage of a man educated in the English system in Ghana, and steeped in American and African literature, who had never lived in a country where English was the first language and who read as much of it as he heard.

One evening, transfixed by a Chinua Achebe novel, he came into the room where I was lying under a mosquito net and intoned:

"When I touched her hand she brushed me away, when I put my arm around her shoulder she said, 'Don't touch me!' But when I began to play with the little beads around her waist she pretended not to notice, because—silence . . . means . . . consent. *Shilensh*"—the slur was for prurient effect—*"meansh conshent!"*

Then he laughed—or rather, a laugh erupted out of him, shaking his shoulders, roiling up from his thick belly into the throat and out of the mouth in small explosions that involved not just his whole body but me as well. And for weeks after he only had to come up to me and murmur, "Shilensh meansh conshent," and immediately we were both in cahoots and stitches.

Simon Tamekloe's showmanship was put on at least partly for the benefit of the Americans he had to spend his summers with. He acted out the Africa and the African he expected them to expect, making fun of himself, of other Africans, and (though they weren't always aware of it) of the foreign whites being treated to his wit. "When an African tells you 'No problem,' " went one of his refrains, "that's when you begin to worry." It could seem like self-mockery, or racism turned against his own people, or ridicule of white anxieties—a little joke from whose hidden edges no one, least of all you, was quite safe.

I got an insight into his showmanship when I learned that, even though Peace Corps continued to hire him for teacher training, he'd quit teaching after sixteen years and was trying to start his own business. He wanted to run a tour agency. He had already printed up business cards in raised type: "Livingstone Tours. Simon K. A. Tamekloe Esq. (Voodoo Tours Specialist)." But for now, without a business license, he had to content himself with occasional commissions from the Togolese government when English-speaking groups arrived in Lomé. His descriptions of the tourists mixed affection, amusement, and disdain:

"Twenty-five black Americans, direct from Chicago and Detroit. They come to Africa singing, 'We shall overcome!' They ask to see the slave forts, the Bé voodoo market, the artisanal center in Kpal-imé, and, since it is the extended version, big game up in the Keran Reserve. I show them everything, and they say, 'Ooh! Look at that,' and do you know what? The entire trip I want to tell them, 'You shall never overcome this way. You say we are your brothers, but to us you seem like whites.' Ha-ha!"

Simon Tamekloe always delivered the goods. He was among the best English-speaking guides in Togo; his knowledge of African religion and ritual was almost scholarly—partly learned in universities here and in Ghana, partly self-taught—and the eloquent monologues kept his groups enthralled. But the routine of the tour guide hid layers of complexity that seemed to peel away in his humorous accounts. He liked the tourists and relished his own performances, but he was aware of being asked to sell them a fraction of the truth of Africa, of the Africa he had to live in. The foreigners came to buy a privileged glimpse, sighed over the Africans' simplicity, and then went home, never realizing that Simon Tamekloe had worn masks out of economic necessity, or that he had been wearing masks at all.

The first time I knew I was seeing the real face came one evening toward the end of the summer. He had arrived late at the communal dinner table, and since most evenings his voice and laughter animated the meal, tonight his silence was conspicuous. He fixed his eyes straight ahead as if no one else were at the table with him, and left as soon as he'd finished eating—rudeness in Africa. Then he disappeared for two days. When I saw him again I asked where he'd gone. His answer was brief and unadorned with metaphor.

"I have lost my new son. I went to my village to bury him."

Later he described to me, without a trace of his tour-guide hype, the ceremony he'd gone to perform. The newborn's hand had to be cut off before the burial; that way its spirit, now unintact, wouldn't return to the mother's womb, be born again, and die again, a perpetual curse to haunt his parents.

After that Simon Tamekloe and I stopped being African instructor and American trainee and became friends. He lived, I was beginning to learn, under the influence of several perpetual curses. In Ghana he'd passed his O levels, completed a correspondence course with the University of London, and taken a degree from a local teaching college; but he never received his bachelor's degree because of financial difficulty. Now, at age forty, with ambition still burning and a wife and five children to provide for, he'd enrolled in the Université du Benin for a B.A. in literature. But a new regulation forbidding teachers from studying in the university had been thrown in his path about a year before I met him. Simon Tamekloe requested, and got, a meeting with the minister of education.

"I listened to him for a long time while the man told me what a superb teacher I was. He said that the country had an urgent need for its best teachers to stay in the field. Finally, when he was finished, I asked him if his own career took him straight from teaching to the cabinet without benefit of higher degrees. Then he became angry and told me he wasn't there to listen to the arguments of CEG teachers. Why did he agree for me to come in, then?"

He quit the profession and stayed in the university. Shortly afterward he found a job as public relations officer for one of the beachfront luxury hotels in Lomé. It meant overwork to the point of exhaustion, and didn't pay even as well as teaching, but it brought in enough to support his large family while he continued his studies. Through the hotel he designed and led "Go to Togo Tours," a series of cultural excursions for English-speakers, in the city, around Togo, and across the border into Benin. But he was still on the government's string, making less than fifteen dollars a day from commissions.

All of this he recounted for me over the last weeks of training. In his eyes two decades of teaching English to kids had been enough;

he owed no more debts to his country, and the arguments of the education minister were a cover for the resentment and fear high officials always felt toward talented, ambitious underlings. With a relation in the ministry, Simon Tamekloe might have been able to win support, but he had none and now he had to go it alone. A foreigner, he said, might wonder why Africans like him couldn't be happy with having any job at all. But no European would be happy, he answered himself, and the minister of education hadn't been happy, living like that, without a future, without goals. Why should he?

"For so many years," he told me, always able to invent new ways to laugh at himself, "I've been like a chicken that eats its own eggs."

After training I didn't see Simon Tamekloe often, and between visits the intervals got longer. Things continued to work against him. With the economic crisis threatening to bankrupt Togo, the government was ceding more control to foreign investors, including control over the hotel that employed him. But whites, even neo-colonial ones, still didn't have all the answers for Africa. Under the tight management of a French company, the hotel cut back, laid off, and began to lose its luxury-loving European clientele until, after a year, occupancy was down to about 20 percent. And Simon Tamekloe was out of a job again.

He scraped by on the odd tour arranged through one company or another. He had to drop out of the university for a semester because of lack of money, and for several months counted on the largesse of a younger brother. A business license would have solved many problems. The hundreds of thousands of francs the government made from the tours they counted on him to give would have been his if he could have run them privately. But the down payment on a license to start his own operation, he'd been informed, was twenty million francs.

"I sat there looking at this petty official, thinking, 'You sitting there with your big fat ass, have you saved twenty million? You're paid better than me and you haven't saved a sou.' They give a license to any Tom, Dick, and Harry who comes in off the street with contacts or a few million. But they go on sucking me when they need me, and then spit me out. It is the purest hypocrisy." His reputation among foreign tour groups was growing, but his personal fortunes didn't change.

Then, overnight, everything changed. A miracle descended in the shape of an eighty-year-old black American woman on one of his tours who invited him to give some talks to the Freeman's Afro-American Genealogical and Historical Society in Houston. At last he had a ticket to the country for which so much of his life had been a preparation.

Several months after his trip I saw him in Lomé. He brought out a suitcase full of proof that incredible things had happened to him. What a scene at the Houston airport, where he arrived in a full-length royal-blue embroidered *bubu*, carrying two suitcases, one packed with African shirts and robes (in Lomé he always wore designer jeans and pullovers, but as an African in the U.S. he put on nothing but traditional clothing), the other with bottles of coconut oil mixed with crushed pepper and shrimp, and pillowcases full of *gari*, the grated manioc Togolese sprinkled like Parmesan on every dish.

"The customs man was as tall as an ostrich and as white as corn flour. He orders me to open my suitcases, and sees the bottles of coconut oil. 'Wut's thi-yus?' he says, the way they talk in Houston. I tell him he can taste it if he wants, but he won't like it. One sniff and now he's as white as boiled yams. Then he starts squeezing my pillowcases and when he opens them, oh Lord, George, you should have seen his face change. He's running all over the airport with my sacks of *gari* asking every Tom, Dick, and Harry if they think it is cocaine. Oh Lord!"

Lectures at colleges in Houston, colleges in Louisiana. Write-ups in the local black newspapers. While he was gone I got a letter: "Since arriving on the 9th I have been performing this noble and honorable assignment with great success. . . . As a result of my success, I have been exposed to some high personalities including the honorable mayor of the City of Houston."

More engagements arranged through new contacts in California.

Days spent as the guest of a couple on their houseboat in San Francisco Bay, where a stream of Marin County residents came to pay for divination and magic ceremonies. Seminars with psychologists, parapsychologists, healers. "There I am," he exclaimed to me, "with my big apelike body, receiving every manner of local charlatan. Such social confusion!"

We spent two hours on the suitcase of relics he'd brought back from America. Then he fell silent.

"I came back here," he said finally, "and I didn't have a sou to show for the trip. Nothing changed."

Simon Tamekloe was still out of regular work, still renting three rooms around a sandy yard in a compound near the ocean without electricity. His wife had just given birth to their sixth child. His latest scheme, African Cultural Studies Tours (he'd printed up a prospectus on a red letterhead, with a logo he'd designed), was stalled for lack of foreign investors. Letters arrived from Americans he'd met; a philanthropic woman in Arizona wrote that she would try to help him but was more interested in India and in fact was about to take a trip there. He had me decipher the letter word by word.

"What does she mean when she says this? Two months ago she wrote that she was very interested in me. Does this sentence mean she will really try to help? Is India more important than Africa?"

A Chicago doctor and a Detroit judge who'd come on a tour had promised to provide room and board if he went to study in the U.S. They didn't want money to get in the way of such an impressive man's prospects. Now the judge was being investigated for misconduct on the bench, and the doctor had stopped answering Simon Tamekloe's letters. I noticed on his desk, next to a pile of used paperbacks—Achebe, Hardy, Twain—a thick stack of business cards. He'd collected them from everyone he came across, tourists in Togo and Americans on his pilgrimage to the U.S. On the back of each card he'd written reminders and instructions to himself: "A young Afro-American lady in the group of East-West Holidays that came to Togo on the 8th and left on the 9th November. She shows interest. Write to her for business."

The cards were messages in bottles that had washed up on his desert island, tantalizing signs that rescue was near. The vision of the West had always haunted Simon Tamekloe. There was the correspondence course with the University of London, the afternoons reading college brochures in the American Cultural Center, the Peace Corps Volunteers, the tourists. Then, for a couple of months, he was rescued, and perhaps it was more fantastic than he'd ever imagined. But on waking up in Lomé again he found that the rescue had been a dream and hadn't left a trace. He was exactly where he'd been.

"I don't worry for myself, but what will become of them?" he said, closing his suitcase and motioning outside the door, where his kids were skipping and clapping in the sand. "What am I making for them? What prospects do I have?"

By this time even the sympathetic Americans who whirled through his life and left him with promises and business cards, and then were reincarnated as letters from overseas, their promises now more tentative, their letters more infrequent, until their existence dwindled to the cards in his stack—even they had begun to try his faith.

But it wasn't gone; it seemed to me it would never go completely. The last time I saw Simon Tamekloe in Lomé he was sending his résumé to the doctor in Chicago and the judge in Detroit. Chockfull of projects he'd undertaken on his own, the résumé was a twenty-year record of initiative and hard work, enough to impress any college admissions dean. Then he spent an hour painstakingly addressing the two manila envelopes.

"I'm like a puppet dangling on a line," he said as we went out to mail them, "manhandled and manipulated this way and that for the pleasure of onlookers." And his body shook with laughter.

Yawovi Mensah never got as far as Simon Tamekloe. When my "lawyer" in Lucien's trial and partner in the health campaign was still a *lycée* student, his father—an old farmer and herbalist in a village south of Kpalimé—told him it was high time he quit school and started working to support his parents. Mensah, who didn't have enough money to support himself, had to drop out of school and took a job as a primary school teacher. Ten years earlier his level of education would have been enough to teach in a CEG (twenty years earlier teachers were so scarce that you only needed to have completed a level to teach in one); but now with the glut of civil servants and the deepening *crise économique*, he was lucky at age twenty-eight to be teaching French and arithmetic to eight-year-olds in a school outside Kpalimé that consisted of four thatch huts.

Someone else might have cursed his fate, and sunk into the sullen and occasionally sadistic ennui in which many minor functionaries dragged out their years scattered up and down the country. But Mensah had other plans. "I never lose faith in my future," he once told me.

Slight and frail, with a goatee, vaguely Oriental eyes, and a domed forehead that receded high up his scalp, he had the look of an Italian philologist, or a Buddhist priest, either one an oddity in West Africa. Even his voice was anomalous, pinched and nasal rather than the usual hoarse baritone. He wore jeans and Peace Corps T-shirts, played the Beatles on a guitar that was missing one string, and wrote autobiographical novels that would never get published in Togo. A place in the West was already set for him: the grad student in English or philosophy, wry, undernourished, drinking coffee in all-night cafés. In Togo all of this made Mensah an exotic creature, and potentially an undesirable one.

There was trouble with his father. The son revered the father's knowledge of plant remedies and Ewé aphorisms, but the father never understood the son's pursuit of education or his living away from the village. And when Mensah brought home the twenty-year-old seamstress who shared his cramped room, to introduce her as his future wife, the old man refused to let a girl from another village, one he himself hadn't chosen, into his house. Mensah went ahead with the marriage, and his father cut off all ties.

Mensah's health was always bad. Malaria ravaged him, subsided, flared up, and ravaged him again. One morning I visited his room on the edge of Kpalimé, with its books, guitar, secondhand black-and-white TV, and wallpaper bizarrely patterned with American colonial figures. Sylvie was making tea; Mensah lay naked and sweating under the mosquito net, emaciated from the disease and a nearly lethal dose of chloroquine he'd gotten at Agou. He didn't recover for weeks.

He could hardly afford to support a child, but Sylvie, who'd quit school after *4ème* to take up sewing, refused the pills he bought for her. A difficult pregnancy ended in the stillbirth of a son. She had been Rh − and Mensah Rh +, but doctors only tested the fetus in the last weeks and by then it was too late for the immune globulin; Sylvie's antibodies had begun to destroy its blood. Within three months, against a doctor's advice, she was pregnant again. This time the infant, delivered through Caesarean section, lived, but the wound opened up four days after the birth and Sylvie nearly died from infection.

By then Mensah was broke. An uncle to whom he'd signed over future paychecks had blown it all in a binge of drunken generosity. Mensah faced four months without salary and years of debt. "In Africa, when a relation comes for a favor," he said, "you don't even ask, you trust him. I trusted my uncle, and he did this to me."

On top of everything else, he had a series of run-ins with his superiors. Some of Mensah's idiosyncratic ideas came from the Peace Corps training he'd received, on his own initiative, in health education, and which he'd gone on to turn into instructorships at other Peace Corps training programs. But his approach to education, I thought, had more to do with his own gentleness and intelligence than with the "progressive" theories of the American manuals.

He never beat the kids. "If you whip them," he once said, "they will obey you today but forget everything you teach them. Then you'll have to whip them again tomorrow. But if you can keep yourself from using the whip, eventually they will love you and love what you teach them." Instead of the goatskin, he used moral pressure and heavy doses of punitive homework. He encouraged his pupils to ridicule classmates who violated the rule against using Ewé. It may not sound especially enlightened to an American, but it was a radical change from the way Togolese children expected to be taught. He knew, as an American wouldn't, how far to go; he knew that a softer tactic would be disastrous. He also had the advantage of dealing with primary school kids, who brought their home rearing to school but not an indelible experience with a sequence of Dickensian teachers.

And his method worked. His classes quickly showed the highest test scores and best grades, and the eight-year-olds became devoted to the thin young *maître*. His success attracted attention, and his technique was subversive enough to rile the principal, who insisted that Mensah use the whip like other teachers. When he refused, the principal took his damaged vanity to the Inspector for Education in the First Degree in Kpalimé.

Mensah had already bumped up against this man once, in an incident he related to me with a wry smile.

"The inspector had us all assembled at his office for a conference on conduct in the classroom. He began by telling us that if one of the children falls ill in the classroom, we have the authority to give out medication. Nivaquine, for example. I raised my hand. There was a case of a nurse who gave chloroquine to a child without a diagnosis, and when the child subsequently died the nurse was held responsible and thrown in prison. I asked the chief if we teachers would be protected from this kind of charge.

"He answered, 'I said nivaquine, not chloroquine.' I said, 'Well, nivaquine, chloroquine, they're both of a base of quinine. But would we be protected?'

"Now he got angry. 'Mensah,' he said, 'I don't need a medical lesson from you. If you and I were in medicine, I would be a doctor and you would be a nurse. Don't teach me about medicine. I, too, have eaten at the table of Europeans!'

"After that I was silent. I have learned to be silent at these meetings, since questions are taken this way. But even my silence is interpreted as criticism. You have to be *for* this man."

His extracurricular Peace Corps work, far from winning points with the inspector, was taken as a sign of arrogance and insubordination. The encounter had been like a warning; and already the principal was trying to have him transferred to another school.

An alternative path had been cut off when he took and failed the CAP, the exam that might have led to certification as a primary school principal. Having prepared for months, he was crushed; he suspected fraudulent results. When the lists of passed and failed were made public his name was on neither, and he only found out he had failed when he went to the Education Ministry in Lomé. An oversight, he was told. Given the other tales I'd heard of fraud and cheating on exams, his suspicions didn't seem paranoid. Now he was asking himself if education, for which he was so naturally suited, was the best line of work to be in. He had begun to form a new image of himself: that of a farmer, in his old village, studying law and philosophy, raising coffee and cacao, and writing things that his children, and a few others, might read someday.

Then the same authority that spent so much of its energy frustrating the plans of people like Yawovi Mensah inexplicably changed its mind. He passed the CAP on the second try, and was promoted by the primary school inspector—the same one who'd played doctor to his nurse, who'd enjoyed a few meals at the white man's table— to be principal of an important primary school in Kpalimé. There was no explanation; power was still unquestionable.

"Now this inspector loves me like a son," Mensah wrote me. "He has finally understood my value and has told me that I'm his best principal. He invites me over often. Only he can't apologize, because he's a Chief."

Sometimes authority in Africa doesn't change for better or worse, but simply leaves a life dangling like a side of beef on a butcher's hook. Then the dilemma becomes less practical than existential, raising paradoxical and perhaps unanswerable questions about what use such a society has for such a life.

This story starts with an African archetype: a boy, raised by a family of cacao farmers in a tropical village, sees school as a way out of hard labor and poverty, the only way. His parents keep him working in the fields until several years past the normal school age, but once in class he quickly overtakes his peers through intelligence and hard work. A priest at a monastery near the village notices him; and when the father, out of need or jealousy or fear, threatens to take his talented son out of primary school and send him back to the fields, the boy runs away from home to the monastery. The priest takes him in and begins sponsoring his education. The boy sends word to his parents that he is safe; within a few months he is visiting them; but he never lives in the village again. At ten he has already made the first leg of the long journey away—only a matter of ten or twelve miles, but irrevocable.

When the boy is in his early teens the priest takes him to France, where he spends four years near Rouen being disabused of the notion, so hard to shake for most Africans who have never left Africa, that the white man's country is a paradise. The school has new textbooks and glass windows, but his classmates taunt him. He finds the French aloof and arrogant toward their former subjects, an impression later confirmed at university, where even the ones who become friends never seem entirely sincere, and hold back from real intimacy.

The boy and the priest come back to Africa. But the priest's sudden death in a car accident leaves the boy, at sixteen, alone in his own country. His parents in the village no longer have any idea of his life; he finds he is speaking a different language. He leaves the countryside and comes to the capital without a sou, enrolls at the best *lycée*, and works his way toward the *bac* by washing dishes and writing the papers of wealthier students. His room has no electricity, and at night he studies outside under streetlamps.

The American version of this story takes the boy from his humble origins through school on just two pairs of pants, to a college scholarship and a career as a judge, during which he pays back the poor people who helped him along the way and rights the social wrongs that he struggled so hard to overcome, enjoying his reward of a two-acre lot in the suburbs.

The African variant follows the story line up to a point. Kwamé Amekufui passed his *bac* on the first try, won a regional scholarship to the Université du Benin, and enrolled in the department of philosophy. Through friends at UB he met Americans around the city, volunteers and others, to whom he began giving French lessons, and soon he was making good enough money with this network of students to rent two rooms with electricity and buy himself a petrol burner.

I met him through this network not long after arriving, and very quickly made my closest friend in Togo after Christine. We talked about his mother and father, whom he hardly ever saw now, about Camus and Malraux, African politics, and finally Togolese politics. Apart from an infection that left his sad eyes red and filmy, and his father's heart ailments, which were draining away most of his savings, he was at ease that summer, speaking about the life he was preparing for himself with an introspective calm and a liquid accent that came from northern France.

Here the story shifts a little. Instead of sailing through his exams at the end of his third year, Kwamé failed them. This meant not only repeating the final year on a dwindling scholarship, but missing his first chance to enter the job market and start earning a living. He suspected fudged results. In his classes he'd been outspoken— blurring his opinions with the required indirections—about African underdevelopment and its origins in corruption; as a leader in a student organization he'd offended a professor. This man sat on his examination panel and alone among the three members voted to fail him. There was nothing to do but take the courses and exams over again.

The next year, with his antagonist off the panel, Kwamé passed with flying colors, and at once submitted his name at the Ministry of Education for a teaching job in the high schools. A month went by with no word, then another, and another. Because of the *crise économique* it was the worst time since independence to be looking for a civil-service job, but his record was superb and he could count on recommendations from his American students. Still nothing came. He was living in his student's quarters, grilling suppers on his petrol burner and stretching out what was left of his scholarship money. He made the rounds of private schools, checked in periodically at the ministry, quizzed everyone he knew with education contacts, and tried to add to his French pupils. And still nothing came.

Lomé wasn't my favorite place to visit, and some practical or psychological need to stay close to the source of jobs tied Kwamé there. When I did go, it was almost impossible to track him down, without a phone, in the Tokoin district just north of the city center, a maze of look-alike concrete-and-iron box houses that had no numbers, on sandy streets that seemed to have no names. So during my first year we lost each other, and only exchanged rare letters with promises of visits.

A few weeks after getting back from Kenya, I ran into Kwamé near the Grand Marché. We sat for two hours outside a beer shack, on a road crammed with money changers behind the market. I was struck by the change that had come over him. He was still looking for work—harder than ever—but as he described his predicament a piece of him seemed to step aside and to look on with a sort of detached cynicism, as if it no longer really believed the things he was saying.

"Friends from UB, ones who have found work, treat me differently now," he said bitterly. "They've dug a pit between us. Before we called each other Kwamé, Kossi, and so on. Now it is: 'Hey! Young man! Want to share a pot of beer with us? It'll do you good.' Sometimes I want to spit in their face, but I hold back. *C'est la vie, George.*"

But when I asked how he was holding up, he assured me, "I'm at peace with myself." Alienation, a divided self—these barely had names, much less acceptance, among the Togolese, even the Togolese who'd eaten at the table of whites. A spell of unemployment and poverty after college didn't qualify as a major grievance here. And so Kwamé didn't expose to me the anger, despair, and self-contempt I sensed he was starting to feel; perhaps he didn't expose them to himself. The concealment became one more constraint on his life.

He had, however, identified a cause of his limbo. When I asked why he thought he was having such bad luck, he smiled and pointed to the scars that ran diagonally across both cheeks. Just after I first met him, he'd told me he wore the tribal marks proudly—they weren't a brand, he'd explained, but a badge of his ancestral heritage. Now he was saying that his bad luck lay in being an Ewé.

"I know of Kabyé, Moba, others who have completed their exams this year and are already out in the schools." He cited other proofs that tribalism and his mildly political career at the university were keeping him out of work. As he spoke his voice rose in anger. None of the big Moslem merchants and Yoruba moneymen around us seemed to notice. But I took the lack of circumspection as a bad sign.

"You know," he said finally, dropping his voice now, "my mother is Kabyé."

"You never told me."

"No, I never did. If it were my father and not vice versa, my problem would be solved." He smiled at the irony.

Somewhere in the middle of his second year of unemployment, reading the handwriting on the walls at home and looking, like millions of West Africans with or without degrees, for work abroad, Kwamé sent a query to the government of Mauritania. And when a favorable reply came back, he didn't hesitate to mail, as requested, his papers and degree. Mauritania was a desert country, a desolate place, but he wasn't in a position to be picky.

A week later Kwamé received a summons to go to the local *gendarmerie* in Lomé. The police had intercepted his letter and confiscated his documents. They gave them back to him, with a warning: no one left Togo without permission.

The reason became clearer when he tried to leave again. This time his destination was Libya. Acquaintances from the university had gone there and come back, after a few years, well off by Togolese standards. Kwamé and a group of friends decided they would try the same route and made plans to take a plane from Lomé to Ouagadougou, which by then had come under Captain Thomas Sankara's brand of African revolution and had regular flights to Tripoli. Qaddafi was offering jobs and easy immigration to black Africans, probably with an eye toward influence south of the Sahara; already he was having some success with Ghanaians and Voltaics. Kwamé didn't care about Sankara or Qaddafi one way or the other; he wanted the work his own country wouldn't give him.

He visited his family the week before departure, fell ill in the village, and came down to the capital a day late for the rendezvous and the flight at Lomé-Tokoin International. He was tracked down by a friend; the others had met at the airport and promptly been arrested and carted off to prison. They were charged with plotting another coup "attempt" with Libyan spies.

Kwamé didn't try to catch the next flight to Ouagadougou. He visited his friends in prison, who told him they were not being ill-treated but warned him not to visit again. He lay low for a while. By now he'd moved out of his rooms in Tokoin to less expensive quarters in a family compound on the northern outskirts of Lomé, a half hour by taxi from the center—"where there is calm," he told me.

The French lessons kept him alive, but they were thinning out. Passing a construction site near the city center one day, he asked for work as a mason's helper and, at a little over a dollar a day, made the month's rent in two weeks. He took a job as a night watchman for a rich Nigerian near the beach and caught malaria from sitting up outdoors all night. Hearing that the government had assembled a crowd of students at the university to express their spontaneous support for the regime, and had flung fifty million francs in wadded bills at them as a reward, he remarked that if he'd known about it he would have been there in the middle of them, jumping up and down, raising his hands, cheering the required cheers.

He said, "You must abandon one personality for another."

The regime became a kind of impotent obsession with Kwamé, like the memory of a soured love. "I have dreams of him," he said to me on a visit to his far-flung lodging, where it was easier to talk than in the bistros and restaurants around the Grand Marché. Even here he spoke of Eyadema in pronouns. "Sometimes we are talking, sometimes fighting. I have cut his throat, and woken up feeling victorious."

In the next moment he was acknowledging the state's power and his helplessness in the face of it. "I used to think of resisting, but what can one do? I am prepared to live my life under that man."

Kwamé was at wit's end. He couldn't leave, but he had nothing to stay for. He idled his time away, made money as he could. But he lacked Simon Tamekloe's natural exuberance, and the fickle god or functionary who had smiled on Yawovi Mensah continued to smirk at him. The last time I saw him he mentioned, half apologetically, as if it were absurd enough to be embarrassing, that the thought of suicide had crossed his mind.

He had been educated to the ears, and sixteen years of school had cut him off from the life of his village. Now the promise of his sacrifice had been broken, and he was trapped in Lomé with a headful of knowledge and nowhere to go. He must have wondered if it wouldn't have been better never to have left the fields.

When I was back in the U.S. his letters reached me, after the usual delay of weeks or months, with assurances that he was surviving.

"I stay in my lodging," he wrote, "writing stories, above all on the subject of my education, which, it seems to me, is now useless. George, I must tell you that just now I am living a period of revolt within myself. And it's a tragedy. Nonetheless, we live. I am in the middle of making a big decision, that of going back to the land in my village and farming it. I have tried many times the route of foreign countries like Gabon, the Ivory Coast, but in vain, for these countries also adopt a policy of protectionism of their people which shows that things are difficult everywhere.

"Above all among us Togolese, working here, there is a fight— a fight where one tries even to harm his neighbor in order to make himself seen by the authorities and gain a position. It's really a shame, George. I have lost everything, everything has become a jungle where the strongest win out. All I can hope for now is to find something better in order to abandon this *box* that is becoming poison to me. So, each day, I think I have to withdraw to the village, work, and live the philosophy of the cicada, which is to say: 'To live happy, live hidden.' "

The idea that once seemed to promise freedom—education, public service, a life of the mind—now had him trapped; the trajectory that had led him so far from the village and the fields was circling round and dragging him back there; the piece of himself he'd cut off turned out to be the piece that might allow him to survive. I tended to see these things in political terms, but Kwamé's dilemma was both more limited and larger than that. He was one African in hard economic times who had a degree and couldn't get work. But his failure was also the failure of his faith in the new world; and he had abandoned a personality for that.

"I have the air of a great pessimist, don't I, George?" the letter went on. "No, not at all, I am very confident of my future, I know that all will go for the best. I'm sure of it."

Dieu est là, ça va passer: the African optimism of bush-taxi slogans and teachers' aphorisms. He still wasn't at ease with being ill at ease. The persona of a malcontent would have no meaning there—would seem like cowardice. But he said next: "My intellectual life is now empty, I spend most of my time looking for money to get by. My spirit isn't fruitful anymore, it doesn't produce.

"You can imagine, then, what the city of Lomé has become."

There were many Kwamés rotting away in the capital—internal exiles, victims of the contradiction Togo had become under Eyadema. *Development* was the watchword all over Africa—the one word, whatever it meant, that everyone agreed was good. When Eyadema built the Université du Benin, he declared it a proud step in Togo's development. But in a country where any idea not originating within "the walls of the RPT" was snuffed out, the intellectuals produced by the university found no use for their minds. The state, far from wanting them to think and act, made itself the biggest obstacle against doing so. Then they became the *préfet*, bureaucratic bolts and fixtures, duly carrying out the borrowed ideas of the one man who could speak. And when even that opening was closed to them, as to Kwamé, they became offal.

The frustration of a class of educated, alienated young people was the only internal threat to the regime. Kwamé and the hundreds like him, to whom much had been promised, but who found themselves unwanted by their society and unable to leave, seemed the only hope for change from within Togo. Already in Lomé you could smell, along with women's cooking oil, the fetid air of discontent.

But the revolution is not at hand. Eyadema might well rule for another twenty years, provided the French and Americans don't decide he is no longer in their interest and stage a successful Sarakawa. No African government has ever undergone a genuine revolution. A handful of middle-level officers assassinate the president, seize the radio tower, execute ministers after show trials, and declare a revolution; they have only added another coup d'état to Africa's endless list. Meanwhile, the vast majority of villagers in whose name the "revolution" was staged continue to break their backs in the fields, and look up one day to find that their children must now have new names and the *animation* songs have changed.

The average Togolese, whether peasants who hoe their yam fields or teachers who complain about their bush posts, don't yet have a political consciousness. Until they do, there can be no democracy in Togo. For them the government remains a fact of life, like rainfall (though much less important). Some seasons the rain is good, some seasons sparse, but each year whatever it is has to be lived with. It would be foolish to throw down your cutlass and stop farming altogether, for then you'd only go hungry. Western leftists who long for the outbreak of Third World revolutions may have to wait years for the spectacle of throngs in the empty lot below the 2 Février pulling down the bronze image to cries of *"Liberté! Mort à Eyadema!"* And when it does crash to the asphalt desert, it will probably be replaced by another statue, another embodiment of the people in one hero; a different face, perhaps, but the same extended hand.

CHAPTER 14

Barcelona

HE LAST WEEKS OF NOVEMBER AND THE FIRST OF December were my happiest in Africa. Not that anything objectively improved in the village; in fact, things were getting worse. We were on the downslide of the circle of village time, the segment of the arc that brought dust and boredom and shortages. The year's work was over, the crops that had been delayed and then stunted by dryness at the start and rotted with rain at the end were harvested, even more meager than last year. The male half of Lavié was entering its four-month cycle of unemployment, and the village was slipping into the doldrums. From the north of Togo came rumors of an impending famine and deaths from starvation, but Lavié looked as if it would be spared high drama, just beaten down again in the old unspectacular way of the dry season.

All the same, I was happy. My third-year classes were reading a story I'd cribbed from *The Merchant of Venice* and Africanized: kings from Mali and Morocco chose among wicker baskets to try to win the hand of Ashra, Princess of Togo. I was paying Christine to cook my supper twice a week, and finding that I actually looked forward to the bowls of stiff corn mush lathered with pungent okra goo. On weekends I hiked up to the *hoëkpe*, the grotto that the brush fires had bared on the plateau and that had immediately filled up with Ewé warriors, panthers, and pythons. Despite the plans of some village boys, it hadn't panned out as a major tourist attraction, and I was usually alone up there, with a book or note pad, in the cool tubercular Sahara dust clouds, looking out over the dying bush and exhausted fields and the road that led to the maze of iron and grass roofs among palms and banana trees. Trails of woodsmoke rising between the huts indicated there was life. And for now, it was enough.

A week before the Christmas holidays and the trip I was planning to France and Spain, the village assembled to celebrate the old Ketekou woman's death. She'd been buried in September, three months of mourning were over, and it was time, a student explained, to come out of grief and reenter the stream of life. Ama and Faustus had spent a lot of money on gaudy invitations—a photo of their deceased mother from at least ten years back, looking grim, superimposed over a white cross soaring in a sunburst out of black clouds, with a list of villagers who'd sent condolences, a verse from one of the Psalms, and an announcement that the all-night wake was scheduled for Saturday in the Ketekou quarter. I gave Faustus fifty francs to cover the cost of printing and promised to be there. Christine and I made plans to go together.

Saturday night, just after dark, the drums started up in the Ketekou quarter, faint, without singing, a low warning rumble like distant thunder. At nine I changed into khakis and the green-and-orange *bubu* I'd just had made by a tailor in Kpalimé, embroidered in gold spirals and arabesques. I passed through the yard, which was dark, and heard water splashing behind the screen by the Agbelis' wall, where the adults bathed. Someone was taking a shower. A woman's form suddenly emerged and was visible like a shadow against the wall. Christine was holding a *pagne* pressed to her stomach for a towel, but aside from that she was naked. Her wet skin glistened in the moonlight, the only light in the yard, and her body came out of its shadow and took on color and texture, a brown smoothness that lost its sheen in each place the *pagne* passed over. I had never seen her legs. Unlike her breasts, she had kept them hidden, and now I understood why. They weren't suggested by what I'd seen above them, the wife's and mother's ruined belly and pulled, withered breasts. Her legs were long, slender, muscled in the thighs and calves by all the work, but unmarred; they still belonged to the girl or sexual woman she had stopped being years ago.

A warm desire was passing through me. It startled me, but immediately I realized it had always been there, only kept hidden even from myself because of the danger of our closeness. And it changed nothing; there was nothing to do even now but turn from this glimpse, which had lasted no more than five seconds, as the sense of taboo grew deeper than desire, and move away toward my door.

"*Meka?*"

Her voice rang out sharp, the way she talked to the kids.

"Oh! Christine. It's me—Fo Georgie."

"Fo Georgie." The voice softened. I could see she was covering herself, but she spoke with a soft pleasure. "You're ready now? Wait ten minutes."

Wrapped in her *pagne*, she went up the stoop and inside. When she came out I was sitting on the log bench under the bougainvillea, and I waited for her to approach. She was wearing a Dutch wax *pagne*, sea green, miraculously elegant, shiny, and unbleached by the sun. She must have put it on once a year. The same material was tied turban-style around her head, and she had on rouge and lipstick too; she could have passed for the wife of a government bureaucrat, except for the lack of a bored face, the rubber flip-flops, and Aku sleeping on her back. I complimented her, she smiled modestly, and we started for the road and the sound of drums. And as if to say she knew that something had passed between us a few minutes before, she took my hand. We didn't say a word all the way to the Ketekou house.

The courtyard was packed. The dead woman's family had rented at least a hundred folding chairs and strung up a dozen fluorescent tubes from the bamboo and palm-frond roof they'd built between huts over the entire yard; an enormous, antiquated generator, also rented, squatted next to the thatch kitchen hut and powered the lights. If Lavié ever got the electricity the chief wanted, it would look like this: harsh, white, with a machine buzz drowning out the buzz of the bush.

The chairs were arranged roughly in concentric circles around a table. Women in their best *pagnes* sat nursing babies on their laps; girls and boys were milling around excitedly. Ama, sitting in the front row near Faustus among the relatives, called out in her husky voice. A couple of farmers circled all the way over from the other side to thank me for coming and give me a shot of *sodabi*. Then Christine pulled me away, and we went to sit with a seamstress she knew. In one corner of the yard I noticed the frail old chief, sitting in a sort of deck chair with a cloth cover, wearing the floppy Buster Keaton hat and clutching his cane. I imagined him being borne in on the chair to watch and preside like a king.

None of the teachers had showed up. Lavié wasn't their village, the state had sent them here, and next year it might be elsewhere; the old Ketekou woman wasn't their kin. Kwamé Amekufui once showed me an essay he'd composed on the custom of all-night wakes like this one. He ridiculed the huge expense, the exhaustion and idleness that followed, the way villagers looked forward to the next death so they could spend another night drinking, revelling, and avoiding work. The traditional value of wakes was gone by now, he wrote; they served no purpose but drunken degradation, and they should be abolished. Wakes stood in the way of development.

The essay might have raised a riot in the Ketekou compound tonight. At the table in the center of everything the musicians were rolling their drums like a band warming up. As usual, the men wore anything at all; the women sang gospel. A boy from my *4ème* class stood and carefully conducted his schoolmates in slow, missed harmonies. The drums went on in their own loose rhythms.

Enough gospel had been sung to make me think of going home when one of the relatives at the center table stood up and began a story. He was young, a farmer, and he told it with drama and verve, enjoying the attention of the villagers, who had gone silent as if everyone knew an important moment was at hand.

"There was a chief of a certain village," he narrated, "who didn't love the words of God, and his people hated and feared him. Two boys in this village loved God, and one of them he killed by magic. But the other boy escaped, and as he grew up everyone said how wise he was. The chief heard of him and was jealous. He called him in and put him to the test to find out his wisdom. 'You are a wise youth—tell me how many stars there are.'

"The youth could think of nothing to say, but then God came to him and put these words in his mouth: 'Count the hairs on a horse and you will know the number.' The villagers were so stirred by his wisdom that they set on the wicked chief and shook him until he died. The youth who loved the words of God became chief, and he ruled for a long time, and everyone loved him.

"When it was time for him to die, the villagers were crushed with their sadness. They didn't want to lose him. When he was dead, they began to take apart his body. They took patches of his skin and put it on their own, and put his heart and liver and other organs into their bodies, and his blood and muscle, so that they could continue to have him with them and feel all his moods and thoughts as they used to. Finally the body was nothing but a skeleton, and then some villagers took apart his bones, too, and set them inside their own flesh. Then there was nothing left of the chief. One man took so much of the chief into himself that when he went that night to possess a girl, and the spirit passed from his body into hers, people said it was the power of the dead chief that shook him and made the girl cry out!"

At the last words a roar of laughter erupted from the crowd and didn't die down for five minutes.

After the story the gospel started up again, and I got bored. I heard other drums from behind one of the huts, livelier than the music here, and left Christine to investigate.

Something different was happening off the main courtyard, out of the fluorescent light. A small group, made up of children, old folks, and drunken men, was standing around a fire. Five drummers thumped out the beat, up-tempo—a couple of smaller drums with skin stretched taut, the others long and open on the far end, giving out a deep bass that went straight through the gut with each beat.

To me this group seemed less than licit, wilder than the big public gathering, its dark underbelly.

Motley, drunk men took turns dancing around the fire. An old man stuck out his buttocks and put down his head and danced a sort of chicken walk that he seemed to invent as he went along—stopped, listened for the rhythm, moved again, as if his dance were a solution to a problem posed by the drums. He spun away to cheers and clapping, and another old man came in, half naked in ruined corduroys, folding and snapping at the waist, staring head down, then up, pointing to the night sky, snapping again. A big young man—smashed on *sodabi* or palm wine, in a wool cap with earflaps and a long black coat with epaulettes, black Napoleon consecrated to Dionysus—staggered around the flame and almost fell in it, entered the rhythm for a few steps, then collapsed back into the crowd. Jeers, whistles, ridiculing laughter. Palm wine passed around in calabashes. The rhythms changed, drums opposed each other, ran under, over, greeted, answered.

Giddy, I went back to the main assembly. The drums had picked up and the men and women were dancing in a circle around the table. It was Akpessé, a simple two-step—bent over at the waist, arms working between the knees, facing and edging forward counterclockwise, first left two shakes, then right two shakes, in the great circle around the drums. Jubilant voices swelled and plummeted:

> *Ne Mawu a de gbe la*
> *Ama deke matenyui o*
> *Ama deke matenyui o*
> *Ama deke matenyui o*
> *Ne Mawu a de gbe la*
> *Ama deke matenyui o*

> If God gives his command
> No one can challenge it
> No one can challenge it
> No one can challenge it

> If God gives his command
> No one can challenge it

Then someone pulled me by the wrist into the circle. I stumbled forward, tripping into the generous buttocks of a woman bent in front of me; above them, on the sloping back, a baby, almost horizontal, clung for life and slept. The mother turned, laughed, cried "Fo Georgie!" From behind me another voice sang out, *"Bien dansé!"* and Christine's echoed it, and then scarves that signified praise fell across my shoulders. Somewhere in the second time around the circle I stopped stumbling and found the rhythm and was brought to the verge of what I'd craved as long as I'd been in Lavié, of leaving my separate thoughts, my own unreality here, going outside myself among them; and I mouthed the words that just now seemed full of joy:

> *Ne amewo zidodui ha la*
> *Ne amewo zidodui ha la*
> *Ne amewo zidodui ha la*
> *Ekema djifofe Mawu la ana be kpewo a do yli*
> *Ekema djifofe Mawu la ana be atiwo a do yli*

> Even if people keep quiet
> Even if people keep quiet
> Even if people keep quiet
> Heavenly God will make stones shout
> Heavenly God will make trees shout

I reach Europe in a cold drizzle. At the Lyons airport the line marked *"Douanes/*Customs" moves briskly; an official in blue, behind a Plexiglas screen, stamps passports after a minimum of questions.

"What is your purpose in coming to France?"

"Vacation."

"How many days are you going to spend in France?"

"One day."

"And then you are going . . . ?"

"To Barcelona."

"*Bon.* Go ahead."

No visa, no banter, no bribe. Signs affixed to sheet-glass partitions are counterparts of his tone: they indicate luggage and rest rooms in international symbols with sleek, simple lines.

I've come badly unprepared, with only a sweater and a windbreaker. Shopping in Lomé and then packing in my house in Lavié, the thought of December in the temperate zone occurred to me and I tried to plan for it. But in the early harmattan, after a year and a half of African heat, I couldn't really believe in winter. Stepping through the automatic glass doors into the night and seeing my breath cloud upward in the rain, I realize that winter has been blotted out of mind. Before I'm off the express bus into the city center my throat is tingling. And throughout the time I spend in Europe, a head cold explodes behind my eyes and occasionally leaves me dizzy on my feet.

The next day brings a rapid and yet interminable train ride (in Africa such a ride would take twenty-four hours and produce countless anecdotes, but this one takes six and produces none): down the Rhone Valley, fields green with rain, past stony medieval towns, into dull gray and brown fields lying fallow near the coast; then west to the edge of the Pyrenees, the land here rocky and harsh, Perpignan, the border, railway signs now in Spanish and Catalan, the babble in the provincial station that of Catalonians who sew words together out of French and Spanish, so that I am always on the verge of understanding everything and understand nothing; a change of trains, the final stretch down to the sea, and Barcelona.

The city looks bigger and richer than I thought possible. The metro, crowded and fantastically sleek, disgorges me in the heart of town, the Plaça de Catalunya. I emerge on the street just as a woman in a fur coat rushes past, frantically waving a gloved hand for a taxi. All around me are great buildings from a hundred years ago, wrought-iron balconies and windows with stone pediments, the heavy cornices, the pitched roofs; above everything else advertisements flash in neon. I find a cheap hotel, a narrow walk-up sandwiched between two larger buildings, near the Barrio Gotico. My room, with its dark varnished reading table and onionskin hotel paper and desk light I can actually read by, after a year and a half of kerosene lamps, strikes me as the height of luxury.

The idea was twenty days of comfort and fun with the Peace Corps money I'd put aside, a European break from the rigors of Africa before my last five months. I've been to Europe but never to Spain, and the cheap flight from Ouagadougou to Lyons put me within easy distance. I've been a tourist before, I know what tourists do. So I go to the Museo Picasso and see the Gaudí cathedral and eat *churros con chocolato* on the Ramblas.

In an electronic goods shop near the Ramblas, I hear a quarrel between the Spanish shopkeeper and a group of black men who are trying to force boxes of merchandise on him. I guess that he buys cheap and resells, that the goods are hot. They seem to be arguing prices, the shopkeeper uncompromising and cool, the other men alternately angry and imploring. They are short and very black, their trousers tight around the thighs and too long—the European cut that doesn't fit Africans but that Africans wear anyway. I think I hear the heavy African lilt in their Spanish; they might come from Equatorial Guinea, Spain's only black colony. I've seen other blacks in the city, invariably hawking sunglasses, snakeskin purses, and watches as if these are a traditional African trade like jewels among Egyptians or silk among Indians. Around the Grand Marché in Lomé men like these shouted among themselves and hissed and dogged customers; here they wait silently at their sidewalk tables, quick to hold up merchandise at the slightest glance of a passing Spaniard or tourist: *"Barato, señor, señora!"*

The Guineans in the electronics shop raise their voices, but the outnumbered shopkeeper controls the moment, with his silence and folded arms; the more heated the men become, the less he says. Finally they stalk out. He smiles at me and shakes his head, as if to say we both know how unreasonable these people are. An urge to follow the Guineans comes over me, but I find that the sentences I am preparing are all in Ewé.

In the streets the winter air, actually mild here along the Mediterranean, stings in my nostrils and eyes and aggravates the head cold. Indoors, the radiators dry up my eyes and my head seems to float in some muting medium. I try to fill up the days, like a fanatical tourist with little time and a long list of must-sees. Yet as I walk around the city the feeling comes that I am going through motions, pursuing an idea of myself as a tourist, without any sense that I am one or want to be. I'm at a loss to say exactly what I think myself to be here. When I wake up in the hotel room in the mornings my pulse is racing, and only in that first unguarded moment of the day does the trip back to Africa, the months ahead, come to me, before I shut it out.

On Christmas Eve I go to a movie, an American one, Woody Allen's *Zelig*: a mock-documentary about a man who takes on the characteristics, chameleonlike, of anyone he happens to be around. I was counting on the relief of English and laughs. But everything is dubbed into Spanish, which I barely understand; except, for some reason they haven't dubbed the taped conversations between Zelig and his female psychiatrist; these have subtitles, keeping the original voices. So for me this American movie, with the familiar faces of Woody Allen and Mia Farrow emitting Spanish voices that—like the Catalan—it seems I should understand, turns into long passages of incomprehension broken up by brief scenes where Woody Allen, in his nasal Brooklyn accent, is saying things like "Help me, help me! I'm falling, falling!"

At the hotel there is a man who always sits at the same corner table for breakfast. It is hard not to stare at him: he carries an enormous bulk on a pair of ostrich-thin legs, one of them bent sharply inward at the knee, and under his short beard most of his chin and one jaw seem to be missing, so that the face looks like a bird's. Nonetheless, every morning he smiles and says *"Buenos días"* in a gravelly Spanish accent. And one morning he invites me to join him.

His handshake is iron, the big torso more muscle than fat. He introduces himself in flawless English as Juan, then apologizes and says he can't use English, using only enough to whisper that he is CIA, new station chief in Barcelona, just back in Spain from years in Miami, security prohibits English.

From then on, making it up as we go, Juan and I talk in a bastardized babble of Spanish, French, and Italian. Juan does most of the talking. He has strength, wit, self-assurance; he is one of those men with a nose for vulnerability who don't converse with people but master them. Part of the mastery comes from his candor, for he is amazingly candid, if anything he says can be believed. And, listening, I have no will to discriminate; I am prepared to believe everything.

His life is organized around the pieces of his body he's lost. Combat in Vietnam (in Miami he gained U.S. citizenship), where half his face was shattered by a grenade; CIA work in Angola in '75, where he trained UNITA guerrillas with illegal funds and had a finger severed by a jeep accident, later sewn back on; Teheran, '79, where he was the CIA's number two man. During the storming of the embassy a stray bullet destroyed his knee. He escaped, and hid for weeks with friends in the city; a sympathetic doctor implanted a steel plate to hold his leg together. Finally he slipped out of Iran in an Arab costume with a Saudi passport; Arabic is one of his dozen or so languages.

He reaches into his wallet and brings out a souvenir snapshot, taken before his escape. A man in a *kafiyeh*, eyes hidden behind sunglasses, the beard, the bird face. He smiles complacently at me.

"Could you tell me from a sheik?"

I can't.

Eventually Juan's monologue, slipping among three languages within a single sentence, comes around to my own work.

"Ah, Peace Corps. Many of our agents in West Africa are Peace Corps Volunteers."

I protest: I've never met a single one.

"Well, of course, they're not going to *tell* you. But we've successfully infiltrated Peace Corps and other groups in Africa. As a matter of fact, one of our African agents is an advisor to Captain Sankara in Upper Volta."

I register my surprise.

"Oh, yes. Nothing is as it seems, my friend. You lived in a village, you only saw a tiny fraction of things. You couldn't get the big picture. CIA has the big picture. It looks very different."

The mention of Sankara and Upper Volta is setting loose images I've kept at bay for days. The train back to Lyons, the flight to Ouagadougou, the rear of a *baché* ten hours through the desert, and a hotel room near the border in Dapaong with a single light bulb; another *baché*, the choking dust, strangers' stares, the stop at Niamtougou with its swollen-headed beggar boy; and then Lavié, sunk in harmattan torpor, and five more months as the village *yovo*, loved and unknown, the hot silences, the goats and roosters at midday, nights alone with kerosene lamps . . .

Juan goes on, in his genial way, crushing any idea of Africa I have to offer after a year and a half there. And as he does I begin to think of him in a new way. I see him as Sakpaté, the forest spirit who has a face scarred with smallpox and clops across the road at night and makes travelers lose their way. I lost mine in going to Africa; I lost it more than once there. Europe was meant as a respite, but Sakpaté has followed me even here; in Barcelona he has become brazen; and finally he has embodied himself in this disfigured gimcrack adventurer.

Somewhere in the middle of Juan's babble I have an unwanted moment of lucidity. I have come to Europe to get away from physical discomfort but also from the mental strain, the isolation, of Africa. Throughout my time there I held the idea of the return home as a simple, fixed thing: once in the West the anxiety of so much strangeness and discovery would go away and I would be returned to myself. Now, here, I have no place or purpose. I am more like the Guineans than the tourists. And yet in the relative familiarity of a European city, the strain of these many months, which in Africa I always had to keep to myself and overcome, is finally slipping loose, weakening my knees, tearing me, as Dr. Jakobi said, in two. Like Zelig, I'm falling.

I say, *"Adíos, ciao, au revoir"* to Juan. I spend the rest of the morning, no longer even a fake tourist, lying on the bed next to the dark varnished reading table. At noon I reach over and call the airlines. Pan Am has a flight via Lisbon to New York tomorrow morning.

New Year's Eve. Around the subway stop at Fourth Street the bars are overflowing drunkenly onto the sidewalks. Big yellow taxis hurtle by, neon blinks red on the dirty snow piled at the sides of streets. The city is cold, and mad: figures in costume rush past each other as if in an old movie going double-time. At a sidewalk table a bearded man is selling scarves, hats, and gloves. I still have nothing but the sweater and the windbreaker. I buy a wool cap and a pair of wool gloves, and hand the man a few dollar bills. Something—the Cameroon Airlines bag, the color of my skin—catches his eye.

"Where ya comin' in from?"

"You really want to know?"

He smirks. "That's what I asked ya for, buddy."

"Africa."

"Africa! Jesus."

Raucous gangs roam the canyons under the giant buildings, stoking themselves for the magic moment. I realize that hundreds of thousands of them are already converging on Times Square. Clothes look unfamiliar and faces grotesque, the glittery jackets, the heavy purple makeup, the hair peroxide-white or oil-black.

I sit up late in my sister's apartment and go back in my mind to Lavié, from room to room in my house, conjuring up the objects in each one. Already they seem a paltry few; already the months there hardly seem to have happened. I write out a list of everything I own, a sort of living will of the still-not-dead *yovo*. Clothes and kitchenware to the Agbelis, my maps to Dossavi, the petrol burner to Koba, the wicker baskets to Ama, cushions to the old chief . . . During the writing I lose track of time and the city, and so for me the year 1983 ends in a suspended place, at an indeterminate moment.

When I wake up, I have no idea where I am. Then, remembering, I sit up and struggle for a way to undo everything and get back to the village and the people who are waiting for me. But the thought of Barcelona returns, the explosion behind my eyes, *Zelig*, Juan, falling. I lie down again and try to prepare for the day ahead in the city. It is the first morning of 1984. During the night a snowfall has whitened the streets below the giants.

George Packer was born in the San Francisco Bay Area, where he attended public schools. After receiving a degree from Yale University, he joined the Peace Corps and served in Togo, West Africa, as an English teacher in 1982 and 1983. He now lives in Somerville, Massachusetts, where he is a carpenter and writes. His essays and reviews have appeared in *The New York Times Book Review, The Nation, Dissent,* and elsewhere.

Also available from
Vintage Departures

Fast Company by Jon Bradshaw
Maple Leaf Rag by Stephen Brook
Coyotes by Ted Conover
One for the Road by Tony Horwitz
Making Hay by Verlyn Klinkenborg
The Owl Papers by Jonathan Evan Maslow
The Panama Hat Trail by Tom Miller
Into the Heart of Borneo by Redmond O'Hanlon
Iron & Silk by Mark Salzman
From Heaven Lake by Vikram Seth
Fool's Paradise by Dale Walker